Negotiating the Livelihoods of Children and
Youth in Africa's Urban Spaces

————

Négocier sa vie : les enfants et les jeunes dans
les espaces urbains d'Afrique

This book is a product of the CODESRIA Child and Youth Institute

Ce livre est une compilation des articles issus de l'institut sur l'enfance
et la jeunesse du CODESRIA

Negotiating the Livelihoods of Children and Youth in Africa's Urban Spaces

------

Négocier sa vie : les enfants et les jeunes dans les espaces urbains d'Afrique

Edited by

Michael F.C. Bourdillon

with

Ali Sangare

CODESRIA

Council for the Development of Social Science Research in Africa
DAKAR

© CODESRIA 2012
Council for the Development of Social Science Research in Africa
Avenue Cheikh Anta Diop, Angle Canal IV
BP 3304 Dakar, CP 18524, Senegal
Website: www.codesria.org

ISBN: 978-2-86978-504-5

Typesetting: Daouda Thiam
Cover Design: Ibrahima Fofana
Printing: Imprimerie Graphiplus, Dakar, Senegal

Distributed in Africa by CODESRIA
Distributed elsewhere by African Books Collective, Oxford, UK
Website: www.africanbookscollective.com

The Council for the Development of Social Science Research in Africa (CODESRIA) is an independent organisation whose principal objectives are to facilitate research, promote research-based publishing and create multiple forums geared towards the exchange of views and information among African researchers. All these are aimed at reducing the fragmentation of research in the continent through the creation of thematic research networks that cut across linguistic and regional boundaries.

CODESRIA publishes *Africa Development*, the longest standing Africa based social science journal; *Afrika Zamani*, a journal of history; the *African Sociological Review*, the *African Journal of International Affairs*; *Africa Review of Books* and the *Journal of Higher Education in Africa*. The Council also co-publishes the *Africa Media Review*; *Identity, Culture and Politics: An Afro-Asian Dialogue*; *The African Anthropologist* and the *Afro-Arab Selections for Social Sciences*. The results of its research and other activities are also disseminated through its Working Paper Series, Green Book Series, Monograph Series, Book Series, Policy Briefs and the CODESRIA Bulletin. Select CODESRIA publications are also accessible online at www.codesria.org.

CODESRIA would like to express its gratitude to the Swedish International Development Cooperation Agency (SIDA/SAREC), the International Development Research Centre (IDRC), the Ford Foundation, the MacArthur Foundation, the Carnegie Corporation, the Norwegian Agency for Development Cooperation (NORAD), the Danish Agency for International Development (DANIDA), the French Ministry of Cooperation, the United Nations Development Programme (UNDP), the Netherlands Ministry of Foreign Affairs, the Rockefeller Foundation, FINIDA, the Canadian International Development Agency (CIDA), the Open Society Initiative for West Africa (OSIWA), TrustAfrica, UN/UNICEF, the African Capacity Building Foundation (ACBF) and the Government of Senegal for supporting its research, training and publication programmes.

Contents

Notes on Contributors

Marie-Thérèse Arcens Somé, sociologue, Institut des Science des Sociétés, Centre National pour la Recherche Scientifique et Technologique, Ouagadougou, Burkina Faso.

Okechi Dominic Azuwike, Department of Geography and Environmental Management, Imo State University, Owerri, Nigeria.

Michael F.C. Bourdillon, Professor emeritus in the Department of Sociology, University of Zimbabwe, Harare.

Peter Ezeah, Department of Sociology/Anthropology, Nnamdi Azikiwe University, Awka, Nigeria.

Ollo Pépin Hien, Politologue, chercheur à l'INSS/CNRST, Département de politologie, Ouagadougou, Burkina Faso.

Susan M. Kilonzo, Department of Religion, Theology and Philosophy, Maseno University, Kenya.

Stanford T. Mahati, Forced Migration Studies Programme, University of the Witwatersrand, Johannesburg, South Africa.

Jean-Marcellin Manga, Département de Sociologie de l'Université de Yaoundé I, Cameroun.

Joseph Wasswa-Matovu, Department of Economic Policy and Planning, Faculty of Economics and Management, Makerere University, Kampala, Uganda.

Tabitha Naisiko, School of Post Graduate Studies, Uganda Martyrs University, Kampala, Uganda.

Josephine Atieno Ochieng', Department of Psychology and Counselling. University of Eastern Africa, Baraton, Eldoret, Kenya.

Babatunde Joshua Omotosho, Department of Sociology, Faculty of the Social Sciences, University of Ado Ekiti, Nigeria.

Ali Sangare, Sociologue, Chargé de recherche à l'Institut des Sciences des Sociétés, Centre National de la Recherche Scientifique et Technologique, Ouagadougou, Burkina Faso.

Jean Félix Yekoka, Historien/Sociologue, IGRAC, FLSH, Université Marien Ngouabi, Brazzaville.

Achille Pinghane Yonta, Attaché d'Enseignement et de Recherche, Université de Yaoundé I / Département de Sociologie, Yaoundé, Cameroun.

1

Introduction

Michael Bourdillon

CODESRIA held a month-long institute on 'Negotiating Children's and Youth Livelihoods in Africa's Urban Spaces' (Dakar, Senegal, in September 2009). The twenty participants were senior and junior academic researchers, both Francophone and Anglophone, from universities and related institutions throughout the continent. This book brings together much of the research and ideas that were presented at the institute or resulted from it.[1]

Problems facing children and youth in African cities have been widely documented and have received much recent attention. African populations have high growth rates and, consequently, relatively high proportions of young people. Population growth in rural areas has stretched resources leading to urban migration and a rapid growth of cities. Economies have not grown apace with the population; and in some countries economies have even shrunk. The result is a severe lack of resources in cities to meet the needs of the growing populations, shown in high unemployment, inadequate housing, poor services, and often extreme poverty. All the essays in this book draw attention to such urban environments, in which children and youth have to live and survive. We have specific detail on the problems in Ouagadougou, Burkina Faso. Ali Sangare's research on unemployment (chapter 2) shows the problems typically faced by youth in many African cities, and how they develop means to deal with city life. In particular, degrees and diplomas are no longer guarantees of future employment. Marie-Thérèse Arcens Somé (chapter 3) shows the lack of resources and services faced by families and their younger children in poor areas, and various initiatives taken by families to overcome the resulting problems. While not all those living in urban areas face the same problems, and not all cities are the same, these two studies illustrate the plight of many children and youth among Africa's urban poor.

Who are children and who are youth? International documents like the United Nations Convention on the Rights of the Child (1989) define children as those under the age of eighteen or the legal age of majority. The broader term 'youth' refers to those who are somewhere between childhood and full adulthood, covering an age range from mid-adolescence (around 15) to various upper limits of between 25 and 35. The African Union Charter (1999) defines youth as those aged from 15 to 35. For several legal purposes, such as the age to drive a car, or get married, or obtain employment, or vote for government, the end of childhood and the achievement of responsibility is defined according to particular ages.

While such definitions may be necessary for legal convenience or customary classification, they do not correspond exactly to the growth of competence and responsibility of particular children. In many African societies, a key transition from childhood to adulthood is symbolized by initiation rites rather than a specific age, but classification according to such rites does not always reflect the behaviour and responsibilities of particular children. Moreover, the determination of when childhood ends is invariably made by adults, with little consideration for the opinions and competencies of particular children. In some situations, the definition of childhood appears precisely to assert the control of children by adults. For example, many adults consider it right for children to work in their homes for no pay, but not to work for money (which would give them a degree of independence). Such rules reflect the dominance and control of adults rather than the competencies of children (Levison 2000). Even traditional initiation rites, by which young people are supposed to become adults, can sometimes be understood as a mechanism for patriarchal control (la Fontaine 1977).

In practice, children live in the same world as adults, and learn gradually how to participate in this world through observation and practice. Forces of poverty and exploitation affect adults and children alike, as do the effects of societal economic growth and development. Clearly defined lines of transition must always be in some sense artificial. Children's behaviour and competencies depend on personal characteristics, on the circumstances of their upbringing, on particular experiences, and on gradual learning processes. Particularly significant in developing competencies are cultural practices and expectations (Rogoff 2003:1-24): in Europe and North America, children are protected from danger by being kept away from it, whereas in other cultures they are exposed to risky situations and taught to deal with them; again in Europe and North America, children are kept free of responsibility, whereas in many other cultures children learn to be responsible for young siblings and for family wealth (particularly when herding domestic animals). While in England it would be illegal to leave children under the sole charge of someone under the age of 16, in many African societies children of ten are expected to care for young siblings while their parents work. Responsible behaviour develops more quickly when it is taught and expected. So in this book, we do not specify rigid definitions of 'childhood' and 'youth' as if these can be separated from the world of adults. Nor do we adopt a particular normative ideal for 'childhood'. Various authors use the terms appropriately for their different studies, which are more concerned with patterns of behaviour and status in society than with age-based definitions.

Young people are numerically dominant in Africa, and the future depends on their ability to sustain themselves and the societies in which they live. Yet they have few resources, material or social, with which to meet the threats of poverty in African cities. Material resources are largely in the control of adults; social networks of youth rarely include those in positions of power; and young people's experience of dealing with livelihood issues is limited by their age. Children and youth are therefore particularly likely to suffer from crises arising in cities, and often struggle to maintain even a constrained and deprived livelihood. Some young people migrate to cities in search of better lives, and find themselves so constrained by poverty that when their illusions about city life are shattered, they have no means of returning home.

Cities, however, also provide opportunities. Children and young people generally are shaped by the world they live in, but also to some extent shape this world to suit their interests and needs (Honwana and De Boeck 2005:ix). They use the cities to engage with the wider world (Simone 2005:1). So, in spite of constraints imposed on them by poverty, many young people find livelihoods in cities which they prefer to what is available in rural areas. Rather than submitting passively to poverty, they frequently become a major resource in dealing with urban problems and developing the cities (illustrated in several essays in Tienda and Wilson 2002). Outside Africa, recent studies have pointed to the ways in which young people can improve their lives even through work on city streets (e.g., Burr 2006; Offit 2008). This book looks at poor to middle-class communities in African cities, and illustrates how young people find ways not only of surviving, but also of enjoying themselves. In the face of cramped and uncomfortable homes, and in the absence of public resources for leisure, young people use the streets and find other urban spaces where they can enjoy themselves. It focuses on how young people adapt to the constraints they face, make use of opportunities that cities offer, and find ways of improving their lives.

We see the creative ways that young people find to improve their economic status in a variety of urban spaces in Cameroon (Lebongo, chapter 4). Impoverished child migrants from Zimbabwe show determination in improving their lives by working for income in the South African border town of Musina (Mahati, chapter 5). Children from very poor homesteads earn a living by recycling materials from a municipal rubbish dump in Eldoret, Kenya (Atieno, chapter 6). Handicapped youths have taken advantage of a government concession to create a trading niche for themselves between Brazzaville and Kinshasa in the two Congos (Yekoka, chapter 7). Youths in Onitsha, Nigeria, take on a variety of forms of self-employment (Ezeah, chapter 8). When homes are cramped and uncomfortable, and cities do not provide adequate recreational facilities, young people find ways of creating leisure and entertainment on the streets and other urban spaces. Children combine productive work with fun in night foraging in Owerri, Nigeria (Azuwike, chapter 9). Youths enjoy themselves, earn a living, and open up possibilities for careers in entertainment by forming 'karaoke' groups in Kampala, Uganda (Wasswa-Matovu, chapter 10). Apart from the material side, young people find spaces for socializing and enjoying themselves in informal TV and video lounges in Ado Ekiti, Nigeria (Omotosho, chapter 11); older youths meet in informal tea clubs in Ouagadougou, Burkina Faso (Hein, chapter 12); and young people meet with peers in a youth group in Bugembe, Uganda, for social purposes and to learn skills (Naisiko, chapter 13). The networks created in these social activities can provide livelihood support, in the forms of useful information, influential contacts, and sometimes material support: the youth group in Bugembe also offers oppor-tunities to learn livelihood skills. Some young people use their sexuality for livelihood purposes, whether for immediate financial returns or for longer-term supportive relationships (Yonta, chapter 14). In all these activities, young people develop and utilize social support from peers, kin (sometimes including those in rural areas), and others in the cities, often creating new networks to replace older family networks that are no longer accessible in cities. Far from accepting the passive role of victims, young people use their initiative to take advantage of oppor-tunities offered to them in the midst of city life. They show themselves to be active agents, attempting with some success to take control of aspects of their lives.

Negotiating Livelihoods

Educationalists have long realized that children do not normally learn by passively receiving information and instructions passed on to them by teachers and other adults. They learn reading, writing, and numeracy by practice. They learn social skills by taking part in social activities. They learn sports by playing them. They observe what others do and imitate what works: learning is a kind of apprenticeship in life (see Rogoff 1990). Children experiment to see the effect of different responses to the situation they are in. They are constantly producing their own responses to the environment they face, and normally they learn to take control of their lives through successful responses.

When we find children and youth in stressful situations, in the cities as elsewhere, it is a mistake to assume that they are passive victims to be rescued: rather they comprise a major resource to be encouraged and utilized. Research on street children in the 1970s and 80s showed them finding ways, often innovative and creative, to deal with the oppressive environment in which they lived. The reality of many children choosing to live on the streets challenged common assumptions that all children live under the protection and control of adults (Hart 1997:14-15). These street children have been badly failed by the adult world, but (with few exceptions) are not simply passive victims: rather they have taken their lives into their own hands.

We could think of a continuum between two extremes. At one extreme, some children have virtually no agency or control over their own lives and have little power to negotiate: children in extreme poverty, or working and living in extreme hardship under dominating adults may be in such a position. Indeed, some street children are unable to cope with street life and are destroyed psychologically and physically (e.g., Gigengack 2006:200-213). At the other extreme, the young people take control and are not interested in negotiating, as we see in Susan Kilonzo's account of Mungiki in Kenya (chapter 15, see also Jensen 2008). The majority of children and youth in African cities lie between these extremes. In spite of the constraints that urban poverty imposes, most find some way of coping and even improving their lives. The degree to which they successfully take control of their lives, and in this sense exercise agency, varies. Sometimes young people contest with adults for use of space and time, and do not always conform to adult regulation (illustrated in chapter 9). There is also variation in the degree to which their solutions are socially constructive, or threaten the norms and fabric of society. Often there is tension between the norms and values adopted by young people, and the norms of the dominant adult society (illustrated in chapters 10, 13, 14, and 15). Negotiation usually leads to patterns of behaviour that are tolerated, if not welcomed, by most people.

The title of this book, and the institute on which it was based, speak of negotiating livelihoods. The English concept of 'livelihood' is difficult to translate into French. In development studies in the English language, the concept of 'livelihood' has been adopted to incorporate the social and physical environment together with people's responses to it (see, for example, Bourdillon and Hebinck 2002). It considers not only material but also human and social resources, including local knowledge and understanding. It thus considers the material means for living in a broader context of social and cultural interpretation. These connotations are not readily conveyed in the French translation, 'des moyens d'existence'. Consequently, we found at the beginning of the Institute a difference in emphasis between some Francophone scholars, who initially focused on earning a living, and Anglophone scholars, who spread their interests more broadly to include values and lifestyles. The advantage of a bilingual institute is that such technical terms have to be carefully examined and explained, and agreement was reached in discussion. This book contains chapters that deal not only with material and economic existence, but also with leisure activities and entertainment, and with forms of social life developed in response to the urban environment.

When we speak of negotiation, we are acknowledging the agency of young people in taking control of their lives within the constraints imposed on them. Agency operates not only in practical decisions, but also in developing knowledge and perspectives on the situations they face.

Perspectives and Knowledge of Young People

In the past, society was largely studied from a male point of view. Many assumed that men were in charge of households, and that men could speak for women. If the feminist movement has not yet succeeded in completely abolishing such a male perspective, it has seriously challenged male points of view. Women comprise half the world's population and in practice are not always subordinate to men. In urban Africa, there are numerous households headed by women. Even when women live with men in patriarchal societies, they are usually able to control many areas in their lives. Women have been seen to be important economically: even unpaid work in the home can have significant economic consequences for the family and society. Moreover, women often have different perspectives on life and culture from those of men. Women demand the right to speak for themselves and to have their perspectives taken seriously. It is now generally agreed that any research on women's issues must take into account what women say about them.

It is not yet so widespread that research on young people's issues must take account of what young people say. Children and youth comprise well over half of Africa's population. They are not always under the control of adults. Their activities, especially those that involve peer co-operation, are often outside adult domains. Indeed, many children and more youths have become socially and economically independent of adults, often living on their own, but increasingly also as heads of households in the absence of adults – in which case young people are usually responsible for even younger children.

The future of African cities depends on this large youthful population. They will ultimately determine what the cities will become. It is extremely unlikely that they will simply reproduce the cities of the past. In this volume, we see young people responding in different ways to changing technologies, changing economic structures, and changing social fabrics. They will produce new forms and styles of urban life and the sociology of cities cannot afford to neglect their inputs.

On the material side, young people are economically important. It has been pointed out that, even in the developed world, children's roles as consumers and producers are often understated or even ignored (Zelizer 2002). In traditional rural African societies, children are expected to contribute to families' means of sustenance in a variety of ways, from looking after the home and young children to contributing their labour in agriculture and animal husbandry. The economic importance of children continues in many urban families, where children still contribute to family livelihood in a variety of ways: indeed, the African Charter on the Rights and Welfare of the Child points to the duty of children 'to work for the cohesion of the family, to respect his parents and elders at all times and to assist them in case of need' (article 31a).

On the cultural side, children and youth have their own perspectives on their lives and on their societies, which affect their behaviour and interaction with others. Their new forms of behaviour and interaction will inform the future cultural life of cities, and so cannot be ignored by social researchers.

Their behavioural responses derive from their views of the world around them, which in turn are affected by their particular experiences. This was illustrated at the institute in an address by Moussow Sow, director of Avenir de l'Enfant – an organization dedicated to protecting children from various kinds of abuse. He spoke about the world of children on the streets, and pointed out how, with their very different experiences of life, they often see things differently from the way adults perceive the same material things. He exemplified this with perspectives on graveyards at night. To most people cemeteries are places of fear to be avoided, especially at night; and precisely because of this, street children see them as places where they can sleep, relatively safe from being molested. Another example was pick-pocketing, a crime and nuisance to much of the world, but a highly skilled and rewarding form of co-operative work to the children. We cannot understand their behaviour without first understanding how they perceive their environment, which requires hearing from them.

Also at the institute, Dr Elsbeth Robson reported on a research project on problems of transport that face children in three African countries. This research was planned so that children themselves would have an opportunity to collect information from their peers and report on the problems that faced them: the findings would thus reflect not only the observations of adults, but also the perspectives of children. The children produced some ideas and perspectives that were missed by adults. One noticeable point was that while walking to and from school and in the vicinity of their homes children felt many fears of dangers (real or imagined), such as dangers from snakes, dogs, or malicious people. Another point made strongly by children, and which was largely unnoticed by adult researchers and informants, related to the unpleasantness and harassment children often experienced while moving around in their communities (Robson et al. 2009:475-476). This example illustrates why good research must incorporate the perspectives of the people being researched, however young they may be.

Sometimes, children's perspectives provide a more fundamental challenge to the very way we think. At an international conference on 'Urban Childhood' held in Trondheim in 1997, representatives of working children were invited to speak at the session on 'child labour', alongside academics and representatives of national and international organizations. A thirteen-year-old girl from Senegal, in a short speech which reduced the hall to an awkward silence, had this to say:

> Do you understand how you insult me, when you talk of 'combatting' and 'abolishing' the work that I do? I have worked as a domestic servant since I was

eight. Because of doing this work, I have been able to go to school (which my parents in the village could not afford); I help my parents with the money I earn. I am very proud of the work I do! (Bourdillon et al. 2010:9)

This young school-going worker from Senegal challenged adults in a fundamental way, to re-consider how they thought and spoke about her work and about her. She challenged the concepts of an ideal childhood that many adults took for granted.

These examples illustrate the fundamental point that, on many things, children have their own perspectives deriving from their specific experiences. If we want to understand the lives of children (and therefore the future of cities), we have to include their perspectives. For this, they must have adequate opportunity to express themselves and we must listen to what they say. While their perspectives, like anyone else's, are limited by what they have learned and experienced, they nevertheless form an important part of the whole picture of what is real, and particularly of how and why they respond to the world in the ways they do.

When we pay attention to the perspectives of young people, certain widely held notions have to be modified. Many studies, for example, point to the exclusion and marginalization of youth. While young people may indeed be marginalized in terms of political and economic power, they form half or more of urban populations, making the term 'marginal' seem incongruous: in some circumstances they adopt life styles and culture that deliberately exclude adult control, thus marginalizing adults. Young people are often central to certain aspects of urban life, and particularly to social change in cities. Perceptions that young people fail to integrate into urban life sometimes reflect narrow adult perspectives and ignore the ways in which the young successfully integrate into an urban life that is different from lives of adults. One of the issues raised in discussion at the institute (and in chapters 3 and 13) is that traditional forms of socialization do not work in the cities, and that parents who are relatively new to cities do not know how best to raise their children for urban life. Children are then left to find their own ways of adaptation, which often create tension with the values of older members of society.

Apart from the importance of children's views in our comprehension of urban life, careful attention to the perspectives of children and youths highlights the limited alternatives realistically available to them when they make their choices, and reveals the variety in the lives and responses of young people. Constraints at home, or the poor quality of available schooling, can lead to the choice of alternative activities outside the home – especially in the streets, which do not always meet the approval of adults. Reasons behind young people's choices frequently reveal rational choice and often contest negative stereotypes that adults may form of 'irresponsible' youth. If youth are indeed irresponsible, policy and intervention is likely to focus on control, which reflects interests of adults. Careful attention to the perspectives of young people produces a better understanding of their plight and ensures that policy and intervention attend to their interests.

This is well illustrated by activities that go against life styles and values accepted broadly by adult society. Early in the institute, consideration was given to children's work, which can be exploitative and abusive (as it is often depicted in high-income societies and communities), but which can also positively contribute materially to the livelihood of children and their families, and in various ways to children's development (see Bourdillon 2009). Children working on the streets have been shown to work for economic reasons, but also to get out of their homes for entertainment and experience (Oloko 1989; 1993). In spite of the poverty and insecurity of many people in African cities, young people sometimes improve their lives by leaving impoverished rural homes to work in cities, even when they have to live and work on the streets (see Mahati, chapter 5). Josephine Atieno (chapter 6) describes young people scavenging from municipal rubbish: while adults were fearful of and for the youngsters involved, these were creative in recycling usable materials for sale, co-operating and socializing with peers, and contributing to stretched household budgets in marginalized communities. Another activity that contests stereotypes is prostitution (see Yonta, chapter 14). At first, some members of the institute could see nothing positive in such activity, but attention to the perspectives of those involved showed a variety of situations ranging from desperate measures against poverty with little chance to exercise agency in the control of one's life on the one hand, to the deliberate choice of an enjoyable life style in the company of powerful persons on the other – with many gradations between. This is neither to approve nor condemn prostitution: it is to point out that a nuanced approach is necessary to understand why different people do what they do.

Human and Child Rights

I have pointed out that it makes sound research sense to let young people speak for themselves and to listen to them. The United Nations Convention on the Rights of the Child also points to children's rights to be allowed to seek information, to express themselves, and to be heard in decisions that affect them (articles 12, 13: see also the African Charter on the Rights and Welfare of the Child, articles 4, 7). If research hopes to influence policy and intervention that will affect the lives of young people, researchers clearly have an obligation to listen to what the young people say, however young they may be. Apart from being necessary for sound research, this is also a matter of the rights of the people concerned.

What are rights? Historical abuses of people, sometimes approved and encouraged by sovereign states, such as in the institution of slavery and the Nazi treatment of Jews, have resulted in widespread agreement that all humans have certain fundamental rights that are not subject to community customs or decisions by individual sovereign states. The culmination of these discussions was the Universal Convention on Human Rights, passed by the General Assembly of the United Nations in Paris in 1948. Rights specific to children came strongly into international discussion in the 1980s, which resulted in the United Nations Convention on the Rights of the Child in 1989, and the African Charter on the Rights and Welfare of the Child agreed by the Organisation of African Unity in 1990.

In chapter 5 of this book, Stanford Mahati suggests that staff of NGOs trying to help migrant children were committed to international conventions on child rights, but that this commitment led to inconsistencies in their support of the children and did not always work in the best interests of children. Elsewhere in Africa it has been noticed that commitment by organizations to a particular interpretation of child rights can work against children most in need of support (Jacquemin 2006). In both cases, the contentious issue was children's work, but this points to a more general problem: international conventions are agreed by governments, and do not always reflect the thinking and values of particular communities or of the children they are intended to protect.

A perception sometimes emerges in Asia and Africa (see, for example, Burr 2006:16-19) that human rights, and child rights in particular, are a Western concept based on individualism and negating more communitarian principles according to which the interests of individuals are subordinate to those of the community. Rights do not have to be interpreted in this way: in particular, the African Charter links children's rights to their responsibilities towards their families, their communities, and their societies (article 32).[2] The preamble to the Convention on the Rights of the Child speaks of 'taking due account of the importance of the traditions and cultural values of each people for the protection and harmonious development of the child'. The rights of individuals, therefore, do not negate the rights of others in the community, nor do they normally negate values of the community.

Moreover, international conventions and supporting government legislation express only those rights that are widely agreed. In practice, the rights of children and young people to protection and harmonious development are largely contained in cultural values and practices. These apply to what they can expect materially and socially from their families as they grow and the support and inheritance they can expect in the future. Such expectations are often referred to as 'moral rights', which are not legally binding but are supported by communities and their cultures.

With respect to children's rights, some people argue that since children are dependent on adults, and since they are in the process of becoming citizens of the future under the guidance of adults, there are problems in talking about children's rights, and that it is more useful to speak of obligations towards children, and of the care and protection that is due to them.[3] Such arguments assume an absolute division between childhood and adulthood. If, on the other hand, we see children as already participating in their families and communities, with responsibilities and duties while they learn, it is appropriate also to consider their rights as they continuously and actively develop their lives.

Rights refer to the fact that all humans have a status and dignity, which cannot simply be subordinated to the economic or political expediency of others. While few of the chapters in this book explicitly engage the language of rights, all accept the premise that children and youth have a fundamental right to basic resources for livelihood, and to be treated with respect as human beings. One fundamental right, related to respect, is to have a say and be heard on matters that affect one's life. While this right is widely acknowledged for adults, it is often overlooked for children when adults (often wrongly) think that they know best what is good for children under their charge (Twum-Danso 2003). All the chapters in this book include information on perspectives of the young people they describe.

We look at young citizens, therefore, as people determined to make something of their lives, and who work to make space available for their activities. The future of our cities depends on them.

Outline of this Collection

After this introduction, Dr Ali Sangare draws from research into unemployment in Ouagadougou, Burkina Faso. He points to the growing number of youths in the city who cannot count on degrees or diplomas to find employment. Instead, they have to rely on a variety of self-employment strategies.

In chapter 3, Marie-Thérèse Arcens Somé considers the livelihoods of families in a poor community in the same city, and the poverty of resources available to them. Without professional qualifications, families have to take on work that may endanger their health and children have to contribute to the fight for livelihood.

Besides seeing African cities as places where young people are excluded and marginalized, Jean Marcellin Manga Lebongo, in chapter 4, considers cities of Cameroon as settings that create advantageous opportunities. He considers economic, agro-pastoral, and cultural activities of young people in which they express their creativity.

The South African border town of Musina is host to a large number of young migrants trying to escape extreme poverty in Zimbabwe. In chapter 5, Stanford Mahati examines how the efforts of children to make a living are sometimes in conflict with norms of organizations that have been established to give them care and shelter. Care workers are inconsistent, in some situations showing appreciation for the efforts of children and in others being very critical of them.

Chapter 6 moves to Eldoret in Kenya. Josephine Atieno describes how children earn a living and establish friendships by recycling garbage at a municipal dump. Here the perceptions of the children of themselves and their work differ from the more negative and fearful perceptions of adults living in the nearby communities.

The governments of the Democratic Republic of Congo and of Congo-Brazzaville agreed to allow disabled persons to trade freely across the river between Brazaville and Kinshasa. Jean Félix Yekoka describes in chapter 7 how physically disabled youths occupied this niche to overcome the cultural and material disadvantages arising from their disability.

Dr Peter Ezeah conducted a survey of youths in a township of Onitsha, south-eastern Nigeria, to examine how they cope with urban life under constraints of poverty. In the absence of opportunities for formal employment or access to social support, youths adopt various forms of economic activity in the informal sector. The majority perceive their livelihood strategies positively despite the constraints they face in negotiating livelihoods in the city.

Okechi Dominic Azuwike describes in chapter 9 the night-time hunting of termites and snails on the streets of Owerri, Nigeria. These activities are undertaken largely for fun, but have an important productive element, both to improve household diet and for income. Although children's hunting is largely outside adult control, produce is usually controlled by parents or guardians. The activity sometimes involves contestation over public space, and can cause tensions with parents or guardians as well as a variety of hazards.

In chapter 10, Dr Joseph Wasswa-Matovu describes how some young people in Kampala, Uganda, join 'karaoke' entertainment groups to earn a part-time living, and sometimes to establish a career in entertainment. The groups, using high-sound technology, establish a space for themselves beside the more formally established entertainment centres that serve the elite. Their work involves a variety of hazards as well as offering opportunities to young people.

Chapter 11 looks at another kind of semi-formal entertainment, this time focussing on the the clients who spend to enjoy it. Dr Babatunde Joshua Omotosho studied informal video and television parlours in Ado Ekiti, south-western Nigeria. These attracted a largely young population, over half of whom were studying in a number of surrounding tertiary institutions. The main motive for visiting the parlours was to watch football matches around the world on large television screens, but the venues also served a variety of social functions.

Returning to Ouagadougou, Burkina Faso, Ollo Pépin Hien in chapter 12 describes tea clubs. Since older, kin-based networks are not easily accessible, young people create new social groups. The chapter describes how groups of young people meet regularly to drink tea together, an activity which provides a focus to discuss and to share information and ideas on issues ranging from entertainment to politics. The clubs also provide a social network for material and social support.

In chapter 13, Tabitha Naisiko uses Bugembe Youth Group in a peri-urban setting in Uganda, to consider the role of socialization in negotiating livelihoods. In the absence of traditional forms of socialization adapted to the urban environment, a parish Youth Centre provides leisure and social activities, as well as training in skills that will be useful economically to the youths. According to the concerns of the both the youth and adults involved in the study, this kind of socialization is considered important to the youth. There are, however, sometimes tensions with adults in the community, and such groups need to be strengthened by combining public and private resources.

The last two chapters deal with activities of the young that are in conflict with dominant values and sometimes with the interests of wider society. In chapter 14, Achille Pinghane Yonta discusses prostitution among young girls in Yaoundé, Cameroon. Apart from the standard sex for pay, he discusses 'semi-prostitution' in which girls use sex to establish longer-term relationships that provide livelihood. He looks at factors that favour this kind of activity, including various categories of clients that utilize it.

Dr Susan M. Kilonzo considers a different kind of youth activity in chapter 15. She describes the organization of Mungiki in Kenya, which started as a youth movement for social justice, but through various transformations and with some political support, became a sponsor of violence and extortion. Although it claims to support traditional cultural values, many of its activities are clearly criminal in nature.

Ways Forward

The essays in this volume illustrate a wide diversity of urban situations and an equal diversity in responses by young people to these situations. There is no single strategy that will improve livelihoods of all. Nevertheless, taken together, the essays suggest certain principles for research if this is effectively to feed into interventions to improve livelihoods.

The first is that the people we are trying to help comprise a major resource. They are already finding ways to help themselves. There are two reasons why sustainable development should build on these initiatives. First, initiatives that are owned and desired by the persons concerned have a better chance of success than those imposed from outside. Second, in the personal development of young people, self-esteem and decision-making ability arise from perceived successful practice; it therefore helps to emphasise and build on their own successes.

Academics can contribute to this approach by more and thorough, respectful research on the numerous ways in which young people perceive and respond to the environments they face in growing African cities. The essays in this volume provide suggestions for a vast field that needs to be explored.

Notes

1. Unfortunately, not all presentations became available in the time scheduled for the production of this book.
2. The African Charter on Human and Peoples' Rights, approved by the Organisation of African Unity (which later became the African Union) in 1981, also refers to the duties of individuals to their communities, to ensure that rights of individuals do not supersede or negate the rights of others. See articles 29 and 27(2).
3. For fuller discussion and critique of these points of view, see Freeman 1997; Archard 2004.

References

Archard, David, 2004, *Children: Rights and Childhood* (2nd edition), London & New York: Routledge.

Bourdillon, Michael, 2009, 'A Place for Work in Children's Lives?' Plan Canada. Download from http://plancanada.ca.

Bourdillon, Michael and Hebinck, Paul, 2002, 'The Concept of Livelihood', in Michael Bourdillon and Paul Hebinck, eds, *Women, Men and Work: Rural Livelihoods in South-eastern Zimbabwe*, Harare: Weaver Press, pp. 1-12.

Bourdillon, Michael, Levison, Deborah, Myers, William and White, Ben, 2010, *Rights and Wrongs of Children's Work*, New Brunswick, etc.: Rutgers University Press.

Burr, Rachel, 2006, *Vietnam's Children in a Changing World*, New Brunswick: Rutgers University Press.

Freeman, Michael, 1997, *The Moral Status of Children: Essays on the Rights of the Child*, The Hague: Luwer Law International.

Gigengack, Roy, 2006, 'Young, Damned and Banda: The World of Young Street People in Mexico City, 1990-1997', School for Social Science Research, Amsterdam: University of Amsterdam. Vol. Ph.D.

Hart, Roger, 1997, *Children's Participation: The Theory and Practice of Involving Young Citizens in Community Development and Environmental Care*, London: Earthscan Publications.

Honwana, Alcinda and De Boeck, Filip, eds., 2005, *Makers and Breakers: Children and Youth in Postcolonial Africa*, Oxford & Dakar: James Currey & Codesria.

Jacquemin, Mélanie, 2006, 'Can the language of rights get hold of the complex realities of child domestic work? The case of young domestic workers in Abidjan, Ivory Coast', *Childhood*, Vol. 13, No. 3, pp. 389-406.

Jensen, Steffen, 2008, *Gangs, Politics & Dignity in Cape Town*, Oxford: James Currey.

la Fontaine, Jean, 1977, 'The Power of Rights', *Man, New Series*, Vol. 12, No. 3/4, pp. 421-437.

Levison, Deborah, 2000, 'Children as economic agents', *Feminist Economics*, Vol. 6, No. 1, pp. 125-134.

Offit, Thomas A., 2008, *Conquistadores de la Calle: Child Street Labor in Guatemala City*, Austin: Texas University Press.

Oloko, Beatrice Adenike, 1989, 'Children's work in urban Nigeria: a case study of young Lagos street traders', in William E. Myers, ed., *Protecting Working Children*, London: Zed Books, pp. 11-23.

Oloko, Beatrice Adenike, 1993, 'Children's street work in urban Nigeria as adaptation and maladaptation to changing socioeconomic circumstances', *International Journal of Behavioural Development*, Vol. 16, No. 3, pp. 465-482.

Robson, Elsbeth, Gina Porter, Kate Hampshire and Michael F.C. Bourdillon, 2009, '"Doing it right?": working with young researchers in Malawi to investigate children, transport and mobility', *Children's Geographies*, Vol. 7, No. 4, pp. 467-480.

Rogoff, Barbara, 1990, *Apprenticeship in Thinking: cognitive development in social context*, New York: Oxford University Press.

Rogoff, Barbara, 2003, *The Cultural Nature of Human Development*, New York: Oxford University Press.

Simone, A., 2005, 'Introduction: Urban Processes and Change', in A. Simone and Abouhani, eds, *Urban Africa Changing Contours of Survival in the City*, Dakar: CODESRIA. 1-28.

Tienda, Martin and Wilson, William Julius, 2002, *Youth in Cities: a Cross-National Perspective*, Cambridge: Cambridge University Press.

Twum-Danso, Afua, 2003, *Africa: A Hostile Environment for Child Participation?*, ECPAT International Monitoring the Agenda for Action Report, Bankok: Ecpat International (End Child Prostitution, Child Pornography and Trafficking of Children for Sexual Purposes).

Zelizer, Viviana A., 2002, 'Kids and commerce', *Childhood*, Vol. 9, No. 4, pp. 375-396.

2

Chômage et conditions d'existence des jeunes de la ville de Ouagadougou

Ali Sangaré

Introduction

Selon le Bureau international du travail (BIT 2000), le chômage se définit statistiquement comme la situation d'une personne sans travail rémunéré, disponible pour occuper un emploi et effectuant une démarche de recherche d'emploi. Sont donc considérés comme chômeurs, ceux qui sont dépourvus d'emploi et qui en recherchent activement un.

Avec un taux de chômage de 1,90 pour cent en 1995, le Burkina Faso s'est retrouvé en 2004, soit 10 ans plus tard avec 18,97 pour cent (Some 2004 : 2) ; le taux du chômage étant défini comme le rapport entre le nombre de chômeurs et la population active. Ce chômage est un phénomène essentiellement urbain quel que soit le type de chômeurs considéré. Le taux de chômage dans les zones rurales ne dépasserait pas 0,5 pour cent alors qu'il serait de 11,8 pour cent en milieu urbain avec 14,3 pour cent pour les deux grandes villes de Ouagadougou et Bobo-Dioulasso, selon les données de l'Institut national de la statistique et de la démographie (INSD) en 2007. Dans la capitale, le taux de chômage concerne surtout les jeunes, car 65,3 pour cent des chômeurs ont moins de 24 ans et la plupart d'entre eux sont à la recherche d'un premier emploi.

Pour lutter contre le chômage et d'une façon générale la question de la pauvreté, l'État burkinabè a entrepris depuis la fin des années 80, de vastes réformes économiques sous les auspices des institutions de Brettons Woods, à savoir la Banque Mondiale et le FMI. Ces politiques et programmes axés essentiellement sur l'emploi, entrepris jusqu'ici, n'ont pas freiné la tendance, ni fait reculer l'ampleur de l'exclusion du monde du travail dont ces jeunes font l'objet. En dépit de quelques améliorations sporadiques de l'activité économique, le chômage augmente d'année en année et prend des proportions inquiétantes. Ce chômage est demeuré élevé notamment celui des jeunes en milieu urbain. C'est au regard de cette situation sur l'ampleur du chômage que nous avons décidé d'entreprendre des recherches sur ce phénomène dans les deux principales villes du Burkina Faso que sont Ouagadougou et Bobo-Dioulasso. La première étude qui a été effectuée à Bobo-Dioulasso nous a permis de comprendre que le chômage et la pauvreté étaient des préoccupations croissantes chez les jeunes (Sangaré 2007). Ainsi les questions principales auxquelles nous tentons de répondre sont les suivantes :

- quelles sont les caractéristiques du jeune chômeur dans la ville de Ouagadougou ?
- quelles sont les conditions d'existence du chômeur ?

Le présent texte a pour objectif de dégager les éléments susceptibles de mieux connaître le jeune chômeur de la ville de Ouagadougou. Ainsi, il s'articule autour des paramètres suivants : les profils des chômeurs qui font ressortir les caractéristiques principales des jeunes, les causes et les conséquences de ce chômage mais aussi les stratégies d'existence de ces jeunes. Cette analyse tient du fait que toute action initiée en faveur des jeunes exige la connaissance de ces paramètres qui, du reste, dépendent les uns des autres. En ce sens que les solutions aux problèmes de chômage des jeunes découlent des causes et des conséquences de ces problèmes, mais également nécessitent une bonne connaissance de ces jeunes chômeurs.

Démarche méthodologique de l'étude

La présente étude a été menée dans le cadre d'un des programmes de recherche de l'Institut des sciences des sociétés (INSS) au Centre national de la recherche scientifique et technologique (CNRST) à Ouagadougou. Elle s'appuie d'une part sur une enquête par questionnaire qui a concerné 200 jeunes en situation de chômage de la tranche d'âge 18-35 ans, toutes catégories confondues. Cette enquête a été réalisée en mai-juin 2009 et porte essentiellement sur les profils du chômeur à Ouagadougou, c'est-à-dire, son âge, sa scolarité, sa situation matrimoniale et son expérience professionnelle. Le choix de ces jeunes a été fait au niveau des lieux où on les rencontre fréquemment (« grins de thé[1] », universités, « maquis »), mais aussi dans des concessions durant les heures de travail.

D'autre part, à l'aide d'un guide d'entretien, 5 focus-groupes ont été organisés avec des jeunes, notamment au sein des « grins » de thé, mais également dans le milieu universitaire, cela afin d'apporter des informations complémentaires sur certains aspects du chômage des jeunes à Ouagadougou. La technique du focus-groupe est bien indiquée pour recueillir des informations enrichissantes sur les conditions de vie des jeunes burkinabè. Car les jeunes au Burkina Faso se retrouvent très souvent de façon formelle ou informelle et dans des cadres précis pour débattre des situations qui les concernent. Les focus-groupes ont concerné 48 jeunes (en raison de 8 à 10 jeunes par groupe) dont une majorité de jeunes garçons et de jeunes hommes. Cette importance majoritaire de garçons s'explique par le fait que les formes de regroupement de jeunes que nous avons ciblées et plus particulièrement les « grins » de thé sont souvent composées de jeunes garçons et de jeunes hommes, chômeurs ou étudiants ayant ensemble des relations d'amitié, de camaraderie, de voisinage ou de parenté. Ces groupes ont abordé les causes et les conséquences du chômage des jeunes en milieu urbain, mais aussi les conditions d'existence de ces jeunes.

L'étude est également fondée sur une revue de littérature sur les questions du chômage, de l'emploi et de la pauvreté des jeunes en milieu urbain burkinabè. Ainsi, divers documents d'institutions internationales (BIT, Banque Mondiale…), de l'administration publique burkinabè ont été consultés, sans oublier les publications scientifiques sur ce sujet. Cependant, il n'a pas été possible d'avoir une bonne connaissance de la situation du chômage au Burkina Faso (notamment les données récentes), du fait de l'inexistence d'un système d'information sur le marché du travail au Burkina Faso. Les documents consultés nous ont quand même permis, non seulement d'avoir une idée de cet état et de l'ampleur du chômage des jeunes au Burkina Faso, mais aussi de cerner les principales actions mises en œuvre par un certain nombre d'acteurs dont l'État et les municipalités pour combattre ce phénomène.

Ainsi, cette étude est à la fois de type quantitatif et qualitatif, privilégiant la recherche d'une meilleure connaissance du chômeur à Ouagadougou. Elle s'articule autour des points suivants :

- les caractéristiques du jeune chômeur ;
- les causes et les conséquences du chômage à Ouagadougou ;
- les stratégies d'existence du jeune chômeur.

Les caractéristiques des jeunes chômeurs

Statut matrimonial et chômage

Selon les résultats de l'enquête, les jeunes célibataires représentent 77 pour cent des enquêtés contre 15 pour cent de mariés et 8 pour cent de ceux qui sont divorcés ou séparés. Les célibataires qui constituent la grande majorité des enquêtés sont ainsi considérés comme les plus vulnérables sur le marché du travail en termes de chômage. Les raisons qui ont poussé le jeune à rester dans ce célibat et qui l'ont exposé au chômage sont le manque d'opportunité d'emploi et les nombreuses charges familiales. Au niveau des mariés, le nombre de femmes est plus élevé que celui des hommes (17 contre 13). Les femmes ne disposent pas d'assez de temps pour exercer des activités. Mais pour certaines femmes (3 sur 17), c'est leurs maris qui n'acceptent pas qu'elles travaillent. Ainsi, les difficultés pour concilier la vie familiale et les obligations professionnelles, de même que le comportement des maris vis-à-vis du travail féminin sont les raisons qui poussent la femme à rester à la maison afin de s'occuper des enfants et des tâches ménagères. Il faut noter que le faible niveau d'instruction des femmes qui est constaté dans le pays explique également le nombre élevé de ces jeunes au chômage.

Scolarité, âge et chômage

L'enquête montre que les jeunes non scolarisés (32,5%) sont moins nombreux au chômage par rapport à ceux qui sont scolarisés (67,5%). Cette incidence est surtout marquée dans la tranche d'âge de 15-29 ans que dans celle de 30-35 ans. Cela est certes dû au fait que les jeunes non scolarisés s'insèrent plus facilement dans le marché de travail par le biais de l'apprentissage et de la formation sur le tas, mais surtout au fait que beaucoup d'entre eux ne sont pas exigeants dans la recherche de l'emploi. Concernant les jeunes scolarisés, le nombre de jeunes ayant des niveaux primaire et secondaire (70%) est plus important que ceux qui sont au niveau supérieur (30%). Pour les chômeurs au niveau supérieur, la tendance est toujours à la recherche d'un premier emploi salarié principalement dans les secteurs public et parapublic.

Les chômeurs de la tranche d'âge 30-35 ans sont ceux qui ont perdu leur emploi à la suite d'un licenciement ou qui sont en situation de fin de contrat. Il s'agit aussi bien de jeunes lettrés, comme illettrés. Les jeunes lettrés sont de niveaux primaire et secondaire. Cette frange de population n'est pas nombreuse (20%) en situation de chômage. Cela signifie que le taux de chômage décroît avec l'âge. L'existence de chômeurs de cette tranche d'âge montre qu'à tout âge, le jeune est exposé au phénomène du chômage, surtout, lorsque l'emploi est précaire. Ainsi, la non-scolarisation, le manque d'expérience et l'instabilité de l'emploi sont des facteurs qui peuvent rendre les jeunes plus vulnérables sur le marché de travail.

Expérience professionnelle, insertion sur le marché du travail et chômage

Les jeunes qui s'insèrent pour la première fois sur le marché du travail représentent 52 pour cent des chômeurs, selon l'enquête. Ils représentent 95 pour cent des jeunes scolarisés. Le nombre de ces jeunes scolarisés est quasi égal tant aux niveaux primaire et secondaire (52%) qu'au niveau supérieur (48%). Le déséquilibre entre les aspirations de ces jeunes et les possibilités d'emploi d'une part, les conditions pour l'obtention d'un emploi, notamment l'acquisition d'une expérience professionnelle, d'autre part, expliquent en grande partie cette situation. Le retard observé dans l'obtention du premier emploi rémunéré chez les jeunes scolarisés reflète une difficulté grandissante à intégrer le marché du travail après les études.

Cependant, pour ce qui est des jeunes ayant des niveaux secondaire et supérieur, les possibilités d'emplois (stages, contrats à durée déterminée, enseignement dans le privé) qu'offrent de plus en plus les structures, réduisent énormément la durée de l'attente pour une proposition d'emploi, notamment chez les jeunes étudiants en fin de cycle. Avec le manque d'expérience professionnelle de beaucoup de jeunes étudiants, à la fin de leurs études, certaines structures se voient obligées de recruter pendant une période d'essai, des stagiaires ou des contractuels qui auront la possibilité d'être définitivement embauchés. Près de la moitié de ces jeunes scolarisés (45%) ont déjà eu des propositions d'emploi, essentiellement dans les secteurs informels et privés. D'ailleurs, ce taux est élevé (72%) au niveau de l'ensemble des enquêtes. Mais les propositions d'emplois ne signifient pas une embauche. En plus, il faut noter qu'en dehors des enseignements dans les établissements privés, les stages de formation tout comme les apprentissages non rémunérés (particulièrement pour les chômeurs ayant une formation technique et professionnelle) ne sont pas généralement rémunérés. Ces stages et ces apprentissages non rémunérés constituent tout de même une étape importante pour l'insertion professionnelle des jeunes scolarisés.

Par rapport au type d'emploi recherché, la grande partie des jeunes chômeurs scolarisés (95%) aimerait trouver un emploi qui corresponde à leur qualification. Parmi ces jeunes, près des 2/3 d'entre eux, c'est-à-dire 88 sur 135 enquêtés scolarisés recherchent en priorité un emploi salarié permanent à plein temps. Le travail salarié est principalement recherché parce qu'il est censé procurer une sécurité de l'emploi. En effet, 70 pour cent des jeunes recherchant un travail salarié mettent en avant la sécurité de l'emploi et 22 pour cent d'entre eux pensent pouvoir y gagner plus. Une grande partie de ceux qui pensent à la sécurité de l'emploi souhaiterait travailler dans des structures publiques. Tandis que ceux qui recherchent des salaires élevés espèrent surtout trouver un emploi dans des structures parapubliques ou privées ou encore dans des institutions internationales.

Un peu plus d'un tiers des chômeurs scolarisés (47 sur 135) pensent plutôt à créer leur propre entreprise. Parmi eux, certains ont déjà monté leurs projets et sont dans l'attente de leur financement. D'autres guettent des opportunités d'affaires pour s'y lancer.

Par ailleurs, les jeunes chômeurs sont nombreux (85%) à ne pas se baser uniquement sur ces emplois correspondant à leur qualification. Sur 135 chômeurs scolarisés enquêtés, 105 d'entre eux (soit près de 4/5) sont indifférents au type d'emploi recherché. Ce qui montre que pour ces jeunes, le plus important, c'est de trouver du travail. Beaucoup de ces chômeurs se déclarent être prêts à réviser à la baisse leurs prétentions salariales si la durée de chômage se prolonge.

Quant aux chômeurs non scolarisés ayant une qualification, tous disent être à la recherche d'un emploi ou de crédit pour financer leur projet d'entreprise. La plupart de ces chômeurs ont, après leur formation, déjà travaillé ; mais pour des raisons de désaccord avec l'employeur, ils ont dû abandonner ces emplois et en recherchent d'autres. C'est le cas de certains chômeurs qui ont perdu leur emploi à la suite d'un licenciement ou qui sont en situation de fin de contrat. Ceux qui n'ont aucune qualification recherchent du travail dans n'importe laquelle branche d'activité. Paradoxalement, compte tenu de leur profil de chômeurs non scolarisés et sans qualification, ils ont parfois de petits boulots, mais qui ne leur apportent pratiquement rien. Au fait, la situation de ces chômeurs est très critique, car, ayant atteint un âge assez avancé et à cause de leur profil (chômeurs non scolarisés et sans qualification), ils ont de sérieuses difficultés à décrocher un véritable emploi.

La recherche d'emploi s'effectue essentiellement à travers deux canaux : les concours (48%) et les réseaux de solidarités familiales (28%). Ils sont peu nombreux (16%) à prospecter directement auprès des employeurs ou à recourir aux annonces des médias (8%) tels que les journaux et les radios. Il faut souligner que les chômeurs non scolarisés s'appuient surtout sur les réseaux de solidarités et la prospection directe auprès des employeurs pour rechercher un emploi. Tandis que ceux qui sont diplômés ont principalement recours aux concours et aux annonces des médias comme moyen principal de recherche d'emploi.

L'enquête a également porté sur l'Agence nationale de la promotion de l'emploi (ANPE) qui est la principale structure publique d'embauche des jeunes au Burkina Faso. Interrogés sur cette agence, les jeunes, notamment les chômeurs non scolarisés ne sont que 12 pour cent, à s'y être inscrits. Plus de la moitié de ceux qui s'y sont inscrits déclarent ne pas compter sur cette agence pour avoir un emploi. C'est pourquoi, beaucoup d'entre eux disent continuer, après une inscription à l'ANPE, à rechercher du travail. Ce qui veut dire que les pouvoirs publics doivent œuvrer à rendre plus visible le rôle et l'importance de cette structure, notamment par l'information sur les opportunités de travail qu'elle offre.

Par ailleurs, l'enquête s'est intéressée aux charges qui incombent aux chômeurs. Il en ressort que les chômeurs qui sont sans enfant représentent près de la moitié de ces jeunes (44%). Ceux qui ont 1 ou 2 enfants constituent 40 pour cent de ces chômeurs contre 16 pour cent pour ceux qui en ont plus de 2. Cela signifie que plus de la moitié des jeunes chômeurs enquêtés ont à leur charge des enfants, ce qui prouve les difficultés réelles auxquelles ils sont confrontées. En outre, la plupart des enquêtés disent être pris en charge par la famille et par des parents collatéraux. Seulement 14 pour cent d'entre eux vivent de leur épargne. Ces derniers sont ceux qui ont déjà travaillé. Il s'agit de ceux qui ont de temps en temps des contrats de travail et de ceux qui étaient auparavant occupés par un emploi et qui l'ont perdu.

En résumé, l'analyse de ces données de l'enquête montre que les jeunes chômeurs ouagalais sont généralement des célibataires scolarisés, de la tranche d'âge de 15-29 ans. Ils sont de différents niveaux d'instruction: primaire, secondaire comme supérieur. Pour les chômeurs du niveau supérieur, ils sont surtout à la recherche d'un premier emploi salarié principalement dans les secteurs public et parapublic. Beaucoup de ces jeunes ont déjà exercé des activités mais sont dans l'attente d'obtenir un véritable emploi. Compte tenu de la durée du chômage, ces jeunes sont de plus en plus indifférents au type d'emploi recherché. L'enquête révèle également qu'une grande partie des jeunes chômeurs ont des charges familiales, en dépit des difficultés qu'ils rencontrent dans le chômage. Cette analyse a permis de mieux connaître le jeune chômeur ouagalais et de comprendre que ce phénomène est une préoccupation majeure, car il touche la frange la plus active mais aussi la plus vulnérable de la population. Ceci nous amène à nous interroger sur les causes de ce phénomène et ses conséquences sur la jeunesse et sur la société toute entière.

Les causes du chômage des jeunes

Il est vrai qu'il y a plusieurs manières d'expliquer les problèmes du chômage des jeunes. Il y a entre autres, la demande globale, le manque de compétence, les règlements du marché du travail, les lois de protection de l'emploi, le faible développement du secteur privé qui permettent de comprendre d'une façon générale les raisons qui sont à l'origine du chômage des jeunes.

Mais l'importance et le caractère chronique du chômage des jeunes au Burkina Faso peuvent s'expliquer à première vue par la demande globale et l'employabilité des jeunes. La demande globale se traduit par l'accroissement du nombre de diplômés qui sortent chaque année des établissements d'enseignement supérieur publics (dans les universités), privés, des écoles inter-États et également dans des nombreux lycées et collèges disséminés dans tout le pays. Cette demande demeure très élevée par rapport à l'offre d'emploi dans les différentes branches d'activités économiques. Les postes à pourvoir au niveau national sont largement en dessous du nombre d'offreurs de travail. Selon des données du Ministère de la fonction publique et de la réforme de l'État (MFPRE), citées par Seglaro Somé (2004 : 13), de 4,77 pour cent en 1995, le taux d'emploi est passé à 3,92 pour cent en 2004. Cette situation fait que chaque année, le nombre de demandeurs de travail s'accroît de plus en plus. Quant à l'employabilité des jeunes, elle se rapporte aux types de compétences et d'attributs qui peuvent faciliter l'insertion dans le marché du travail. Elle inclut le niveau et la qualité de l'instruction et de la formation d'un individu. Il est évident que, pour trouver des solutions au chômage des jeunes, il faut pouvoir déterminer l'importance relative de ces différents facteurs. Des informations issues de l'analyse documentaire et des focus-groupes, nous pouvons dégager les différentes raisons qui sont à l'origine du chômage des jeunes : le manque d'expérience professionnelle, l'inadéquation entre la qualification des demandeurs d'emploi et les besoins des employeurs, le faible taux de scolarisation, le manque de dynamisme.

Manque d'expérience professionnelle

Le marché du travail est de plus en plus exigeant, de sorte que les employeurs préfèrent les demandeurs d'emplois qui possèdent une expérience professionnelle dans des domaines bien précis pour pouvoir bénéficier d'économies de formation. Les jeunes ne possèdent pas ces qualifications requises pour postuler à un emploi, en dehors de celles acquises dans les établissements secondaires d'enseignement général et dans les universités. Au sein de tous les groupes de discussion, cette question d'expérience est ressortie comme la grande barrière pour décrocher un premier emploi. L'acquisition d'une expérience professionnelle est considérée comme la principale cause du chômage des jeunes. Un diplômé en droit explique ceci :

> J'ai déposé des dossiers d'embauche à divers services il y a 2 ans ; à chaque fois, on me dit que je manque d'expérience. Or, pour avoir de l'expérience, il faut travailler. Même pour décrocher un stage, c'est difficile. Tous les ans, je me présente aux concours, mais ça ne marche pas. Nombreux sont ceux qui passent par du copinage, des relations pour obtenir du travail. C'est sincèrement très difficile.

Comme réponse à cette question d'expérience professionnelle, des étudiants proposent d'une part, que des volets « stages » en fin de cycle soient intégrés dans tous les programmes universitaires afin d'initier les étudiants à la vie professionnelle. D'autre part, ils voudraient que les pouvoirs publics adoptent des lois pour imposer aux services d'intégrer des périodes d'essai ou de formation (3 à 4 mois par exemple) dès l'embauche. La grande majorité des jeunes diplômés pensent que le manque d'expérience est le nœud du problème du chômage parce qu'il limite sérieusement leurs chances sur le marché du travail.

Inadéquation entre la qualification des demandeurs d'emploi et les besoins des employeurs

Une grande partie des structures de formation des jeunes ne sont pas orientées vers la professionnalisation, dans le sens de l'adaptation des modules d'enseignement aux besoins des employeurs. À ce sujet, plusieurs jeunes au niveau des focus-groupes tiennent des propos similaires. Selon eux, l'État est responsable de leur situation :

> Si des formations ne sont pas adaptées au marché de l'emploi, pourquoi ne pas les supprimer ? C'est un faux problème. Ces politiciens nous proposent du travail à la veille des élections, ils vous lâchent dès qu'ils sont élus. Ceux qui ont pu décrocher un emploi avec eux sont généralement leurs propres parents », raconte l'un d'entre eux.

Mais il faut noter que ces dernières années, plusieurs structures d'enseignement s'orientent de plus en plus vers l'enseignement technique et professionnel. C'est le cas de certaines structures d'enseignement public et privé et surtout de l'université de Ouagadougou dont la refondation a eu lieu en 2000. Aussi depuis 2009, des réflexions sont en cours dans la plupart des établissements d'enseignement supérieur public et privé, afin de les intégrer dans le système LMD (licence-master-doctorat) qui est plus orienté vers la professionnalisation. Par ailleurs, des jeunes diplômés se sont prononcés sur la formation technique et professionnelle dans les établissements d'enseignement privé. Ils voudraient bien se former dans ces écoles, mais n'en ont pas les moyens nécessaires. C'est ainsi que l'on pouvait entendre les propos suivants : « ces écoles coûtent très cher », « pour accéder à ces écoles, il faut débourser 500 000 F CFA minimum par an, pour au moins 2 ans de formation ; où pouvons-nous trouver cet argent ? », « on peut opter pour la formation technique ; mais après la formation, il faut créer son entreprise. C'est la croix et la bannière pour avoir un crédit ».

Le problème de l'accès aux crédits pour financer des projets est également l'une des causes du chômage des jeunes. En effet, les structures d'appui à la création des entreprises ont une capacité d'intervention encore limitée face à l'immensité des besoins de financement exprimés par les jeunes promoteurs. Il convient également de souligner que les conditionnalités d'octroi de crédits de financement imposent des exigences, notamment en matière de garanties qui sont inadaptées aux moyens propres d'un grand nombre de jeunes. Un étudiant raconte à ce propos :

> Ce n'est pas la peine d'aller vers les structures de crédits pour chercher à avoir un prêt. Je connais beaucoup d'étudiants en fin de cycle qui ont tenté leur chance à ce niveau mais on leur a demandé tellement de choses comme garantie qu'ils ont fini par abandonner.

D'autres jeunes disent connaître des bénéficiaires de ces crédits qui ne sont pas arrivés à gérer correctement les fonds octroyés et qui, en fin de compte, se sont retrouvés à les rembourser durant des années. Au sujet de ces crédits, beaucoup de jeunes, notamment les étudiants, estiment que l'État doit initier de façon régulière des sessions de formation en entreprenariat et mettre en place des structures de conseil et de suivi des bénéficiaires de crédits. Cela, afin que les jeunes réussissent le démarrage de leurs projets et qu'ils puissent ainsi rembourser les crédits qui leur ont été accordés. Il s'agit donc de mettre en place une véritable politique d'accompagnement des jeunes.

Faible taux de scolarisation

Les effectifs et les taux de scolarisation sont très faibles en dépit des efforts de l'État. En effet, selon des études menées par Kobiane J.F. (2007), dans ce domaine, moins de 40 pour cent des enfants burkinabè ont franchi les portes de l'école primaire en 2004. Aussi, la plupart des jeunes sans qualification et des diplômés issus du système éducatif en milieu rural ne sont plus satisfaits du mode de vie en campagne. Ils deviennent des candidats aux emplois dans les centres urbains où les offres d'emplois sont de plus en plus limitées et sélectives. À ce sujet, au sein d'un des focus-groupes, un jeune migrant arrivé sans qualification de son village il y a 14 mois explique sa situation à Ouagadougou :

> J'ai fait 6 mois de formation en menuiserie et en soudure ; après, j'ai travaillé avec quelqu'un qui ne me payait pas, j'ai décidé de partir. Depuis lors, je cherche du travail mais en vain. Si j'ai l'occasion d'aller en Europe ou aux États-Unis, j'irai tenter ma chance là-bas.

Il est vrai que la scolarisation des jeunes nécessite de gros moyens financiers, mais ce problème pourrait être comblé par des programmes de développement qui viseraient à former sur le tas les jeunes sans qualification. Des directions de formation professionnelle existent certes, mais elles ne disposent pas d'assez de moyens pour organiser des formations à grande échelle pour les jeunes. D'ailleurs, ces directions sont très peu connues du public. Pour apprendre des métiers, les jeunes sans qualification prospectent généralement auprès de réseaux de parents et d'amis. Ce qui conduit souvent à des situations d'exploitation. Car, le plus souvent, ils sont exposés quotidiennement à des risques divers, étant donné qu'ils travaillent sans aucune mesure de protection sociale et suivant un volume horaire journalier important.

Manque de dynamisme

Certains jeunes se laissent aller à la facilité et recherche le gain facile. La plupart d'entre eux ont du mal à obtenir un emploi, surtout avec ce marché du travail exigeant. Dans de nombreux cas, il s'agit des jeunes chômeurs sans qualification. Mais on trouve aussi dans cette catégorie de jeunes, des diplômés qui ne cherchent que des emplois correspondant à leur qualification. Ces jeunes qui ont choisi la facilité sont souvent dans un état de mendiants, à la charge de leurs parents ou dans la rue. Beaucoup de jeunes rencontrés dans les groupes de discussion ont abordé ce manque de dynamisme de certains chômeurs. Selon eux, certains jeunes sont naturellement partisans du moindre effort. Mais pour d'autres, cet état de faits est plutôt une des conséquences d'un chômage de longue durée. Ainsi, découragés et désespérés, ces jeunes se laissent aller dans une telle situation.

En plus, il y a ceux qui évoquent des cas de sorcellerie pour justifier leur situation de chômage. En effet, il ressort de certains focus-groupes que des personnes, généralement âgées, cherchent à nuire aux jeunes qui commencent à réussir, notamment pour des raisons de jalousie. Ceux qui tiennent de tels propos disent avoir été victimes ou témoins de telles situations. Ainsi, l'on pouvait entendre dire que « la sorcellerie existe toujours dans nos villages », « je me donne pour réussir, mais je n'y arrive pas, je pense donc que c'est le fait de la sorcellerie », « nous sommes victimes de notre temps où les pratiques de sorcellerie sont encore vivaces ». La catégorie de jeunes qui avance ces propos est surtout celle dont les parents résident au village. C'est donc dire que ce phénomène de sorcellerie au Burkina Faso mérite d'être étudié et compris.

Les conséquences du chômage des jeunes

Quelle qu'en soit la cause, le chômage des jeunes entraîne des conséquences graves, surtout lorsque le chômeur reste longtemps sans travailler ou s'il se retrouve au chômage plusieurs fois de suite. La durée du chômage tend à être plus courte dans le cas des jeunes travailleurs que dans celui de travailleurs plus âgés. La différence n'est cependant pas très grande. Plus un travailleur reste au chômage longtemps, plus il lui est difficile de retrouver un emploi car il perd ses qualifications professionnelles, le moral, et son équilibre psychologique sont atteints. Le chômage des jeunes peut conduire à un certain nombre de problèmes qui agissent aussi bien sur le chômeur lui-même que sur sa famille et la société toute entière. Les conséquences du chômage des jeunes selon les propos des enquêtés sont l'expatriation des jeunes, la dévalorisation des diplômes, la déviance sociale, le poids du chômage des jeunes sur la famille.

Expatriation des jeunes

La plupart des jeunes ruraux qui ont migré en ville à la recherche d'emplois et les diplômés, vont travailler ailleurs en Afrique ou dans les pays développés, dès qu'ils en ont l'occasion. Bien que les conditions d'accueil ne soient plus favorables comme avant, ces jeunes sont toujours tentés de migrer. Certains jeunes qui étudient à l'étranger préfèrent y rester au lieu de revenir servir leur patrie. Cette question de départ des jeunes à l'étranger a été largement débattue au sein des groupes de discussion. La majeure partie des jeunes de ces groupes raconte que l'expatriation est la solution au problème de chômage des jeunes, faute de mieux et se présente donc comme un pis-aller. Les jeunes non scolarisés sont plus prêts à partir que les jeunes scolarisés qui manifestent de la réticence. Un jeune non scolarisé disait ceci : « cela fait la 3ᵉ année que je chôme alors que j'ai ma femme et mes 2 enfants à nourrir. Dès que j'ai l'occasion de partir, je partirai, et étant à l'étranger, je pourrai autrement servir mon pays ».

Dévalorisation des diplômes

En raison du nombre très limité des emplois offerts sur le marché du travail, les jeunes diplômés dévalorisent leurs diplômes pour pouvoir accéder à un emploi. Ainsi, on peut trouver des diplômés nantis du Baccalauréat et du Brevet d'études du premier cycle (BEPC) se présenter aux mêmes tests de recrutement ou concours. En faisant cas de ce problème de dévalorisation des diplômes, plusieurs jeunes scolarisés estiment que c'est une perte pour ceux qui sont dans cette situation, mais surtout pour l'État qui investit pour assurer la formation des titulaires de ces diplômes. Au sein de tous les groupes de discussion, on rencontre des jeunes diplômés qui ont vécu ces situations. L'un d'eux rapporte ceci :

> Avec ma licence en sciences économiques, j'ai fait plusieurs fois des concours de la fonction publique où c'est le BEPC qui est demandé, et parfois même le Certificat d'étude primaire (CEP) : le concours de la police ou de la douane par exemple. Et toujours, ça ne marche pas.

La dévalorisation des diplômes est un problème réel au Burkina Faso. Pour s'insérer dans la vie professionnelle, beaucoup de jeunes diplômés notamment dans certaines disciplines des sciences sociales (comme la sociologie, la psychologie, la démographie) qui ne sont pas enseignées au niveau du secondaire, sont confrontés à ces situations. Non seulement ils ne peuvent pas poursuivre leurs études faute de moyens, mais également, ils ne sont pas en mesure d'exercer de petits boulots tels que des enseignements à domicile, des prestations de services à des particuliers. Ils sont obligés de dévaloriser leurs diplômes pour accéder à des concours de la fonction publique. Cependant, avec les ONG et les projets de développement, les plus chanceux arrivent à décrocher des emplois. Mais il faut noter que c'est au niveau des ONG et des projets que les recrutements sont plus rigoureux car l'accent est mis sur la maîtrise des postes à pourvoir et sur l'expérience professionnelle du demandeur d'emploi.

Déviance sociale

Il existe un lien certain entre le chômage des jeunes et certains problèmes sociaux graves tels que le banditisme, la toxicomanie, l'oisiveté et la délinquance. Le chômage, s'il perdure, pousse les jeunes désespérés à la déviance sociale et à des comportements néfastes à leur santé. Dans les grands centres urbains du Burkina Faso, face à la montée de ces phénomènes, et plus particulièrement le banditisme et la prostitution, les parlementaires se sont penchés sur ces questions afin d'y apporter une réponse. En évoquant cette question de déviance, plusieurs jeunes au sein des groupes de discussion affirment qu'elle est une réalité. Pour ces jeunes, si le chômage perdure, cela peut pousser le jeune à la perte de l'estime et à l'adoption de comportements déviants. Un enquêté désespéré raconte : « quand je vois que ma situation se dégrade d'année en année, avec toutes les charges que j'ai, il m'arrive d'avoir envie de me lancer dans des activités illicites ».

Poids du chômage des jeunes sur la famille

Les jeunes au chômage, s'ils ne sont pas dans la rue, sont contraints de vivre avec les parents qui, malgré leur faible revenu, doivent les prendre en charge. Le manque d'opportunité de travail allonge cette période de dépendance économique vis-à-vis des parents et du reste, retarde le mariage ainsi que l'accès du jeune au logement. L'incapacité de certaines familles à remplir ces fonctions de soutien et de protection des jeunes est source de conflits, d'incompréhension et de tension avec les parents. Le poids du chômage des jeunes sur la famille a été partout soulevé dans les focus-groupes. Beaucoup de jeunes chômeurs ont raconté leur propre situation. C'est ainsi que l'on pouvait entendre certains d'entre eux dire ceci : « ma conjointe m'a abandonné », « mes parents me traitent de paresseux », « je sors de la maison, toujours les matins de bonheur et je rentre tard dans la soirée ».

Les conditions d'existence des jeunes chômeurs

Les jeunes chômeurs adoptent des stratégies alternatives endogènes pour faire face à leur situation. Par rapport à ces stratégies, les avis recueillis dans les groupes de discussion et les données de l'enquête par questionnaire sont quasi similaires. Chaque catégorie de jeunes développe sa propre stratégie d'insertion dans la ville.

Dans le domaine de l'emploi, les données collectées révèlent qu'une partie des jeunes urbains scolarisés, et plus particulièrement les étudiants, dispense des cours à domicile à des élèves ayant des difficultés dans certaines matières précises. Les étudiants dans les matières techniques ou scientifiques comme les maths, la physique et la chimie sont plus nombreux à dispenser ces cours par rapport aux étudiants des sciences sociales. Plusieurs étudiants expliquent que ces revenus sont très insignifiants mais peuvent satisfaire quelques besoins vitaux. Ils s'établissent entre 20 000 et 45 000 F CFA / mois. D'autres jeunes scolarisés ou qui ont déjà travaillé, ont créé des associations informelles. Ou bien, ils se retrouvent pour passer le temps ensemble en échangeant souvent sur des problèmes qui les concernent. Ces regroupements de jeunes se font également à partir des relations de voisinage ou de parenté. C'est ainsi qu'ils parviennent quelquefois, par les échanges, à monter ensemble des projets d'entreprise.

Les jeunes urbains déscolarisés et non instruits s'orientent très vite vers l'apprentissage de métiers ou trouvent une occupation dans le secteur informel. Face à l'essoufflement de l'économie nationale, ce secteur informel constitue un refuge et un rempart contre la marginalisation d'un grand nombre de jeunes. Cependant, ceux qui se replient vers le secteur informel exercent souvent des activités considérées comme vulnérables et précaires et ne leur procurent que des revenus très modestes. Ainsi, il ne s'agit pas ici des activités illicites ou illégales succeptibles de favoriser le profit et l'accumulation de capital, exercées dans un but d'évasion fiscale ou en marge de la législation, mais d'activités de survie qui procurent des gains mais immédiats. Selon les jeunes enquêtés concernés, ces emplois sont occasionnels ou saisonniers. Il s'agit des emplois de ramassage de sable pendant la saison pluvieuse, de garde d'engins à deux roues ou à quatre roues, de vente de journaux ou de crédit téléphonique minimes, de cigarette, de cola, etc. Le financement de ces initiatives reste souvent très lié au réseau familial, et de ce fait assez minime. Ces jeunes qui font preuve de débrouillardise sont plutôt dans une situation de « marginalité active ».

Une autre catégorie de jeunes qui regroupe aussi bien les scolarisés, les déscolarisés et les non instruits affirment de temps en temps aider leurs parents dans leurs activités. Il s'agit là d'activités commerciales ou artisanales dans le secteur informel. Tous les jeunes enquêtés de cette catégorie, filles comme garçons, travaillent avec leurs parents qui, non seulement les forment, mais aussi les aident financièrement. C'est dans ce cadre d'ailleurs, que beaucoup de jeunes embrassent la carrière empruntée par leurs parents. Mais la plupart de ces jeunes pensent abandonner ces activités dès qu'ils trouvent un emploi qui correspond à leurs profils. Par ailleurs, les jeunes filles qui ont participé aux groupes de discussion sont, pour la plupart, scolarisées. En dehors de celles qui aident leurs parents dans leurs activités, aucune n'est occupée par un emploi. Cependant, la question de la prostitution a été évoquée par un certain nombre d'entre elles. En effet, elles avouent qu'elles sont nombreuses à se sentir obligées de se livrer à la prostitution avec le chômage qui perdure. De nombreux cas de prostitution ont été soulevés par ces filles qui disent avoir connu des étudiantes qui s'adonnent à ce métier, non pas par plaisir, mais pour pouvoir assouvir leurs besoins. Elles expliquent que généralement les filles qui s'adonnent à la prostitution n'en font pas un métier. C'est pourquoi, ces filles guettent la période des fins de mois (période de paiement des salaires) ou se dirigent vers des clients censés être riches (les expatriés par exemple) pour se prostituer. C'est ainsi que pour elles, plusieurs étudiantes cherchent à sortir avec des hommes riches pour leur argent ou pour qu'ils les aident à trouver un emploi. Certaines filles n'ont pas écarté cette hypothèse en ce qui les concerne, si l'occasion se présentait à elles.

Par ailleurs, ce qui est perceptible, lorsqu'on aborde la question de la prostitution, c'est la réticence des filles. Si elles ne s'adonnent pas à la prostitution, elles reconnaissent que ce phénomène est réel dans leur milieu, notamment en ce qui concerne celles qui ont des niveaux d'instruction élevés et qui sont au chômage.

Conclusion

La présente analyse avait pour objectif de mieux connaître le jeune chômeur de la ville de Ouagadougou. Ainsi, l'on peut retenir de cette analyse qui précède que les jeunes chômeurs ouagalais sont généralement des célibataires de la tranche d'âge de 15-29 ans, ayant des charges familiales. Ils sont de tous les niveaux d'instruction. Les jeunes non instruits s'insèrent plus facilement sur le marché de travail, surtout par le biais de l'apprentissage et la formation sur le tas, que les autres jeunes. Mais ces derniers ont la chance d'exercer des activités mais sont dans l'attente d'obtenir un véritable premier emploi principalement dans la fonction publique. Compte tenu de la durée du chômage, ces jeunes sont de plus en plus indifférents au type d'emploi recherché. Ils adoptent souvent des stratégies alternatives endogènes afin de faire face aux problèmes auxquels ils sont confrontés. Il s'agit des activités exercées temporairement pour subvenir au minimum vital qui leur fait défaut.

Il ressort aussi de cette analyse que les jeunes de la ville de Ouagadougou sont très exposés au chômage dont les causes sont multiples et sont souvent attribuées à plusieurs facteurs. Au nombre de ces facteurs, il y a surtout l'accroissement du nombre de demandeurs et l'employabilité des jeunes qui contribuent à exacerber la crise économique. Pour ce qui est des causes évoquées par les jeunes, la plus importante, selon eux, est le manque d'expérience professionnelle. Les enquêtés semblent d'ailleurs apporter des éléments nouveaux par rapport à la vision des pouvoirs publics des causes du chômage des jeunes. En effet, pour remédier à ce problème du chômage des jeunes, les stratégies mises en œuvre par les pouvoirs publics portent essentiellement sur le renforcement de la scolarisation des jeunes et l'adéquation de leur formation à l'emploi notamment dans les structures d'enseignement supérieur. Les résultats de la présente étude indiquent qu'une importance capitale doit être accordée à la question de l'expérience professionnelle, mais en accompagnant les jeunes dans la recherche de leur premier emploi.

Cette étude démontre également que le chômage a des conséquences sérieuses sur la vie des chômeurs. La vulnérabilité des jeunes les pousse à l'appauvrissement, à la perte de l'estime, à des sentiments de frustration par rapport à leur situation et au rejet de cette frustration sur les parents et sur la société entière.

L'enquête qui a été réalisée traduit non seulement un sentiment de marginalisation et d'exclusion du marché du travail, mais également un sentiment de désespoir des jeunes. La situation alarmante de cette jeunesse urbaine, qui représente la frange la plus active mais aussi la plus vulnérable de la population, contribue à aggraver la crise sociale urbaine que connaît la ville de Ouagadougou. C'est donc dire que le chômage des jeunes constitue l'un des phénomènes les plus aigus auxquels le pays est confronté. Dans cette perspective, l'on peut dire que la problématique du chômage liée à la lutte contre la pauvreté est une question d'une telle importance qu'elle nécessite des réflexions approfondies mais aussi des actions concertées en vue d'y apporter une réponse adéquate.

Note
1. Les « grins de thé » sont des formes de regroupement, des réseaux de sociabilité de jeunes qui se retrouvent souvent autour d'un thé pour échanger sur des questions d'actualité et de ce qui les concerne.

Références

Bureau International du Travail, 2000, *Les jeunes au travail : promouvoir la croissance de l'emploi*, Symposium interrégional sur les stratégies à adopter pour lutter contre la marginalisation et le chômage des jeunes, 13-14 décembre 1999, 1re édition 2000, Genève, BIT.

Institut National de la Statistique et de la Demographie, 2003, *L'emploi, le chômage et les conditions d'activité dans l'agglomération de Ouagadougou*, Burkina Faso.

Institut National de la Statistique et de la Demographie, 2007, *Résultats préliminaires*, Ministère de l'Économie et du Développement, Bureau Central du recensement, Burkina Faso.

Institut pour la Recherche et le Développement, 1997, *Actes du Séminaire « Jeunes, Ville, Emploi », bilan et perspectives*, tenu du 27 au 29 février 1997 à Ouagadougou, Burkina Faso.

Godfrey, Kanyenze, Mhone, Guy C. Z., et Sparreboom, Theo, 2000, *Strategies to combat youth unemployment and marginalization in Anglophone Africa*. OIT/SAMAT document de réflexion n°14 Harare.

Kobiane, Jean François, 2007, « Ethnies, genre et scolarisation au Burkina Faso », *Les Cahiers de l'INED*, collection dirigée par ROHRBASSER J.-M., Paris, p. 221-237.

Lachaud, Jean Pierre, 2003, *Pauvreté et inégalité au Burkina Faso : Profil et dynamique*, septembre 2003, version 1.0, PNUD, INSD.

Ministère de l'Emploi, du Travail et de la Jeunesse, 2004, *Emploi et pauvreté au Burkina Faso*.

Ministère de la Jeunesse et de l'Emploi, 2006, Rapport sur les besoins des utilisateurs potentiels des produits de l'Observatoire national de l'emploi et de la formation professionnelle (ONEF), étude conduite par Yaméogo C.R. et Koalaga-Onadja E.

Ministère de la Jeunesse et de l'Emploi, 2008, *Politique nationale de l'emploi*, Burkina Faso.

Sangaré, Ali, 2006, « Le travail des enfants en milieu urbain. Étude de cas de l'agglomération de Ouagadougou », *Les Cahiers du CERLESHS* n°25, Ouagadougou, Presses universitaires de l'Université de Ouagadougou, p. 273-302.

Sangaré Ali, 2007, Résultats partiels d'une enquête sur les jeunes de Bobo-Dioulasso », *Sidwaya*, n°5807 du 24 janvier 2007, p. 14-15.

Sie Tioye, Antoine-Marie, et al., 2004, *Études sur les expériences du Burkina Faso dans le domaine de la promotion de l'emploi de 1960 à nos jours*, juillet 2004, Ministère de l'économie et du développement du Burkina Faso.

Sévédé-Bardem, Isabelle, 2007, *Précarités juvéniles en milieu urbain africain. Aujourd'hui, chacun se cherche*, Paris, L'Harmattan.

Somé Seglaro, Abel, 2004, *Le marché de l'emploi au Burkina Faso*, série Document de travail, D-T, CAPES, n°2004-18.

3

Familles en survie dans un espace défavorisé à Ouagadougou

Marie-Thérèse Arcens Somé

Introduction

Le Burkina Faso est un pays d'Afrique de l'Ouest, carrefour d'échanges dans la sous-région, pays de transit entre les pays sahéliens (Mali et Niger) et les pays côtiers (Ghana, Togo, Bénin, Côte d'Ivoire).

Aujourd'hui, la commune de Ouagadougou dépasse le million d'habitants (INSD 2007 : 24). À la faveur de la politique de décentralisation (à partir de 1992), la commune de Ouagadougou a été scindée administrativement en 5 arrondissements dans lesquels se répartissent une trentaine de secteurs. L'arrondissement de Boulmiougou (un des arrondissements de Ouagadougou) est administré par un maire et un conseil municipal, élu pour 5 ans.

Le terrain d'étude est le secteur 19 situé en périphérie sud-ouest de la ville de Ouagadougou, dans l'arrondissement de Boulmiougou. La population du secteur est estimée en 2006 à 44 827 habitants dont 21 759 femmes et 23 068 hommes (INSD 2007 : 24).

Le concept « droit à la ville »[1] fait ressortir le droit pour les différents acteurs sociaux d'accéder à l'existant. Pour mettre en pratique ce droit, il faut avoir la capacité de le revendiquer, de s'identifier à un espace donné, de s'organiser et de faire valoir sa place dans la société. Le « droit à la ville » renvoie à la dynamique sociale, à la conscientisation, l'acquisition de capacités et de responsabilisation, dans la transformation de son espace de vie.

Des enfants naissent et grandissent en marge de la ville organisée. Beaucoup parmi eux ont perdu leurs repères familiaux et culturels. Le chômage chronique du chef de famille entraîne bien fréquemment une grande misère et affecte directement les enfants (Marguerat 2003 : 7). D'autres causes comme la séparation des parents, la violence intra conjugale sont autant de facteurs de plus en plus fréquents dans les familles urbaines. Elles déstabilisent l'enfant et le jettent dans les rues des villes (Marguerat 2003 : 7).

Le secteur 19 n'est pas épargné par ce phénomène. Certains enfants très jeunes ne vivent pas avec leurs parents biologiques pour diverses raisons : divorces, enfants confiés, orphelins. Les parents qui en ont la responsabilité privilégient leurs propres enfants et cela aboutit souvent à la maltraitance, à l'exploitation domestique, aux abus sexuels, à l'indifférence amenant une carence affective pour l'enfant (ADLV/B 2007). La rupture partielle ou totale avec sa communauté villageoise a pour conséquence une carence éducative dans le domaine de la socialisation. Les valeurs traditionnelles qui sont inculquées à travers les rites culturels ne se transmettent plus que partiellement. Sans transmission de valeurs et en échec scolaire, certains enfants grandissent sans véritables repères. Les seules issues qu'ils jugent valables sont les voies de la facilité conduisant à la petite délinquance, pour satisfaire leurs besoins élémentaires.

L'une des plus graves difficultés réside dans l'interruption de la scolarisation chez les enfants en bas âge (niveau primaire). Elle génère un sentiment précoce d'exclusion et un désœuvrement dont les conséquences sont les dérapages dans la délinquance juvénile. Selon Tanon Fabienne (2003), les enfants à Abidjan se retrouvent déscolarisés pour quatre raisons essentielles : la peur de l'enseignant, les travaux domestiques, la pauvreté des parents ou le décès du soutien de famille. À Ouagadougou, selon la perception des enfants, les enfants scolarisés représentent la norme et ceux non scolarisés l'exception (Baux 2007). L'analphabétisme devient un facteur de marginalisation, car il empêche de comprendre la règle sociale, particulièrement en milieu urbain.

Au secteur 19, les enfants et les adolescents sont souvent livrés à eux-mêmes, car le père et la mère sont chacun à la recherche de moyens de subsistance. Ils font différentes expériences dans leur quartier, comme la cigarette, la drogue, la prostitution, loin du regard des adultes censés les protéger.

Cette étude a pour objet d'analyser la dimension de la négociation des moyens d'existence chez les enfants et les adolescents vivant dans un espace urbain défavorisé. Après avoir présenté l'espace de vie précaire dans lequel vivent les familles du secteur 19, nous proposerons une analyse des opportunités qui s'offrent à elles, à travers des interrelations, ainsi que les moyens de subsistance qu'elles utilisent pour survivre et permettre à leurs enfants de se construire un avenir.

Dans cette optique, nous posons les questions suivantes : quels sont les moyens qu'utilisent les familles pauvres pour survivre, sans compétences professionnelles en milieu urbain ? Quels rôles jouent les enfants dans la survie de leur famille ? Quelles sont les opportunités qui leur sont offertes et par qui ?

À partir de ce questionnement, nous voulons montrer dans notre analyse que, malgré les grandes difficultés qui se présentent aux familles résidant dans des espaces urbains défavorisés de la ville de Ouagadougou, un certain nombre d'opportunités leur permet de survivre et de scolariser leurs enfants. Les difficultés de la vie quotidienne poussent les adultes à créer des réseaux de solidarité pour s'ouvrir des perspectives d'avenir meilleur pour eux et aussi pour leurs enfants.

Démarche méthodologique de l'étude

Les résultats d'enquête ont été obtenus à partir de différentes sources : des sources documentaires et des sources d'investigation directe. Trois études ont été exploitées, réalisées par une association dénommée Dunia la vie/ Burkina (ADLVB) entre 2005 et 2008. Elles retracent les enquêtes menées sur un échantillon de 140 familles et 165 enfants et la centaine d'associations que compte le secteur. Les enquêtes ont concerné la vie des enfants en famille, la précarité des parents et la recherche des moyens de subsistance, ainsi que la vie scolaire.

Entre janvier 2008 et novembre 2009, nous avons mené une série d'entretiens de type qualitatif. Nous avons dans un premier temps approché quatre responsables communaux afin de mieux cerner les contours de la zone d'étude. Lors d'une série d'entretiens servant de prétests menée en 2008 et début 2009, nous avons eu des entretiens avec trois structures associatives, cinq femmes et un groupe de cinq enfants sous forme de focus groupe. En 2009, nous avons repris les entretiens après avoir revisité les guides d'entretiens. D'octobre à novembre 2009, nous avons eu des entretiens avec 20 enfants et adolescents scolarisés et trois femmes, au sein de la structure associative Dunia La vie/ Burkina. Parmi ces 20 enfants et adolescents, une jeune fille avait 22 ans et était inscrite en classe de 3ᵉ.

L'objectif de ces entretiens, menés sous forme de récit de vie, était de mettre en exergue, l'évolution sociale et les difficultés rencontrées par des hommes, des femmes et des enfants, dans leur quête quotidienne de bien-être. Parmi les enfants et adolescents, 13 sont au primaire et leur âge varie entre 9 et 15 ans. Les sept autres sont inscrits au collège municipal de Boulmiougou ou dans des lycées privés.

Neuf filles et onze garçons ont participé aux entretiens. Les enfants du primaire ont eu plus de mal à s'exprimer en français, ce qui nous a poussé à discuter dans deux langues, le français et le mooré (la langue locale la plus parlée dans la ville de Ouagadougou). Par contre, les enfants du collège se sont sentis plus à l'aise dans l'expression orale. Les entretiens avec les enfants se sont déroulés dans l'enceinte de l'association Dunia La vie/Burkina (ADLV), qui a ouvert une bibliothèque et un centre d'étude encadré par des étudiants, pour pallier l'incapacité des parents à acheter des livres scolaires et à suivre leurs enfants dans les études.

Organiser une vie de famille

Cadre conceptuel

L'urbanisation exprime, à travers la prolifération du tissu urbain, la concentration croissante des populations et des activités sur un espace limité. Elle est un accès à la modernité, en ouvrant la voie au processus de transformation sociale et politique, impliquant plusieurs générations et plusieurs cultures (Arnaud 1993). L'accession à la propriété est une des caractéristiques les plus essentielles à l'intégration urbaine, et la désintégration sociale permet une appropriation plus rapide de la culture urbaine.

Le périurbain se présente comme un espace en perpétuelle évolution (Golaz et Dupont 2004), situé à l'extérieur de l'agglomération urbaine existante, et dans laquelle des changements socioéconomiques prennent place. Selon la définition qu'en fait Jargowsky P. (cité par Golaz et Dupont 2004),

> Les zones périurbaines sont celles qui ont été récemment transformées ou sont en train d'être transformées, de localités repliées sur elles-mêmes en localités qui existent dans une relation continue mais subordonnée à une ville centre importante.

Le secteur 19 de Ouagadougou est situé hors de la ville centre, en milieu périurbain Il se présente comme un espace relié mais en marge de la ville de Ouagadougou. Il se caractérise par une transformation de sa population et une évolution de sa dynamique sociale. En effet, le secteur est constitué en partie d'une population ancienne, du côté de Noosin, ayant construit un habitat en matériaux solides. Dans sa deuxième partie qui vient d'être lotie, la population est mobile, changeante. L'espace est faiblement construit et demeure dans une précarité évolutive.

La notion de « défavorisé » implique un habitat peu dense manquant de structuration et une insuffisance d'infrastructures collectives. Le quartier de Noosin a été loti et aménagé à partir de 1986, à la faveur du programme d'urbanisation mis, en œuvre par le pouvoir révolutionnaire de 1983. Cette partie du secteur est communément appelée Noosin, mais comprend un autre quartier qui s'appelle Nogomikma (ADLVB 2005). Un second lotissement a été réalisé en 1999 et les bénéficiaires ont commencé à construire leur habitat en 2002. Cette partie est communément appelée Rimkieta mais comprend les quartiers de Nonghin, Sogpelcé, Taonsogo, Komdianoré et Nabitinga. Ce sont en fait des sous quartiers de villages proches qui ont été rattachés au secteur 19. À l'heure actuelle, le quartier de Noosin qui est la partie la plus urbanisée du secteur, ne compte aucune route goudronnée, pas de caniveau et aucun poteau électrique.

Conditions de vie des ménages

Sur 140 familles de l'échantillon d'enquête de l'ADLV/B, le lotissement communal a permis à 123 d'entre elles de devenir propriétaires, alors que neuf sont restés en location et huit familles habitent un logement appartenant à un proche. Seulement,

51 familles ont réussi à construire leur maison en matériaux définitifs. 72 familles ont construit en matériaux précaires (argile). 42 domiciles n'ont pas de clôture. Rimkieta n'a pas encore accès à l'électricité et les familles s'éclairent à la lampe à pétrole.

À Noosin, un certain nombre de ménages n'a pas accès non plus à l'électrification. Bien que les ménages du secteur aient bénéficié d'une campagne d'adduction en eau courante, 83 ménages de l'échantillon n'ont pas de robinet privé, par manque de ressources financières.

Le lotissement de Rimkieta en 1999 a consisté à ouvrir des voies en terre et créer des parcelles pour la construction d'habitation. La parcelle revient à environ 30 000 F CFA par famille[2]. Chaque famille a droit à un espace compris entre 150 à 250 m², selon sa capacité financière. Dans d'autres espaces périphériques de la capitale, les parcelles sont vendues entre 2 500 et 5 000 F CFA le mètre carré. Le secteur 19 est un espace d'habitation de bas standing, dépourvu d'infrastructures d'assainissement et d'équipements collectifs dans le domaine socioéducatif. Les populations de Rimkieta accède à l'eau potable majoritairement par des bornes fontaine et des forages. L'ONEA y a installé des conduites pour l'adduction en eau des habitations. Le service est trop couteux pour la plupart des ménages, comme l'explique une résidente de Rimkieta, mère de 6 enfants, « Parfois on va prendre l'eau à crédit ; et le monsieur aussi il se plaint parce que il a besoin d'argent à la fin du mois pour aller payer ses factures à l'ONEA ».

L'environnement physique n'a pas été structuré, même pour la construction d'habitations. Chaque famille construit sa maison avec ses propres moyens. Les quartiers de Rimkieta et Noosin sont séparés par un bas-fond. Des ponts en terre ont été construits pour permettre aux voitures et engins à deux roues de passer d'un quartier à l'autre. Le quartier de Rimkieta constitue une des limites de la capitale et les familles qui sont situées aux confins de ce quartier trouvent plus bénéfiques de recourir aux services de santé du village le plus proche, Zongon,[3] appartenant aussi à l'arrondissement de Boulmiougou. Une femme appartenant à une association[4] témoigne :

> Rimkieta ! C'était un ancien village… Il y a un dispensaire à Zongo et à Nonsin… Il y a une clinique à côté…là-bas c'est cher, parce que la consultation là, c'est 100 F à Zongo. Mais là-bas, c'est 1000 F…tu vas aller prendre 1000 F consulter et payer les produits là avec quoi ?

Il en est de même pour les infrastructures scolaires, qui ont une capacité trop faible pour la population scolarisée du secteur. Certaines écoles publiques recrutent au-delà de leur capacité, souvent avec la complicité de la commune qui leur envoie des enfants pupilles de l'État (orphelins, enfants en grande difficulté, etc.).

Conditions d'éducation scolaire des enfants

De nombreux enfants du secteur sont obligés d'être scolarisés, soit dans des écoles privées, ce qui pose des problèmes d'endettement de leurs parents, soit hors du secteur ; et cela aussi pose le problème de la distance. Une jeune fille de 12 ans explique :

> Je vais au lycée à Gounghin, au secteur 9. C'est un lycée privé. J'ai un vélo. Mon frère est au lycée public Marien Gouaby au secteur 3. Lui aussi a un vélo. Mon lycée est loin de chez moi. Je me lève tous les jours à 5h du matin.

Par manque de place dans les institutions publiques, certains sont obligés de chercher des inscriptions dans les collèges privés, d'autant plus que sans l'entrée en sixième[5] et ayant obtenu le CEP à un âge trop avancé, comme c'est souvent le cas pour les plus pauvres, ils ne peuvent plus avoir accès à l'enseignement public.

Les écoles et collèges privés qui sont installés dans ces espaces précaires ne peuvent pas entrer totalement dans leurs fonds. Les familles payent la première tranche de scolarité et ne peuvent poursuivre le paiement. Certains directeurs d'écoles évitent d'exclure les enfants en retard dans le paiement de leur scolarité. C'est également une forme de solidarité avec les familles en situation précaire. Du même coup, ils ont du retard dans le paiement de salaire des enseignants et certains ne parviennent pas à acheter l'équipement nécessaire pour les classes. Lors de l'enquête sur le système scolaire dans le secteur, menée par l'ADLV/B (2007), un directeur d'école privée témoigne : « Parfois l'école s'endette auprès de certains commerçants pour avancer les salaires en attendant que les familles s'acquittent des frais de scolarité. » Tous n'ont pas cette capacité. Parmi la vingtaine d'enfants interviewés, deux ont été renvoyés de l'école, pour non paiement de la scolarité. Dans un murmure, une jeune enfant m'explique son problème : « Je suis au CM2, je prépare le CEP. Mardi, on m'a chassé de l'école. Mon père est agriculteur. Il m'a dit d'attendre qu'il ait une entrée d'argent pour payer ma scolarité ».

Sur les 165 enfants de l'échantillon, 159 sont scolarisés dans des lycées et collèges environnants et un enfant fréquente une école de couture. Cinq enfants sont déscolarisés (ADLV 2005). Les parents s'obligent à inscrire leurs enfants à l'école, car ils pensent que c'est la voie indispensable désormais pour réussir dans la vie. Mme A., mère de six enfants, témoigne : « J'aide les enfants (pour qu'ils aillent à l'école) ; parce que même le fait de ne pas pouvoir parler (français) nous cause de la peine ; il y a tant de choses qui vous échappent quand vous n'avez pas fréquenté une école ». Son fils aîné a 21 ans, il prépare son BEPC et elle souhaite, s'il réussit à obtenir le diplôme qu'il recherche, il tentera de passer des concours de la fonction publique, afin de permettre à ses autres frères et sœurs d'évoluer également dans leur scolarité. Son second enfant est une fille de 18 ans qui a abandonné l'école pour apprendre la couture. Les autres enfants sont tous inscrits dans un établissement scolaire.

Sur 14 enfants déscolarisés identifiés lors des enquêtes, l'ADLVB en a scolarisé neuf. Parmi eux, deux enfants âgés de 11 ans n'avaient jamais mis les pieds dans une école. Certains parents expliquent qu'ils doivent faire un choix entre leurs enfants pour la scolarisation. C'est le cas d'une mère de famille, en ce qui concerne sa fille qui a abandonné l'école au CM2 sans avoir obtenu le CEPE. Elle a dû quitter l'école parce que sa mère a accouché de jumeaux et avait besoin de son aide pour les entretenir. Son mari est gardien et elle témoigne de leur difficulté pour tenir les enfants scolarisés :

> Elle a quitté l'école au CM2. Elle a échoué au CEP, quand je venais d'accoucher des jumeaux. Ces derniers étaient souvent malades et hospitalisés, donc des conditions difficiles. L'année suivante nous n'avons pas pu payer la scolarité et elle a fini par abandonner…Entre temps, elle a demandé à son père de l'inscrire de nouveau, en cours du soir. Il lui a dit qu'il n'avait pas les moyens.

Les filles sont désavantagées dans le cercle familial. Elles doivent aider leur mère quand cette dernière continue de mettre au monde des enfants. La santé des petits enfants grève l'épargne des familles pauvres. Les filles, aînées ou pas, ont pour rôle d'aider la mère à l'entretien des bébés et de permettre aux autres enfants de construire leur avenir à travers la scolarisation, à condition que le chef de famille puisse les inscrire à l'école. La fille a l'opportunité de s'inscrire de nouveau à l'école après avoir perdu plusieurs années à aider sa mère pour l'entretien de ses petits frères et sœurs. Mme B témoigne :

> Elle faisait le CP1[6] et a abandonné l'école pendant 5 ans, pour m'aider à la maison. Il fallait qu'elle reste à la maison pour m'aider car j'accouchais encore. Après, elle a recommencé dans un CP1 encore. Elle a 19 ans, mais à l'école, elle en a 14.

Ces deux cas montrent combien la pauvreté est un poids pour certains enfants au sein des familles, particulièrement les aînés et les filles. Ces dernières doivent sacrifier un certain nombre d'années de leur vie pour s'occuper de leurs frères et sœurs. Elles n'ont par la suite pas toujours l'occasion de reprendre leur scolarisation. Parfois, les conditions de vie de la famille se dégradent, la santé de la mère se détériore ou le père perd son emploi. Une dame témoigne :

> Il (le mari) achetait des chaussures ou bien des montres, des lunettes, c'est ça qu'il vendait. Mais actuellement il ne fait plus rien, ça ne marche plus…Quand je n'étais pas malade, je partais acheter de la cola que je revendais. Avec les bénéfices, je nourrissais les enfants. Depuis que je suis tombée malade, je n'arrive plus à faire grand-chose ».

La maladie et les grossesses nombreuses finissent par miner la santé des mères de famille. Migrantes passives (Sévédé-Bardem 1997 : 213), ayant suivi leur conjoint, elles vivent leurs activités et pratiques quotidiennes à travers leur culture et leurs connaissances du monde. Elles pensent que le premier rôle d'une femme est la création d'une famille, nombreuse si possible, et l'entretien du foyer. C'est à ce titre, en plus que peu d'opportunités se présentent à elles, qu'elles sacrifient plusieurs années de vie de leur fille aînée, pour l'entretien des autres membres de la famille. Cela participe à l'apprentissage et au savoir faire que doit avoir une jeune fille. Elles ont néanmoins l'intuition que la scolarisation pourrait permettre aux filles d'échapper au cercle de la pauvreté. En effet, à partir d'un certain niveau d'instruction, de nouvelles opportunités s'offrent autant aux filles qu'aux garçons.

De faibles opportunités malgré les obstacles

Il est vrai que l'on rencontre de nombreuses déscolarisations tout au long du cycle primaire, mais un certain nombre d'enfants pauvres, étudiant dans des conditions difficiles, parviennent jusqu'au niveau du CEP. Là est le premier obstacle à surmonter pour la grande majorité, pour plusieurs raisons : l'âge en est une, les ressources financières en sont une autre. Pour pouvoir passer l'entrée en sixième, il y a une limite d'âge (12 ans) que beaucoup d'enfants issus de familles pauvres ont dépassé, à cause d'une part, du retard dans la première inscription, et d'autre part des nombreux redoublements. Les redoublements successifs sont la plupart du temps dus à un manque de concentration à cause de la faim. Ces enfants ont avec beaucoup de peine un repas par jour, qu'ils obtiennent généralement à la fin de la journée. Un jeune garçon résidant dans la partie extrême de Rimkieta, non encore lotie, témoigne :

> Je vais au collège municipal, en 4e. J'ai 15 ans. Mon père ne travaille pas et ma mère est commerçante au marché. Je me lève tôt pour aller au collège car je marche et c'est loin. Le matin, je ne mange pas parce qu'il n'y a rien. J'attends l'après midi pour manger. Je viens à la bibliothèque pour apprendre mes leçons car je n'ai pas de livres.

Certains enfants passent le CEP à plusieurs reprises avant de l'obtenir et doivent rechercher des inscriptions dans des collèges privés. Ils n'en n'ont pas les moyens ce qui leur fait interrompre une fois de plus leur scolarisation, cette fois ci pour rechercher un emploi précaire. Avec de la chance, quand leur emploi et leur patron le permettent, ils peuvent de nouveau s'inscrire, en cours du soir. La scolarisation par ce biais, est devenue pour beaucoup d'enfants et d'adolescents, un moyen d'évolution sociale. Un enfant d'une dizaine d'années donne sa perception de la pauvreté : « Une personne pauvre ne peut pas nourrir ses enfants ou leur acheter des habits. Elle est pauvre parce qu'elle n'a pas de travail. Pour avoir un travail, il faut être allé à l'école ». La majorité des enfants interviewés pensent que c'est grâce à l'école qu'ils peuvent éviter la pauvreté. Ils veulent devenir militaire, enseignant, et même ministre.

Opportunités provenant d'initiatives privées

Certaines opportunités se présentent pour les familles pauvres, comme des miracles de la vie. Le récit de cette dame résidant à Rimkieta le montre :

> On me conseille d'aller voir le fondateur de l'école (privée) pour voir s'il ne pouvait pas m'aider. Il demande à savoir quel est le problème pour lequel nous sommes venus le voir. Je lui dis que c'est à cause de mes enfants, je suis venue voir s'il y a de bonnes volontés qui pouvaient m'aider. Il a reçu les deux (2) enfants, pour les soutenir ; celui qui a obtenu le CEP, ainsi que le petit frère de celui qui était là, qu'il a choisi de soutenir.

Nous l'avons vu, certains directeurs d'écoles et de proviseurs de collèges et lycées privés se sentent quelque peu solidaires des enfants en situation précaire. Un des rapports d'enquête de l'ADLV/B (2007) met en exergue quelques cas difficiles où des enseignants, avec leur faibles moyens, offrent des cahiers aux élèves les plus démunis, car certains élèves, entre la faim et le découragement, peuvent abandonner en pleine année scolaire, comme le montre le témoignage suivant : « Lorsqu'un enfant manque de matériel, le maître peut le réclamer plusieurs fois avec insistance auprès de l'élève. Si cela reste vain, la tension monte entre le maître et l'enfant. Si l'enfant est découragé, trop découragé, il arrête l'école ».

Les enfants les plus démunis obtiennent une aide de la municipalité. En effet, celle de Boulmiougou a un service social qui recense dans l'arrondissement tous les enfants et familles en grande difficulté. Les familles reçoivent à plusieurs reprises au cours de l'année des vivres et des vêtements. Les enfants sont placés dans des écoles publiques, les fournitures leur sont offertes et leur scolarité payée, comme les pupilles de la nation, les orphelins pris en charge par l'État. Les familles doivent faire la démarche pour s'inscrire sur la liste des indigents du service d'action sociale de la mairie. Cette même dame qui a été aidée par un proviseur de lycée privé s'est présentée trop tard à la municipalité pour faire prendre ses enfants en charge. Elle témoigne :

> Un jour que je suis revenue de voyage on avait demandé aux enfants de dire à leurs mères qu'elles sont attendues à l'école. Il était question d'aller à la mairie où une aide avait été prévue pour les enfants de parents démunis ; quand je suis allée à la mairie, on m'a dit qu'il était question de tenues à coudre, mais ils étaient déjà partis. Quand j'ai fait le tour des marchés et obtenu qu'on prenne ses mesures, ils ont dit que son nom n'y était pas (inscrit).

Cette femme n'a pas pu faire prendre en charge ses deux enfants par la mairie. Elle s'est présentée avec du retard pour les démarches administratives, à cause de sa santé défaillante. De plus, pour des analphabètes comme elle, il est difficile d'obtenir toutes les informations à temps, ou de savoir par quel moyen obtenir le service nécessaire. Cela l'a conduit à rechercher de nouvelles opportunités, hors de la sphère municipale. Des personnes à la mairie lui ont suggéré d'aller voir le proviseur d'un lycée situé hors de son secteur, pour lui demander de l'aide. Elle a effectivement reçu un appui de sa part, comme nous l'avons montré plus haut. Dans sa quête de soutiens, elle a montré une grande détermination à scolariser ses enfants. Dans son récit de vie, elle explique que c'est à partir du 4e enfant qu'elle tente de les scolariser car le défi économique était trop rude auparavant pour la famille, dont le chef de famille est sans emploi. Elle s'est rendue compte que ses enfants souffraient de leur analphabétisme. Ils ne parvenaient pas à s'insérer dans le réseau social de ces enfants scolarisés et se sentent mis à l'écart. Une jeune enfant scolarisée m'explique :

> J'ai des copines. Elles sont toutes dans mon école. Je ne fréquente pas les filles et les garçons qui habitent près de chez moi, car ils ne vont pas à l'école. Certains travaillent dans les ateliers artisanaux.

Les enfants sont conscients des appuis qu'ils peuvent recevoir de la famille et font parfois eux-mêmes des recherches pour obtenir de l'aide. Une fille d'une dizaine d'années affirme que lorsqu'elle a été renvoyée de l'école pour non-paiement de la scolarité, elle est allée voir sa tante qui vit dans un autre secteur et qui est tisserande. Cette dernière lui a promis de lui payer sa scolarité dès qu'elle en aura les moyens.

La marginalité de ces enfants, se fait sentir par leurs difficultés de survie. Elle devient dynamique dès lors qu'ils trouvent les moyens de la contourner, grâce au réseau de solidarité. D'autres enfants n'ont pas ce réseau familial autour d'eux. Une bonne moitié de l'échantillon d'enfants interviewés dans le cadre de cette étude, affirme ne pas connaître le village de leurs parents. Lorsque le couple est séparé, la solidarité familiale se réduit encore plus, laissant la place à la construction de nouveaux réseaux sociaux. Un jeune garçon d'une douzaine d'années nous explique qu'il est né et a grandi en Côte d'Ivoire. Ses parents se sont séparés et sa mère est revenue avec ses enfants à Ouagadougou. Le père, resté en Côte d'ivoire, leur rend visite de temps en temps : « Quand mon père nous rend visite, ma mère et lui se disputent car il ne laisse pas assez d'argent pour notre entretien. Je lui demande pardon pour qu'il revienne à la maison ». La fréquentation de la bibliothèque de l'association « Dunia la Vie » est un moyen pour lui de se faire de nouveaux amis.

Opportunité venant de structures associatives

Certaines associations participent de façon aussi active, sinon plus, que les relations individuelles, à créer des opportunités aux personnes ayant besoin d'appuis. C'est le cas de l'ADLV/Burkina qui, depuis 2006, tente de recenser à travers les enfants avec lesquels elle travaille, les familles en grande difficulté de survie. Elle offre un appui au niveau scolaire, en vivres et en vêtements. Des associations dans d'autres domaines, sont également sollicitées par ces acteurs, en rupture culturelle et sociale. Ces derniers négocient avec des structures de santé communautaire. L'Association African Solidarity (AAS) au secteur 11 de la ville de Ouagadougou, le centre de santé islamique Ahmadiya au secteur 8, ECLA (Être Comme les Autres), sont très sollicités par les personnes démunies en quête de soins de santé.   Ces centres apportent des appuis sous forme de soins médicaux (médicaments, perfusion, prises en charge diverses) ou de distributions de vivres et de vêtements. Mme A explique :

> Je n'ai pas pu aller voir quelqu'un à la mairie pour qu'on m'aide, et c'est la première fois que je viens ici (ADLV/B). Là où j'ai été c'est AAS. Là, là-bas on me donne seulement des comprimés, ce qu'ils ont sur place ; si je viens avec une ordonnance, ça ne marche pas ; une ordonnance, ils ne donnent pas. Mais s'il y a des produits qu'ils ont là-bas, c'est ça qu'on me donne.

Le dispensaire de ECLA est basé au secteur 19, dans le quartier de Noosin. Il appartient à une association qui œuvre pour la promotion des handicapés, considérés comme une catégorie vulnérable au sein de la population. Le médecin du dispensaire témoigne[7] :

> La plupart du temps, c'est au cas par cas ; c'est nous-mêmes qui constatons que l'individu n'a même pas d'argent pour payer la consultation. Il y a beaucoup de gens qui ne savent pas qu'il faut aller à la mairie pour prendre un certificat d'indigence pour bénéficier de la gratuité au niveau des structures, des services publiques et même privé ! Si le papier est là, on ne peut pas te refuser. Il y a un enfant, son père est aveugle, sa mère, c'est elle qui, je crois, se débrouille pour pouvoir s'occuper de la famille et c'est elle qui a amené l'enfant. Tout le temps l'enfant a des problèmes digestifs. Nous avons fait l'échographie et nous avons constaté que c'est une appendicite en voie même de perforation. Nous on a appelé un autre jeune, un étudiant et on lui a dit d'amener l'enfant à l'hôpital (Yalgado) parce que la maman ne pourra même pas faire les soins ; donc j'ai fait un papier pour dire qu'il est indigent, j'ai désigné des gens qu'il faut aller voir à l'hôpital. Ils ont fait comme ça et l'enfant a été opéré. 10 jours après, ils sont revenus ici avec la maman j'ai dit aux infirmiers, faites son pansement gratuitement .

Opportunités provenant de l'assistance municipale

En plus de l'aide que peuvent apporter les élus municipaux, à des associations ou à des individus, il y a l'assistance, la plus régulière et la mieux organisée, provenant de la mairie. Malgré la faiblesse des moyens, tant humains que matériels, la municipalité a mis en place un cadre institutionnel pour assister les plus pauvres dans l'arrondissement. Un service social est installé à la mairie, avec une éducatrice sociale qui en est responsable. Elle reconnaît la faiblesse des moyens de la mairie, mais plusieurs dizaines d'enfants survivent grâce à cette aide. Elle prend en charge un certain nombre d'enfants et d'adolescents, orphelins qui vivent seuls au domicile de leurs parents, sans électricité et sans eau. Elle leur rend visite au moins une fois par trimestre à domicile, pour leur déposer des vivres. Son grand handicap est la vétusté du véhicule de son service qui est utilisé également par d'autres services municipaux, et surtout le manque régulier de carburant.

La responsable du service de l'action sociale de la mairie se déplace également dans les établissements scolaires dans lesquels elle a fait placer les enfants en grande difficulté. Au début, elle donnait les kits de fournitures aux établissements directement pour qu'ils fassent la distribution. Beaucoup d'orphelins et d'enfants démunis n'obtenaient pas leurs fournitures. Pour toucher directement les enfants, elle fait une fois par trimestre, le tour des trois circonscriptions scolaires (Boulmiougou, Ouaga 7 et Ouaga 8, qui comptent une cinquantaine d'écoles primaires).

Certains enfants sont orphelins d'un parent ou des deux. Parfois ils ont pu être placés en famille d'accueil mais ce n'est pas le cas pour tous.

La mairie a prévu une aide financière pour les enfants scolarisés, en situation précaire. Cette aide leur est octroyée lors d'une cérémonie, dans l'enceinte de la mairie. Le maire fait une remise de fournitures aux enfants les plus méritants. Sont concernés les premiers de chaque classe du primaire, des écoles publiques et certaines écoles privées. Un arbre de Noël est également organisé au profit des enfants en difficulté de l'arrondissement, scolarisés ou pas.

À la recherche de moyens d'existence

La recherche des moyens d'existence diffère selon que l'on soit un enfant, un homme ou une femme. Elle s'avère difficile pour tout le monde car les acteurs sociaux au secteur 19, n'ont pas de compétences professionnelles et de formations qui puissent leur ouvrir des perspectives d'emplois permanents et bien rémunérés. Les femmes s'activent dans le petit commerce, c'est-à-dire la vente d'arachides, de fruits, de beignets, font le concassage de cailloux et le tamisage de sable. Mme B. témoigne : « Je balaie le sable ; je vends le sable (aux entreprises de construction) ».

Les hommes construisent des briques en banco dans les bas fonds, vendent des biens de consommation courants (lunettes, casquettes, etc.), ou offrent leur service comme aides-maçons, manutentionnaires, etc. En ce qui concerne les enfants, les garçons vendent au détail sur les trottoirs ou sont des apprentis dans des petites entreprises du secteur informel :

> Je suis en deuxième année de collège. En fin d'année scolaire, mon père m'emmène chez mon oncle qui a un atelier de menuiserie au secteur 21 et j'y travaille durant toutes les vacances.

Un autre enfant explique :

> Je suis au CM2. Pendant les vacances, j'achète les cartes de crédit de téléphone et je vais au centre ville pour les revendre. Je n'ai pas d'endroit précis ou les vendre, je déambule dans la ville jusqu'au soir.

Ces activités sont précaires, parfois quotidiennes et ne permettent qu'une survie, sans projection sur l'avenir. Pendant la saison des pluies, les familles s'adonnent à la culture de céréales ou de légumes autour de leur concession : mil, maïs, gombos, aubergine africaine, haricot, etc. Le quartier de Rimkieta se transforme à cette période de l'année en un village, où il est difficile de retrouver sa route quand on n'y réside pas. L'avantage de cette activité saisonnière est qu'elle donne à de nombreuses familles périurbaines des moyens temporaires de subsistance. Une jeune scolaire nous dit :

> Mon père est agriculteur. Pendant l'hivernage, il cultive dans les champs situés après Rimkieta. Je vais l'aider avec mon frère pour cultiver, mais ma mère ne nous accompagne pas car elle est commerçante au marché de Baskuy (au secteur 11).

Très peu d'activités lucratives sont offertes aux jeunes filles sans formation. Avec le niveau de fin d'étude primaire, elles peuvent proposer leurs services comme domestiques, aide coiffeuses, couturières ou dans les télé centres.[8] Certaines activités sont difficiles à recenser ou à mesurer. C'est le cas de la prostitution, qui existe bel et bien au secteur 19. Le maire de la commune de Ouagadougou a lancé une grande campagne de répression, donnant un délai pour la fermeture des maisons closes, jugées inquiétantes du point de vue sanitaire. La plupart de ces maisons reçoivent des filles dans des chambres exigües et insalubres, avec comme seul mobilier des nattes posées sur le sol. Elles sont trois ou quatre par pièce. Il est difficile au secteur 19 d'approcher ces filles car aucune n'avoue publiquement exercer cette activité. Les femmes de l'association Ratamanégré s'expriment sur ce sujet :

> Il y en a mais ce n'est pas beaucoup (les chambres de passe) ; ça vient un peu un peu… est-ce que ce n'est pas en construction seulement ? Non il y en a pas ; moi-même j'ai entendu parler de ça mais c'est vers….Noguin… (Rimkieta) vers la cité là aussi… sinon il y a quelques maisons mais ce n'est pas encore beaucoup…ça doit être le seul coin d'ailleurs…l'autre c'est au temps du non loti que ça existait. Celle qui existe aujourd'hui est collée avec une école même ! Donc vous voyez que ce n'est pas normal !

Autant certaines activités, aussi illicites puissent-elles être, sont avouables, autant d'autres ne le sont pas. Mais elles figurent parmi les activités auxquelles les femmes en particulier auront recours en cas d'extrême nécessité. De plus en plus de jeunes adolescentes, scolarisées ou pas, s'adonnent à la prostitution et cela n'implique pas toujours un paiement en argent. Le service peut être payé en nourriture, en vêtements ou même en produits de toilette (Sévédé-Bardem 1997 : 177). La prostitution offre à ces adolescentes, des opportunités pour échapper à la monotonie de leur vie faite de privations et de frustrations. Elle n'est dérangeante que par le regard que lui jette la société burkinabé, évoluant dans le puritanisme, et qui en fait un délit à partir de 1983 (Sévédé-Bardem 1997 : 176).

Le ramassage de sable et le concassage de gravillons se mènent dans les bas-fonds. La poussière soulevée, causant des maladies et les risques réels d'éboulement en ont fait une activité interdite. Malgré cela, les femmes, les plus pauvres, n'ayant aucun autre recours, les pratiquent au vu et au su de tout le monde, même du service de l'action sociale de la mairie. Cette dernière a parfois envoyé des femmes pour mener ces activités, faute de n'avoir rien à leur proposer.

Ces activités précaires offrent aux familles la possibilité d'obtenir un repas par jour. C'est important, car beaucoup d'enfants vont à l'école à jeûn. Un jeune élève du primaire donne son témoignage :

> Je me lève à 6 h du matin, je me lave, je mange quand il y a des restes de la veille. Sinon je pars à l'école et j'attends midi pour manger. Mes copines me donnent à la récréation une partie de leur goûter.

Les repas sont insuffisants, qualitativement et quantitativement. Les enfants se battent pour en avoir la plus grosse part, et une maman interviewée exprime son désarroi et son déchirement à voir ses enfants se disputer à longueur de journée à cause du repas insuffisant de la journée. Cela est un moyen de survie, plutôt que de subsistance, offert à la famille, dans sa quête quotidienne, dans un milieu urbain défavorisé.

Conclusion

La famille constitue pour beaucoup d'enfants et d'adolescents, une opportunité non négligeable pour négocier des moyens d'existence. Quels que soient les obstacles qui s'érigent devant eux, les enfants ont la capacité de les contourner et de créer des opportunités qui les amoindrissent. Ces opportunités, aussi petites soient-elles, leur permettent de se socialiser par la scolarisation ou le travail, afin de survivre dans un milieu urbain difficile.

Dans ces espaces urbains défavorisés, on y trouve de plus en plus de femmes, chefs de famille, avec un certain nombre d'enfants sous leur responsabilité. Pour s'en sortir, elles tissent des relations avec des individus ou des structures, et développent ainsi des réseaux de solidarité dont leurs enfants sont le centre. Des directeurs d'école, des enseignants, des associations, des dispensaires, des conseillers municipaux et également la municipalité, font partie de ce cadre de réseau relationnel qui se tisse autour de ces familles marginalisées par une précarité tant économique que sociale. En effet, le manque de ressources a poussé un bon nombre de ces familles à quitter leur communauté, pour au final se retrouver dans cet espace urbain défavorisé. En rupture totale ou partielle du lien social et culturel, sans ressources économiques, ces acteurs sociaux, autant enfants qu'adultes, n'ont de cesse de recréer autour d'eux un espace vital. C'est un fait inhérent à la condition humaine, qui refuse la marginalisation, en se reconstituant de nouveaux liens de solidarité et d'entraide. En effet, lorsque la marginalité d'un acteur social perd sa dynamique, le phénomène de la déviance sociale s'exacerbe à son plus haut point, dans la délinquance, voire la folie.

Les enfants et adultes vivent dans ces espaces urbains défavorisés, recherchant des moyens de subsistance, en complément de ceux que leur réseau d'entraide leur fournit. Par manque de formation et de compétences spécifiques, les activités qui s'offrent à eux sont précaires, temporaires et souvent dangereuses, ou illégales. Certaines de ces activités contribuent à détériorer la santé de ces acteurs sociaux, comme par exemple la prostitution ou le ramassage de sable. Dans un autre quartier de la ville de Ouagadougou, des jeunes hommes et femmes traitent le granit en brûlant des pneus usés sur le rocher, faisant fi de l'intoxication qu'ils s'imposent quotidiennement. Le plus souvent, les autorités municipales interviennent peu, faute de n'avoir pas trouvé un moyen efficace d'éradication de la pauvreté. Parfois sous forme « d'opérations coup de poing », elles réagissent pour pointer du doigt la prostitution de ces pré adolescentes et ces jeunes garçons, ou le danger que courent ces femmes qui raclent le sol à la recherche de sable et de gravillons, risquant de se faire ensevelir sous les éboulements.

Nous avons voulu dans cette étude montrer qu'il existe des moyens de subsistance et des opportunités pour les familles en situation précaire, pour survivre en milieu urbain, mais le prix à payer pour y accéder est souvent lourd. Les enfants jouent un rôle à la fois actif et passif dans la recherche des familles de ces moyens d'existence. Ils sont le centre des sollicitudes, mais recherchent avec les adultes, des moyens d'existence, pour la famille entière. Ce sont les petits vendeurs à la sauvette, au coin des rues, ou apprentis dans certaines entreprises du secteur informel. Les conditions de vie sont difficiles. La faim, le découragement ou la recherche de meilleures conditions de vie sont les causes des nombreuses déscolarisations des enfants vivant en milieu urbain défavorisé.

Cette étude ouvre de nouvelles perspectives d'analyse des conditions de vie et d'évolution des enfants scolarisés, en milieu urbain défavorisé, en se concentrant sur leurs rêves et leurs espoirs, à travers leurs propres récits de vie.

Notes

1. L'ouvrage d'Henri Lefebvre, philosophe français, *Le droit à la ville*, est paru avant les évènements de 1968, pour dénoncer la question du logement qui ne prenait plus en compte la problématique de la socialité dans les cités urbaines, mais considérait plutôt la fonction de loger.
2. Information émanant d'un conseiller municipal de la mairie de Boulmiougou.
3. Lors des inondations qui ont touché la capitale du Burkina Faso le 1er septembre 2009, de nombreuses habitations ont été détruites particulièrement dans les quartiers pauvres comme Rimkieta. Le pont reliant Rimkieta et Noosin est tombé et une grande partie des habitations de Zongo s'est écroulée au cours de cette longue pluie qui a duré plus de 12 h de temps.

4. Entretien avec une dizaine de femmes de l'association Ratamanégré de Rimkieta sous forme de focus groupe, en octobre 2008.
5. Il s'agit d'un concours que les enfants du CM2 passent pour obtenir une place dans un collège, un lycée public.
6. Dans le système scolaire français, le CP1 correspond à la grande section où les enfants apprennent à lire, à écrire et à compter.
7. Extrait de l'entretien avec le médecin de l'association ECLA en avril 2009.
8. Ce sont des centres de téléphonies privées qui fonctionnent de moins en moins bien depuis le développement du téléphone portable.

Références

Arnaud, M., 1993, *L'urbanisation en Afrique de l'Ouest. Mécanismes et logiques*, Ministère de l'Écologie, du Développement et de l'Aménagement durable, Centre de documentation de l'urbanisme (CDU), France.

Baux, Stéphanie, 2007, « Discours sur l'école et représentations du système scolaire à Ouagadougou », *La question éducative au Burkina Faso, Regards pluriels*, Félix Compaoré , Maxime Compaoré, Marie-France Lange et Marc Pilon (dir.), Paris-Ouagadougou, IRD/CNRST.

Golaz, V., et Dupont, V., 2004, *Dynamiques périurbaines : population, habitat et environnement dans les périphéries des grandes métropoles*, Compte rendu de l'atelier de Delhi (25-27 août 2004), INED, IRD, CSH. France.

Jargowsky, P., 1997, *Poverty and Place: Ghettos, Barrios, and the American City*, New York, Russell Sage Foundation.

Marguerat, Yves, 2003, « À la découverte des enfants de la rue d'Abidjan : des visages et des chiffres pour les comprendre », Marguerat, Y. (dir.). *Garçons et filles des rues dans la ville africaine. Diversité et dynamique des marginalités juvéniles à Abidjan, Nairobi, Antananarivo*. Rapport de l'équipe de recherche « Dynamique du monde des jeunes de la rue ». Recherches comparatives sur l'évolution de la marginalité juvénile en Afrique et à Madagascar. Paris, EHESS.

Institut National de la Statistique et de la Demographie, 2007, Ministère de l'Économie et du Développement, Bureau Central du recensement, *Résultats préliminaires*, 2007, Burkina Faso.

Sévédé-Bardem, I., 1997, *Précarités juvéniles en milieu urbain africain. « Aujourd'hui, chacun se cherche »*, Paris, L'Harmattan.

Tanon, F., 2003, « L'attribution causale chez les jeunes marginalisées abidjanais. Étude des deux groupes d'enfants de la rue », in : Marguerat, Y. (dir.). *Garçons et filles des rues dans la ville africaine. Diversité et dynamique des marginalités juvéniles à Abidjan, Nairobi, Antananarivo*. Rapport de l'équipe de recherche « Dynamique du monde des jeunes de la rue », Recherches comparatives sur l'évolution de la marginalité juvénile en Afrique et à Madagascar, EHESS, Paris (France).

4

Villes et créativité des enfants et des jeunes au Cameroun

Jean-Marcellin Manga

(…) pour comprendre certaines dynamiques sociales et politiques qui se manifestent dans la vie quotidienne en Afrique subsaharienne (…), il faut aller au-delà des pathologies habituellement recensées et exprimées avec condescendance. Il faut abandonner la lecture paternaliste et superficielle des difficultés de l'Afrique et des Africains, et explorer sérieusement le substrat philosophique et les schémas de raisonnement qui se dissimulent derrière les comportements les plus banals de la vie quotidienne.

Monga, Célestin, 2009, *Nihilisme et négritude*, Paris, PUF, pp. 30-31.

Introduction : Brèves remarques sur les enfants, les jeunes et la ville

Trois observations majeures sont au départ de la présente analyse. Tout d'abord, il est important de rappeler que, pour qui est attentif au développement de la population camerounaise, il ne fait aucun doute que les enfants et les jeunes constituent deux catégories sociales dont la densité démographique permet de défendre l'idée qu'elles exercent un ascendant éminent dans la configuration morphologique de ladite société.[1]

Ensuite, il faut reconnaître que, pour comprendre le Cameroun contemporain et, subséquemment, les enfants et les jeunes qui y vivent, on aurait tort de limiter notre regard à l'effervescence socio-démographique que connaît ce pays du continent noir. En effet, en marge de cette considération, l'autre remarque qui mérite d'être mise en exergue, c'est que l'urbanisation est, après l'inflation démographique, la métamorphose la plus fondamentale qui traverse de plus en plus la société camerounaise (Nguendo Yongsi 2008 : 25). Les enfants et les jeunes sont tout particulièrement au cœur de ces dynamiques urbaines. Au Cameroun, pareillement à plusieurs autres pays d'Afrique, à l'observation, on ne peut manquer d'être frappé par le constat selon lequel, ce sont eux qui pratiquent de plus en plus la ville.

Les enfants et les jeunes ne se contentent donc pas seulement d'être statisquement majoritaires. Ils sont aussi les plus présents dans les milieux urbains (Moriba et Fadayomi : 1993). On peut davantage le vérifier dans les villes de Yaoundé et de Douala. Paradoxalement, et c'est là le sens de la troisième observation qu'il est important de relever. Il faut se presser de rappeler que ces catégories ont, jusqu'ici, été méconnues dans la plupart des domaines de la vie sociale. Pour s'en rendre compte, peut-être faut-il se souvenir que, dans les imaginaires populaires, ils restent ces portions sociales que l'on assimile à des *cadets sociaux* (Bayard 1985 : 233-281). Cela expliquerait pourquoi, en dépit des discours et autres slogans politiques, ils tardent à être responsabilisés. Et si quelques analyses sont repérables, qui soulignent les capacités et les aptitudes d'ingéniosité des enfants et des jeunes dans un écosystème social fait de contrariétés protéiformes,

> les discours dominants et certains reportages ne voient en eux que « des vagabonds », « des vandales », « des irresponsables », « des contestataires », « des déracinés », « des voyous », « des voleurs », « des bandits », « des pyromanes », « des prostitués », « des drogués », « des délinquants », « des chômeurs (Zoa 1999 : 236).

Les enfants et les jeunes sont ainsi très souvent perçus comme un problème social, appréhendés à travers les catégories de la déviance et de la marginalité, présentés par des images réductrices et négatives qui les enferment dans l'étroitesse des paradigmes de la délinquance et de la paresse. Or, en les affichant de la sorte, on a tendance à ignorer qu'au-delà des figures péjoratives et dévalorisantes qui les confinent dans les conceptions du « voyoutisme » ou de la maladie, les enfants et les jeunes apparaissent comme des acteurs qui produisent une nouvelle culture urbaine. Celle-ci est repérable dès lors que l'on s'intéresse à certaines de leurs formes d'expression, ou encore à certaines activités qu'ils réalisent dans les milieux urbains camerounais.

Au cœur des interrogations qui retiennent notre attention tout au long de cet exercice analytique, la ville nous intéresse prioritairement. De cette ville, il ne faut toutefois pas, à première vue, considérer cet espace que l'on exhibe sous une physionomie avilissante, déterminée à partir d'un implicite culpabilisant.[2] Dans ce travail, il ne s'agit pas, non plus, dans la perspective des études de sociologie urbaine, de s'intéresser à la ville en tant que site qui offre aux enfants et aux jeunes la possibilité de s'investir dans des activités informelles. Tout comme il ne nous importe guère de nous intéresser, en questionnant le milieu urbain, à certaines catégories pathologiques où travaillent les enfants et les jeunes. Encore moins, de réfléchir à la ville africaine en tant que celle-ci se donne à voir comme un lieu où les enfants et les jeunes expérimentent diverses modalités de la vulnérabilité comme ont pu le faire de nombreuses analyses.[3] L'itinéraire que nous empruntons dans les lignes qui suivent s'oriente vers un axe qualitativement différent : il s'agit d'interroger l'espace urbain camerounais en tant qu'il est un site offrant aux enfants et aux jeunes des opportunités pour l'éradication de la vulnérabilité.

De façon plus précise, il est question pour nous, dans le présent travail, de rejoindre la ville en Afrique en dehors des lieux de la déviance, de l'exclusion et de la marginalité sociale où l'on tend à l'enfermer pour retrouver comment, à travers les avantages qu'elle présente, elle peut être appréhendée comme un cadre qui permet aux enfants et aux jeunes de s'affranchir de la précarité. En optant, comme nous prétendons le faire, d'explorer la ville urbaine camerounaise comme un environnement social et spatial qui offre des possibilités à un très fort pourcentage des groupes parmi les plus vulnérables du continent, il s'agit, pour nous, de nuancer les analyses qui ne voient – souvent à juste titre – les espaces urbains africains que comme des lieux nocifs pour les enfants et les jeunes. En d'autres mots, il est question de retrouver les jeunes dans leurs tête-à-tête quotidiens avec les occasions propices que leur octroie la proximité d'avec le milieu urbain.

L'objectif de cette recherche est donc de rendre compte des opportunités qu'offrent les espaces urbains au Cameroun. Il est question de savoir de quelle manière il est possible de renouveler le regard que l'on porte sur la ville camerounaise en la décrivant, non plus seulement comme un milieu qui obstrue l'émancipation et les potentialités créatrices des enfants et des jeunes, mais plutôt comme un cadre qui crée et offre des possibilités avantageuses pour cette catégorie d'acteurs. Il s'agit aussi de dire, en fournissant des indications précises, de quelles catégories d'enfants et de jeunes il est question. Outre ces centres d'intérêt, notre travail, dans cette analyse, consistera également à identifier à quels types d'opportunités les enfants et les jeunes ont à faire. Bref, il s'agit d'analyser les parcours de réussite à court, moyen et/ou long terme qu'empruntent les enfants et les jeunes et qui sont rendus possibles du fait de l'existence des milieux urbains.

L'hypothèse-force qui nourrit ce travail repose sur l'idée que, en s'efforçant de porter son regard loin des simplifications abusives et négatives qui confinent la ville camerounaise dans les catégories de la délinquance, de la maladie et de la vulnérabilité, les espaces urbains camerounais apparaissent comme des sites qui offrent des opportunités pour les enfants et les jeunes. Celles-ci sont décelables au travers de certaines formes d'activités économiques, agricoles, pastorales, culturelles, sportives, ludiques et politiques qui mettent en question la coloration, par trop négative, que l'on fait des contextes urbains africains.

Considérations méthodologiques : cadre de l'étude, modèle théorique et technique de collecte de données

La ville de Yaoundé définit le site principal à partir duquel cette étude a été conduite. Il s'agit d'un lieu urbain sur lequel nous avons opté d'exécuter le travail de récolte des informations. Par ailleurs, capitale politique du Cameroun, cette agglomération subjugue par la diversité des enfants et des jeunes qui s'y meuvent. Elle est considérée ici comme un espace dynamique en continuelle fluctuation, point d'intersection d'une multitude de cultures africaines issues, aussi bien des différentes contrées du Cameroun que d'autres pays de l'Afrique. C'est un terrain favorable à l'observation et à l'analyse des pratiques sociales et culturelles contemporaines telles que les nouvelles formes de travail dans lesquels s'investissent les segments sociaux qui retiennent notre attention.

La décision de mener cette étude dans un milieu urbain est guidée par la volonté qui est la nôtre de produire des connaissances nouvelles sur la créativité sociale qui apparaît comme l'un des nombreux phénomènes sociaux, culturels et identitaires contemporains qui s'affichent dans un Cameroun moderne et cosmopolite. La ville est envisagée, tout au long de cette réflexion, comme un macrocosme social et culturel particulier, producteur de codes nouveaux, de pratiques, de valeurs culturelles et de représentations collectives originales, dynamiques et métissées. Ainsi, Yaoundé se décline comme le lieu par excellence de la création et de l'invention de nouvelles pratiques culturelles.

En nous intéressant aux manières de travailler qui se dynamisent chez les enfants et les jeunes, le cadre d'insertion de notre terrain d'étude n'est pas figé. C'est la raison pour laquelle, bien que l'espace urbain *yaoundéen* présente, dans cette recherche, l'avantage de s'offrir comme un espace ouvert, il n'est pas en mesure, pris isolément, de circonscrire la géographie de notre étude. A la suite d'Arborio et de Fournier (2001 : 12), nous concédons, « qu'une activité particulière, des pratiques ou un mode de vie communs permettent de délimiter un groupe à prendre pour objet d'étude ». Pour cette raison, la surface retenue pour effectuer cette recherche ne se restreint guère uniquement au site physique d'une ville. Elle est aussi faite d' « un ensemble de pratiques socialement produites, matériellement codifiés et symboliquement objectivées » (Mbembé 2005 : 16) à l'intérieur d'autres sites urbains au Cameroun. Au cœur de ces pratiques, on retrouve les manières de s'occuper, de créer ou encore de travailler qui sont accessibles dès lors que l'on scrute avec attention les signes, les gestes et les attitudes à travers lesquels les enfants et les jeunes font signe à la vie en milieu urbain.

Pour rendre compte des multiples pratiques à travers lesquelles les enfants et les jeunes des villes au Cameroun investissent les milieux urbains pour capter les opportunités qui s'y dramatisent, cette étude peut difficilement contourner une sociologie des expériences sociales qu'expérimentent ces catégories d'acteurs. La sociologie de l'expérience « vise à définir l'expérience comme une combinaison de logiques d'action, logiques qui lient l'acteur à chacune des dimensions d'un système » (Dubet 1994 : 105). En la convoquant dans ce travail, il s'est s'agi d'examiner d'une part, les différentes logiques qui influencent les comportements des enfants et des jeunes. D'autre part, le recours à cette approche théorique nous a permis de montrer comment, par voie de conséquence, la subjectivité et la réflexivité de ces acteurs se construisent dans le constant mouvement de va-et-vient qu'entretiennent ces logiques plurielles. Mais, le détour par la sociologie de l'expérience, pour cardinal qu'il soit, n'aurait pas valu grand-chose pour cette recherche si nous n'avions fait intervenir le paradigme théorique des « logiques de l'action ». Cette grille se propose de « mettre au jour les « raisons d'agir » des individus en prenant en compte la diversité des mobiles et des rationalités, et en tenant compte des discours que tiennent les acteurs sur leur propre conduite » (Lallement 2000 : 256-257). À partir de l'approche des logiques d'action que avons convoqué, il a été question de montrer que, dans leur affiliation à certaines activités économiques, agricoles, pastorales, culturelles et politiques, les enfants et les jeunes que nous avons questionnés se réfèrent toujours à des logiques d'action plurielles qui font système.[4]

Les techniques de collecte des données utilisées ont consisté en une recherche bibliographique sommaire, une observation directe *in situ*, des entretiens approfondis avec des informateurs privilégiés, notamment certains commerçants, et des récits de vie d'enfants et de jeunes que nous avons approchés dans diverses villes au Cameroun. Les méthodes auxquelles nous avons recouru sont donc essentiellement qualitatives. Elles offrent le privilège de procurer des informations qui apportent un maximum de lumières sur les attitudes, les expériences, les perceptions et les imaginaires qui nourrissent la vie quotidienne de ces acteurs sociaux. En manipulant ces outils, il s'est surtout agi pour nous d'écouter ce que les enfants et les jeunes disent de leurs propres pratiques à analyser.

Précision conceptuelle

Qu'entend-on par créativité ? Cette interrogation nous intéresse. Le terme « créativité » est un mot polysémique difficile à circonscrire. Il tire sa source du verbe latin *creare* qui veut dire « créer ». Au sens strict, créer, c'est donner naissance à quelque chose, inventer, imaginer. Cette signification est assez proche de celle que lui assigne la religion chrétienne.[5] Mais créer veut aussi dire faire, réaliser quelque chose qui n'existait pas encore. Ses synonymes sont alors : concevoir, élaborer, produire.

La créativité sociale peut être rendue comme étant un processus faisant intervenir des éléments cognitifs, par lequel un groupe d'individus (en l'occurrence ici les enfants et les jeunes) extériorise sa singularité dans la façon de lier des choses, d'associer des idées, d'engendrer des situations qui, par l'aboutissement du résultat concret de cette démarche processuelle, change, modifie ou transforme la perception, l'usage ou la matérialité auprès d'un public donné. La créativité sociale d'une catégorie d'acteurs qualifie aussi la capacité dont dispose ce groupe à produire, à une période précise, des solutions, des idées ou des concepts qui sont susceptibles de permettre de réaliser, d'une manière efficiente et inattendue, une action. La créativité sociale peut donc être comprise comme équivalente de l'inventivité ou, pour faire corps avec le titre d'un ouvrage d'Alex Osborn (1971), de *l'imagination constructive*. Allusion est faite ici à la capacité de produire des idées grâce à l'imagination. La créativité sociale fait ainsi appel aux fonctions inventives, à l'imagination créatrice.

Grosso modo, on peut catégoriser les précisions faites autour du concept de « créativité » et de la notion de « créativité sociale » autour de trois grands sens. Premièrement, la créativité sociale renvoie à un acte par et/ou à travers lequel quelque chose voit le jour dans une société donnée. A ce niveau, la créativité est attribuée à des processus cognitifs, à l'influence de l'environnement social, ou encore, à la personnalité. Ce sens est d'ailleurs en harmonie avec ce que suggère Le Bœuf (2004 : 270).

Deuxièmement, la créativité sociale peut, *lato sensu*, être considérée comme la capacité d'apporter ou d'aider à trouver des solutions originales aux problèmes d'adaptation auxquels font face des groupes sociaux. Vu sous ce prisme, la créativité sociale devient une méthode de résolution des problèmes. La démarche créative commence, de ce point de vue, par la reconnaissance d'une difficulté. À partir de là, on peut postuler que l'acte créatif implique une démarche qui se construit sur un désaccord, une contrariété. Lequel désaccord pousse les individus à se mobiliser pour rechercher une nouvelle solution à la difficulté qui surgit. Ce deuxième sens que prend l'expression « créativité sociale » a été régulièrement convoqué dans cette analyse.

Troisièmement, la créativité sociale peut être caractérisée par une volonté ou une intention de transformer son environnement, son « propre monde », ce que nous nommons son « moi social existentiel ». La créativité sociale porte donc, de part en part, c'est-à-dire précisément par quelques bouts qu'on la tienne, l'idée de modification, de changement social. La créativité au sein d'une collectivité peut s'apprécier à plus d'un niveau. Pour nous, notre attention sera davantage portée sur la créativité économique, agropastorale et culturelle (musicale et artistique).

Seulement, « Les notions d'enfance et de jeunesse auxquels nous nous référons ici ne peuvent être fondées sur de simples critères biologiques ; elles doivent plutôt englober des variables sociales et culturelles telles que le sexe, la religion, la classe, le rôle social, les responsabilités, les attentes, la race et l'ethnicité » (De Boeck et Honwana 2005 : 6). Bien que nous avons intégré ces éléments qui permettent une certaine homogénéité originelle, nous tenons à faire savoir que les enfants et les jeunes sur lesquels nous nous appuyons dans cette réflexion, ne font pas référence à une catégorie sociale homogène. En effet, ces enfants et ces jeunes se signalent par les dissemblances de leurs trajectoires existentielles, leurs provenances régionales, linguistiques et sociales. C'est la raison pour laquelle, ils ne sont pas appréhendés, tout au long de cet itinéraire analytique, comme une « classe d'âge », mais plutôt, pour reprendre mots pour mots le propos d'Anne-Sidonie Zoa (1999 : 237), comme « une étape de la vie ». Dans cette réflexion, nous envisageons « les jeunes non seulement comme des proto-adultes ou des êtres en devenir, mais surtout comme des êtres au présent et des agents sociaux à leur présence propre » (De Boeck et Honwana 2005 : 6). En optant, comme nous prétendons le faire, d'être attentifs aux enfants et aux jeunes afin d'apprendre comment ils agissent eux-mêmes, en nous assignant pour objectif de mettre en évidence certaines de leurs stratégies de conquête statutaire, il s'agit, pour nous, d'apporter une contribution dont l'objectif est de désenclaver le monde des enfants et des jeunes en nous intéressant, davantage, à ce qui fait sens, aujourd'hui, pour ces acteurs urbains au Cameroun. En d'autres mots, il est question de retrouver les enfants et les jeunes dans leurs centres d'intérêts, dans leurs attractions, dans leurs préoccupations, pour essayer de pénétrer quelques- uns des modes opératoires à travers lesquels ils négocient leur existence. Car, il convient de l'affirmer avec vigueur, malgré le peu de considération qu'on leur porte, dans notre contemporanéité, « beaucoup de jeunes gens sont engagés en Afrique dans des activités sociales, politiques, culturelles et économiques multiples ; ils démontrent une créativité débordante en se forgeant une vie propre dans un climat de conflit et d'instabilité sociale » (De Boeck et Honwana 2005 : 7).

Enfants, jeunes et créativité dans les espaces urbains

En quoi est-il pertinent de lire la ville comme un milieu qui crée et offre des opportunités pour les enfants et les jeunes au Cameroun ? Ainsi se trouve énoncée la question qui retient notre attention. Pour y répondre, il faut avant tout faire observer que les espaces urbains se présentent comme des cadres sociaux qui créent et offrent des opportunités pour les enfants et les jeunes dans la mesure où cette réalité est démontrable si l'on considère certaines formes d'activités économiques, agricoles et culturelles qui relativisent la description négative que l'on fait des écosystèmes sociaux urbains africains.

Les activités économiques dont nous faisons mention ici ne relèvent pas, *stricto sensu*, du secteur informel – bien qu'on puisse déceler un lien entre certaines de ces activités et le secteur informel. Il s'agit plutôt d'occupations saisonnières que mènent certains enfants et jeunes durant les périodes de vacances scolaires et qui sont supposées leur permettre d'économiser un peu d'argent grâce auquel ils peuvent préparer leurs rentrées scolaires et académiques. Généralement, ces activités économiques (vente ambulante d'arachides, de bananes, d'ananas, de friperie, etc.)

fleurissent dès la fin du mois de mai,[6] période à laquelle l'année scolaire connaît une interruption et marquant « officiellement » le départ en vacances dans la plupart des établissements primaires et secondaires. À cette période , il n'est pas rare de trouver certains élèves qui, comme Olivier, 16 ans, élève en classe de 4e au Collège « CCCS », et venu passer ces vacances à Yaoundé, s'investissent dans des métiers ambulants. L'intéressé, approché le 03 août 2009 et interrogé sur les raisons qui fondent son investissement dans cette catégorie d'activités explique :

Je vends les arachides depuis trois ans.

Que fais-tu avec l'argent que tu gagnes ?

Avec l'argent que je reçois, j'aide mes parents à payer ma pension.

Comment fais-tu pour garder ton argent ?

Je donne à mon grand-frère.

Et avec cet argent, que vas-tu faire ?

Je vais seulement payer la pension.

Est-ce qu'on t'oblige à vendre les arachides ?

Non, on ne m'oblige pas. Je ne peux pas venir en vacances et rester là comme ça à ne rien faire.

Est-ce que tu as également des amis qui vendent comme toi ?

Oui, j'ai aussi des amis. D'autres vendent les arachides, les bonbons pendant les grandes vacances et d'autres vendent même aussi pendant les congés des premier et deuxième trimestres, moi je ne vends pas pendant les congés-là.

Les informations qui sont mises en exergue dans cet entretien appellent à un certain nombre de commentaires. Tout d'abord, à en croire le jeune Olivier, l'activité qu'il mène résulte d'un choix délibéré. En ce sens, on peut donc dire qu'elle s'éloigne de la problématique relative au travail des enfants telle que conceptualisée par ceux qui, très souvent, n'y voit qu'une réactualisation de l'exploitation de ces derniers. Ensuite, les bénéfices récoltés sont soigneusement préservés par son grand-frère à qui Olivier verse quotidiennement une somme. Malheureusement, ce dernier a été hésitant quand nous lui avons demandé de nous dire le montant qu'il versait journalièrement à son frère aîné. En revanche, nous avons appris de la bouche du concerné lui-même que cet argent serait employé pour payer les frais de scolarité.

Ce qui nous semble particulièrement fructueux, c'est l'idée que le jeune Olivier pratique ce petit commerce à l'occasion de son séjour à Yaoundé, chez son frère aîné. Il avoue lui-même travailler parce qu'il n'a pas envie de « se croiser les bras ». Il y aurait donc, dans le choix fait par Olivier de vendre des arachides, un désir de s'occuper. C'est la même volonté que l'on retrouve chez Paul, 19 ans, élève dans la section industrielle, « option : installation des sanitaires » au Collège d'enseignement technique (Cetic) de Sangmelima. En effet, au moment où nous l'avons rencontré, Paul effectuait un stage de vacances depuis trois mois au Bureau camerounais d'affrètement et de voyages (Bucavoyages). Il raconte :

> Je fais un stage à Bucavoyages où je suis laveur de voitures.
>
> *Tu laves en moyenne combien de véhicules par jours ?*
>
> Trois voitures.
>
> *On te paye combien par voitures lavées ?*
>
> Cinq cent FCFA. Donc trois voitures ça me donne 1500 F CFA puisque chaque voiture c'est 500. On se lève à 4 heures et on lave les voitures de transport de l'agence. On a 500 F CFA de ration. Donc par jour, je ne peux pas me retrouver avec moins de 2500 F CFA. En plus, il peut aussi arriver que d'autres voitures viennent, comme celles de l'hôtel, par exemple.
>
> *Que vas-tu faire avec l'argent que tu gagnes ici ?*
>
> L'argent-là n'existe même plus. J'ai déjà préparé ma rentrée scolaire. J'ai déjà acheté tout (cahiers, bics, tenues, etc.).

Nous lui posons la question de savoir *où est-ce qu'il habite ?* Il répond :

> [Au village] Et il poursuit : Si je n'étais pas resté ici à Sangmelima, je serai déjà rentré au village.

Les informations que nous fournissent cet entretien ne s'écartent pas fondamentalement de celles issues de celui qui le précède. Ici, on voit également de quelle manière Paul met un point d'honneur à utiliser les fonds issus de son labeur pour préparer sa rentrée scolaire. C'est dire que l'argent que gagnent les jeunes en travaillant durant les vacances leur est d'un précieux concours dans leur réussite scolaire. A la fin de l'entretien, Paul affirme qu'il réside au village. En réalité, ce qu'il semble vouloir indiquer, c'est que ses parents vivent à la campagne et que la raison qui fonde et justifie sa présence à Sangmelima est essentiellement scolaire. À travers ces indications, se trouve affirmée une faille à partir de laquelle les espaces urbains se dressent comme des lieux qui offrent aux enfants et aux jeunes des opportunités.

En effet, l'opposition « village » et « ville » est une des portes d'entrée qui renseignent le mieux sur le caractère propice des espaces urbains. On s'en rend compte en scrutant avec attention la catégorie d'enfants et de jeunes qui nous intéressent. Dans ce sens, il est important de relever que les enfants et la plupart des jeunes qui quittent les campagnes pour la ville durant les vacances y viennent, pour travailler. En empruntant une catégorie doxique qui a pignon dans le vocabulaire au Cameroun, on dira qu'ils viennent en ville « pour prendre leur part ». Ceci pour désigner le fait qu'ils y séjournent essentiellement pour accumuler un minimum de ressources financières qui leur seront très utiles pour préparer leur rentrée scolaire, aider leurs cadets, etc. À titre d'illustration, au terme des vacances, il arrive souvent que ces jeunes aient de l'argent pour se prendre en charge. C'est donc pour cette finalité que de nombreux jeunes se déploient dans les rues urbaines durant ce « temps-mort » scolaire. Ils viennent souvent, par la même occasion – non sans conséquences – faire concurrence aux acteurs de l'économie souterraine. Même si certains enfants et jeunes avec lesquels nous avons devisé soutiennent qu'ils se livrent à cette activité pour « perdre ou tuer le temps », force est de constater que cette façon de se distraire permet à beaucoup de trouver leur compte car ils y tirent au moins l'argent de leur ration journalière.

Contrairement aux milieux ruraux, l'espace urbain se présente comme un environnement ouvert, porteur de nombreuses possibilités d'activités économiques. Qui plus est, le fait que les villes camerounaises s'étendent de plus en plus positionne les écosystèmes sociaux urbains comme des cadres qui favorisent la créativité sociale des jeunes car ceux-ci, étant entendu qu'ils y évoluent, peuvent exercer certaines activités qui leur permettent de « s'en sortir ». À cause de cela, il n'est pas excessif de penser que, avec l'extension des villes, s'ouvrent plus d'espaces de production et de consommation que les jeunes peuvent saisir.

Le développement récent de certaines activités agricoles (et pastorales) nous en fournit une illustration patente. La forme d'agriculture sur laquelle nous mettons le doigt est l'agriculture périurbaine, c'est-à-dire, celle qui se pratique autour des grandes villes. En effet, l'entrepreneuriat agricole autour des grandes villes est une piste sérieuse qu'explorent certains jeunes. La proximité d'avec le marché est une donnée qui positionne la ville comme un lieu d'opportunités pour ces derniers. Le fait que la ville soit considérée comme le siège de la consommation par excellence apparaît comme une opportunité qui est saisie par ces jeunes et cela justifie l'importance des enfants et des jeunes qui s'y investissent dans diverses sortes d'activités.[7]

Pour voir en quoi est-ce que l'implication des jeunes dans cette activité participe de la créativité, il faut se rappeler que, dans les sociétés africaines contemporaines en général, et dans la société camerounaise sur laquelle nous portons notre regard, en particulier, on ne compte plus l'effectif de jeunes qui se sont établis dans les espaces urbains, soit pour des motifs scolaires ou académiques, soit pour suivre une formation dans tel ou tel secteur d'activité, ou encore, pour chercher d u travail – ou pour d'autres motivations – et qui se meuvent dans l'économie informelle. À côté de cet ordre de personne, une autre catégorie de jeunes prend des proportions inquiétantes : ce sont les jeunes en situation de chômage. S'il est possible pour qui est attentif à ce qui se donne à observer dans le secteur informel d'y voir des faits qui attestent la créativité dont font montre des enfants et des jeunes, notre intérêt porte ici sur les activités agro-pastorales qui sont d'autres types d'opportunités de travail que tentent de saisir un nombre, fut-il encore minime, à l'heure actuelle, de jeunes.

Pour la plupart, il s'agit de jeunes qui ont senti qu'il existe autour des grandes villes des opportunités de s'occuper. En effet, dans les milieux urbains vivent de nombreux consommateurs qui, à cause de la nature de leurs activités, sont dans l'impossibilité de s'investir dans des activités de production. Dans les villes, les produits agricoles et d'élevage sont très sollicités et la demande va toujours *crescendo*. Pour ces jeunes, réunir des moyens nécessaires à la réalisation de la production de cultures maraîchères (légumes, fruits, racines et feuilles), de plants en pépinière, de la myciculture (culture du champignon), de fleurs ou encore de maïs présente des atouts certains : accès facile au marché, clientèle importante et souvent capable de payer le prix. Les jeunes producteurs ont également la possibilité de mettre aisément la main sur des intrants agricoles de qualité ; de profiter des moyens de transport faciles non seulement pour eux-mêmes mais aussi pour écouler leur production ; d'avoir un accès facile à l'information, etc. ; de profiter des services et infrastructures de base ; de démarrer avec peu de moyens ; d'avoir le moyen de s'assurer un emploi stable pour pourvoir à leurs besoins ainsi qu'à ceux de leurs familles ; d'avoir le moyen de gagner de l'argent ; et la possibilité de s'assumer et de de prendre en charge sa vie.[8]

Mais, il n'y a pas que vers l'exercice des activités agricoles que nous devons tourner notre regard. Il existe également des jeunes qui pratiquent l'élevage autour des villes (élevage des porcs, du poulet de chair, des lapins, des poissons, des cailles, des aulacodes, etc.). Tous bien considérés, si ces activités fleurissent davantage autour des villes et non dans les centres urbains, c'est en raison des nombreux inconvénients qui se dressent dans les villes. Parmi ceux-ci, on peut citer, sans être exhaustif, les litiges fonciers, les catastrophes naturelles (inondations, éboulements …), la difficulté à avoir accès à une terre arable, etc.

Pour se convaincre de l'intérêt que présentent les activités agro-pastorales que nous venons de mentionner dans l'épanouissement socio-économique des jeunes, il n'est pas superflu de considérer leurs avis. En tout cas, le sentiment de Jean-Romuald, fleuriste à Nsimalen, semble indiquer que c'est une chance pour lui d'être installé à côté de la ville de Yaoundé. Il témoigne :

> J'ai 23 ans. Après mes études en menuiserie, je n'avais personne pour m'aider à ouvrir un atelier. Mon frère fleuriste à Yaoundé m'a mis en contact avec un agronome qui cherchait un employé pour tenir sa pépinière. Il m'a recruté et m'a formé en production des plants de palmiers à huile et greffage des arbres fruitiers. Avec le temps, le salaire devenant irrégulier, mon frère m'a donné des semences de quelques espèces de fleurs très demandées à Yaoundé et m'a expliqué comment les cultiver. C'est ainsi que j'ai démarré cette nouvelle activité qui m'occupe aujourd'hui. Je fais dans les fleurs de jardin » (in *La Voix du Paysan* 2009 : 9).

Pour justifier son choix de s'établir dans une banlieue de la ville de Yaoundé, le fleuriste répond :

J'ai déménagé pour vivre à Nsimalen où je loue ma chambre à 12 000 F par mois. Étant sur place, j'ai pu trouver non loin de ma pépinière, à côté d'un bas-fond, un terrain de 1/2 hectare que je loue à 25 000 F par an. J'y cultive les légumes, la pastèque, le piment et le gombo. Mes clients viennent de Yaoundé. Il y a des bayam-salam (revendeuses) qui viennent acheter les légumes et les fruits sur place. Parfois, dès que je sors du champ, comme je suis sur un axe goudronné, les voitures s'arrêtent aussitôt pour acheter toute ma production. J'ai déjà compris une chose, mon avenir est dans l'agriculture. C'est une chance d'être à côté de Yaoundé où tout se vend, même les fleurs (in *La Voix du Paysan*, 2009 : 9).

Jean Bakari, producteur de fleurs à Nsimalen a un point de vue similaire. Il insiste tout particulièrement sur les atouts que présentent les écosystèmes sociaux urbains :

J'ai reçu une formation en agriculture mais je me suis spécialisé sur les fleurs à la demande des clients qui m'ont dit que ma proximité avec l'aéroport de Yaoundé-Nsimalen me serait très avantageuse. Je cultive les fleurs de jardin. Par mois, je produis environ 1 000 pieds de différentes espèces. Le prix d'un pied varie entre 150 et 1 000 F CFA. Mes clients viennent de Yaoundé, de Mbalmayo, d'Ebolowa et même du Gabon. Les fleurs les plus demandées sont le Duratan, le Rosier, le Sapin, l'Hibiscus, le Pourpier, le Bégonia. Les périodes où je fais de bonnes recettes sont les mois d'avril, mai, juin et août. Aux jeunes qui voudraient se lancer dans la culture des fleurs, je leur conseille de ne pas trop s'éloigner de la ville où se trouve la clientèle. Au village, ça ne paiera pas (in *La Voix du Paysan*, 2009 : 9).

On aurait tort de penser que les jeunes que nous que nous faisons parler ici ne sont que des jeunes horticulteurs. Cyprien et Christian sont tous deux des maraîchers qui confessent volontiers le succès qu'ils rencontrent grâce à la culture de certains de leurs produits. Voici ce que rapporte Cyprien qui pratique son activité à Nkol Ondom, une localité située à la périphérie de la ville de Yaoundé :

Je suis élève en classe de première. Je fais l'agriculture parce que, depuis que je suis enfant, je vois mes parents et mes aînés cultiver la terre. Le terrain appartient à mon père et il m'a juste donné une petite parcelle pour que je puisse faire mon champ. Je cultive les céleris, les tomates, les poivrons, les poireaux, les carottes, la laitue et autres légumes. Mes clients sont les Bayam Sellam du marché du Mfoundi à Yaoundé. Le prix varie entre 500 et 1 500 F CFA selon les saisons. Le maraîchage est bien rentable. Grâce à ça, j'ai pu construire une chambre dans laquelle je vis et je paie mes fournitures scolaires (in *La voix du paysan*, 2009 : 9).

Christian, la trentaine, apporte des informations qui s'orientent dans une perspective identique à celle de Cyprien. Il confie :

En réalité, je suis maçon de formation. Je suis originaire de Zamengoué (à une vingtaine de km de Yaoundé). Je suis arrivé à Nkol Ondom (5 km de Yaoundé) en 2007 grâce à ma grande sœur qui est mariée dans ce village. C'est elle qui m'a dit qu'il y a de bonnes opportunités dans l'agriculture à Nkol Ondom. J'y suis arrivé et j'ai constaté qu'elle avait raison. Aujourd'hui, je cultive la laitue, les carottes, les céleris, le chou et autres légumes. La terre que j'exploite appartient à mon beau-frère. Mes principaux clients sont les revendeurs du marché du Mfoundi à Yaoundé. C'est une activité qui rapporte. Grâce à mes revenus, je m'occupe aisément de ma femme et de mon enfant (in *La voix du paysan*, 2009 : 9).

Tous ces exemples que l'on pourrait multiplier en donnant la parole à des jeunes qui, autour des villes de Douala, Ngaoundéré, Maroua, etc., s'activent dans des activités agro-pastorales périurbaines indiquent l'inventivité dont ils font montre dans un contexte d'adversité protéiforme. En considérant avec attention leurs itinéraires biographiques, on se rend compte que, pour la plupart, les jeunes qui s'investissent vers ces secteurs sont des personnes qui, suite à leur socialisation scolaire, n'ont pas pu s'insérer sur le marché de l'emploi. Dans un contexte où le « mythe du matricule » structure toujours l'imagination de la réussite de nombreux jeunes, le fait qu'une minorité d'entre eux s'investissent dans les métiers de la terre et y réussissent appelle un commentaire fondamental.

C'est que, parmi les générations contemporaines, l'idée qui se fait de plus en plus jour est que la réussite sociale ne se lit plus uniquement et exclusivement à partir d'un travail bureaucratique. En choisissant de préférer la pioche à la plume (Ela 1971), les jeunes gens prouvent que ce qu'il est important de retenir, c'est que, à défaut de déboucher sur un emploi administratif, l'école donne les moyens de trouver du travail. Un tel éclairage interpelle en même temps les pouvoirs publics qui se soucient très peu du type d'homme dont la société a besoin pour se développer.

À ceux qui pourraient nous objecter le caractère insignifiant ou peu rentable des activités que pratiquent les enfants et les jeunes dont nous parlons, nous répondons, en prenant appui sur *L'éthique protestante et l'esprit du capitalisme* de Max Weber, que ces activités sont en réalité économiquement porteuses. Car l'argent est par essence prolifique et générateur d'argent. N'utilisant pas les bénéfices pour satisfaire leurs jouissances, mais plutôt pour accroître leurs activités, ces enfants et ces jeunes se retrouvent, à la fin des vacances ou dans l'exercice de leurs activités agro-pastorales, avec une somme d'argent qui les met à l'abri d'un certain nombre de besoins, tout en participant, à leur niveau, au fonctionnement de leurs cellules familiales. Cette idée est en harmonie avec celle que défend Weber lorsque, dans son ouvrage précédemment cité, il réussit à manifester l'ascendance du calvinisme sur la propagation de l'esprit du capitaliste. A en croire le célèbre sociologue allemand, en effet, il est possible de jeter un pont entre ces deux éthos du moment qu'ils mettent tous en avant une conduite austère qui sert tant la rédemption de l'âme puritaine que la dynamique de l'accumulation.

Appliqué au contexte camerounais, le raisonnement du théoricien allemand autorise à penser les différentes séquences « professionnelles » des jeunes que nous avons esquissées ici comme différentes trajectoires qui participent, plus largement, d'un parcours vers la réussite sociale. En effet, très souvent, en ce qui concerne les activités que les jeunes élèves exercent durant les vacances, il n'est pas rare d'observer une mobilité professionnelle ascendante. De la sorte, il arrive que les métiers pratiqués par ceux-ci varient en fonction du capital que ces jeunes réussissent à mobiliser au terme de leurs vacances.

Mais ce n'est pas tout. Le milieu urbain ouvre également aux jeunes de nombreuses opportunités culturelles. Dans cette perspective, il faut peut-être accorder une attention particulière aux métiers qu'exercent les enfants et les jeunes dans ces espaces. Ici, il convient de mentionner les métiers d'artistes, de danseurs, de chorégraphes, d'humoristes, de peintres, de sculpteurs, de plasticiens, etc. Pour l'essentiel, l'effervescence de ces métiers qui s'origine dans l'apparition de nouvelles « industries culturelles » s'enracine dans ce que nous avons appelé la dynamique des modèles et des itinéraires de la réussite sociale que prise la jeunesse urbaine camerounaise (Manga Lebongo 2007).

À partir de l'implication de ces derniers dans ces espaces, il est possible de dépasser les lectures qui présentent les villes africaines comme des espaces accessoires, dont les jeunes sont des acteurs passifs face aux impératifs (politiques, économiques, culturels) d'un monde social auquel ils sont régulièrement confrontés. Au regard de ce que nous avons observé, notre point de vue est que, même s'il nous paraît possible de penser la ville africaine comme un cadre au sein duquel se dramatise un certain nombre de déficits, celle-ci se présente comme un haut lieu où s'affirme l'ingéniosité et la vitalité des enfants et des jeunes. En témoigne par exemple les phénomènes aussi divers que le commerce des denrées alimentaires, la pratique des stages de vacances, l'agriculture périurbaine, etc. qui s'y épanouissent. En réalité, en tenant compte de toutes ces activités, il est possible de mettre en évidence la créativité protéiforme dont font montre les jeunes dans les grandes villes d'Afrique, pour montrer ce que l'adversité qu'ils conjuguent au quotidien évoque et provoque en termes d'ouvertures dans les villes camerounaises contemporaines.

Conclusion

Tout au long de cette étude, les questions qui ont alimenté nos réflexions étaient guidées par un souci : interroger d'une manière peu courante la ville de façon à mettre en exergue les activités créatrices qui y sont produites par les enfants et les jeunes dans le contexte camerounais. Pour cela, il s'est d'abord agi de préciser les contours de ce que revêtent dans le cadre de ce travail les notions de créativité, d'enfants et des jeunes. La créativité dont il s'agit dans ce travail, renvoie, avons-nous vu, à un processus faisant intervenir des éléments cognitifs par lequel les jeunes extériorisent leur singularité dans la façon de lier des choses, d'associer des idées, d'engendrer des situations qui, par l'aboutissement du résultat concret de cette démarche processuelle, change, modifie ou transforme la perception, l'usage ou la matérialité auprès d'un public donné. La créativité sociale des enfants et des jeunes qualifie ainsi la capacité dont dispose ce groupe à produire, à une période précise, des solutions, des idées ou des concepts qui sont susceptibles de permettre de réaliser, d'une manière efficiente et inattendue, une action. L'espace urbain, quand à lui se présente comme un milieu qui crée et offre des opportunités pour les enfants et les jeunes dans la mesure où il rend possible le développement de l'imagination créatrice des jeunes grâce à laquelle fleurissent un nombre considérable d'activités économiques, agricoles et culturelles qui relativisent la description négative que l'on fait de cet écosystème social au Cameroun.

Notes

1. Le Cameroun se singularise en effet par la jeunesse de sa population. Selon les statistiques descriptives que fournit Tsala Tsala (2009 : 101), « Le taux de croissance annuelle de la population du Cameroun est passé de 3,0 pour cent en 1976 à 2,9 pour cent en 1987 et à 2,87 pour cent en 2000 selon les projections (DSCN 1987). Toujours à partir des mêmes sources, et suivant les calculs effectués par le FMI en octobre 2000, la population camerounaise est théoriquement passée à plus de 17 106 000 habitants. Les différentes projections donnaient les chiffres de 18 000 000 pour 2005, 23 000 000 pour 2014 et 25 000 000 pour 2020 dont 51 pour cent de femmes et 49 pour cent d'hommes. » D'après les résultats provisoires de la troisième enquête camerounaise auprès des ménages (Ecam III 2008 : 25), « La population camerounaise est estimée à 17,9 millions de personnes en 2007, dont 51 pour cent de femmes et 49 pour cent d'hommes. » Selon les données de cette même source (Ecam III 2008 : 25), « cette population est extrêmement jeune : 43 pour cent des personnes ont moins de 15 ans et 3,5 pour cent seulement sont âgés de 65 ans ou plus ».
2. En portant notamment notre regard sur les jeunes de la rue par exemple. Ou encore, en interrogeant les « vagabonds », les « délinquants », et/ou toute la part de « déchets sociaux et/ou domestiques » qu'on y fait figurer.
3. Voir la tonalité qui s'exhale d'un certain nombre de rapports commandités par le ministère camerounais de la ville et réalisé par des cabinets d'experts (Sasco, 2000 ; Abondo Akomndja, Missi, Emini Ekouma 2002). Consulter aussi Eboko (2002).
4. De nombreuses pistes de réflexion ont été fouillées afin d'interroger les comportements sociaux en termes de logiques d'action. Pour notre part, nous inspirons de la synthèse réalisée par Michel Lallement (2000).
5. Voir dans le livre *Le récit des origines du monde et de l'humanité*. Il y est écrit : « Au commencement, Dieu créa le ciel et le terre ». Cf. *La Bible*, Genèse 1, 1.
6. Ce qui correspond à la fin de l'année scolaire au Cameroun. Les vacances s'étalent sur trois mois. Ce qui donne une idée de la période durant laquelle cette catégorie d'acteurs est mobilisée.

7. Il ne s'agit pas ici seulement d'un regard objectif au regard des acquis de l'ethnologie et de la sociologie urbaine. La ville est également lue, de façon subjective (c'est-à-dire par les enfants et les jeunes eux-mêmes) comme le siège de la consommation par excellence.
8. Pour construire cette partie de notre réflexion, nous nous sommes fortement inspiré des idées développées dans *La voix du paysan* qui se veut, au Cameroun, le *Mensuel de l'entrepreneur rural* n° 217 (2009 : 5-13).

Références

Abondo Akomndja, Vincelline, Jean-Paul Missi, Zéphirin Emini Ekouma, *et al.*, 2002, Projet n° CMR/2000/08/08/56, Document de stratégie de prévention locale de la délinquance urbaine à Yaoundé, document de discussion.

Arborio, Anne-Marie et Pierre Fournier, 2001, *L'enquête et ses méthodes : l'observation directe*, Paris : Nathan, 2ᵉ éd.

Bayart, Jean-François, 1985, *L'État au Cameroun*, Paris : Presses de la Fondation Nationale des Sciences Politiques, 2ᵉ éd.

De Boeck, Filip et Honwana, Alcinda, 2005, « Faire et défaire la société : enfants, jeunes et politique en Afrique », *Politique Africaine* n° 80, décembre, Paris : Karthala, pp. 5-11.

Dubet, François, 1994, *Sociologie de l'expérience* Paris : Seuil.

Eboko, Fred, 2002, Pouvoir, jeunesse et sida au Cameroun. Politique publique, dynamiques sociales et construction des sujets, Thèse pour le doctorat en science politique, Université de Bordeaux, Institut d'études politiques.

Ecam III, 2008, Troisième enquête camerounais auprès des ménages (Ecam III), « La population camerounaise, in *Ecam III, Tendances, profil et déterminants de la pauvreté au Cameroun entre 2001-2007* », Yaoundé : INS.

Ela, Jean-Marc, 1971, *La plume et la pioche. Réflexion sur l'enseignement et la société dans le développement de l'Afrique noire*, Yaoundé : CLÉ.

Lallement, Michel, 2000, « A la recherche des logiques d'action », *in* Philippe Cabin et Jean-François Dortier, *La sociologie. Histoire et idées*, Paris : Sciences Humaines, pp. 256-257.

La Voix du Paysan, 2009, « Agriculture et élevage autour des grandes villes. On y gagne bien sa vie », *Mensuel de l'entrepreneur rural*, n° 217, pp. 1-18.

Manga Lebongo, Jean-Marcellin, 2007, Les dynamiques des modèles sociaux au Cameroun. Esquisse d'une sociologie des imaginaires de la réussite sociale et politique de la jeunesse urbaine de Yaoundé, Mémoire de maîtrise en Sociologie, Université de Yaoundé-I, Inédit.

Manga Lebongo, Jean-Marcellin, 2009, Jeunesse urbaine camerounaise, créativité sociale et contestation politique. Analyse de quelques modes d'expression et d'action d'une catégorie sociale, mémoire de DEA en Sociologie, Université de Yaoundé-I, Inédit.

Mbembé, Achille, 2005, *De la postcolonie. Essai sur l'imagination politique dans l'Afrique contemporaine*, Paris : Karthala.

Mucchielli, Alex, éd., 2004, *Dictionnaire des méthodes qualitatives en sciences humaines*, Paris : Armand Colin, 2ᵉ édition.

Nguendo Yongsi, H., B., Dickens Priso, et Humphrey Ngala Ndi, 2008, « Mutations fonctionnelles de l'espace en milieu urbain camerounais : occupation des fonds de vallées et risques de santé à Yaoundé », in *Annales de la Faculté des Arts, Lettres et Sciences Humaines*, Université de Yaoundé I, Vol. 1, N° 8, Nouvelle série, 2008, Premier et Second Semestres.

Osborn, 1971, *L'imagination constructive*, Paris : Dunod.

Sasco, 2000, Élaboration d'un plan d'insertion des jeunes en difficulté, Phase II, Enquête de terrain (Douala), étude menée pour le compte du ministère de la ville.

Touré, Moriba et Fadayomi, éd., 1983, *Migrations et urbanisation au Sud du Sahara : Quels impacts sur les politiques de population et de développement ?*, Dakar/Paris : CODESRIA/ Karthala, Coll. « Série des livres du CODESRIA ».

Tsala Tsala, Jacques-Philippe, 2009, « Psychologie et développement. Comment la psychologie peut-elle contribuer au développement du Cameroun », in *Annales de la Faculté des Arts, Lettres et Sciences Humaines*, Université de Yaoundé I, Numéro Spécial, *Actes des « Mercredis des Grandes Conférences »* 2006-2007.

Zoa, Anne-Sidonie, 1999, « Langages et cultures des jeunes dans les villes africaines », *in* Gauthier, Madeleine et Guillaume, Jean-François (éd.), *Définir la jeunesse ? D'un bout à l'autre du monde*, Laval : PUL/L'Harmattan, pp. 237-250.

5

The Representations of Unaccompanied Working Migrant Male Children Negotiating for Livelihoods in a South African Border Town

Stanford Taonatose Mahati

Introduction

The recent phenomenon of massive numbers of unaccompanied Zimbabwean migrant children[1] who are working in South Africa is provoking consternation among parents, guardians, child-related organizations, and the governments of South Africa and Zimbabwe. People's concerns about these children revolve around their safety, which is threatened by a range of factors from economic exploitation to denial of fundamental human rights. Their fears are based on reports (e.g., Palmary 2009) that these children are doing work that is harmful or interferes with their development (see United Nations Conventions on the Rights of the Child 1989, Article 32).

In response to this situation, agencies working in the border town of Musina were providing a plethora of services to these children. Care workers' efforts to protect children could be based on the categorization, common in Northern ideologies, of children as innocent victims who are not to blame for their situation (see Burman 2008).

Although various parties assume children's work to be wrong (see Burr 2006:4), children themselves sometimes feel they need to work. The way care workers then go about representing working children, which can either help or constrain their negotiations for livelihoods, deserves particular attention. In addition, the representation of these children has to be interrogated in resource-poor settings, where adults are not able to support children, and there is enormous pressure for children to contribute to family incomes (Bourdillon 2008b:270).

Burman explained that problems start when children violate ideals of dependence and innocence, and that children may then incur the penalty of no longer being accorded indulgences or privileges associated with childhood (2008:190). Consequently, children without the attributes of a proper childhood are often considered deviants and this determines how they are treated (Walkerdine 2001).

This chapter stems from broader research, which considers the predominant representations of unaccompanied migrant children that service providers bring to bear on their interactions with these young people in the South African border town of Musina, one of the busiest ports of entry in sub-Saharan Africa. The chapter examines how the representations of service providers are informed by international child declarations.[2] It specifically focuses on the representations of working boys, when they negotiate for livelihoods. Findings on girls will be presented in another publication.

Migrant working children can experience marginalization and exclusion in the 'new informal economies' (Boeck and Honwana 2005:1) as they are 'not supposed' to work. This view is a consequence of the construction of children as dependants whose main occupations are play and school (Woodhead 2007:23), reinforced by the South African law which forbids inappropriate and hazardous child work as well as any employment below the minimum school-leaving age of 15 (Basic Conditions of Employment Act, 75 of 1997). However, a significant population of unaccompanied minors are working as it is one of the major reasons why they migrate to South Africa (e.g., Palmary 2009).

Whilst literature is abundant on why children work, there is less on understanding how these children are represented, the consequences of those representations, and how the children represent themselves. To unpack the representations of childhood, there is need to consider the influence of social factors like age, gender and class. There is also need to question the structural power imbalances which characterize the relationship between adults and children. Kitzinger (1990:162) noted that an analysis of power, which shapes children's position, is often rejected in favour of a paternalistic approach to children.

This chapter is anchored on the understanding that as working migrant children negotiate for livelihoods, they are active social agents who create meanings about themselves and through their relations with adults (Woodhead 2007:34). The construction of children as passive victims can be attributed to the 'traditional relegation of children to the world of the muted – along with groups such as women, the disabled… and minority peoples' (Twum-Danso 2004:1) and the prevalence of the view regarding children as passive and immature (Burman 2008). Analysing children's views may bring to the fore issues like how these children make sense of their marginalization and exclusion from the workplace.

Generally, migrants from Zimbabwe have been characterized as "economic migrants, and not refugees" (Roelf 2007 cited in Rutherford 2008:39). However, the issues facing migrant children when they negotiate for livelihoods might not simply be economic.

The study contributes to the concerns which Burman (2008) raises: globalization of the West's definition of the child, which tends to see a child as innocent and dependent on adults, can lead to the pathologization or demonization of children whose behaviour repudiates the conventional norms. This chapter follows Burman's (1995) point that the daunting task of supporting children who live in developing countries demands not only a re-conceptualization of how we see those children, but more importantly an assessment of socio-structural factors that determine their positions.

At the centre of the universal child declarations are the principles of the best interests of the child, the right of the child to be heard on decisions that affect him or her, and the importance of soliciting his or her views. The way these principles function and are contested in the context of migrant children in Musina is a further subject of this chapter.

One of the critical areas which are interrogated in this chapter is whether the children see things the same way as the carers; and how they interpret the world may be appropriate to understanding how they interact with interventions. Consequently, Norman Long's (1992) actor-oriented approach was used as an analytical and methodological approach to unpack the life-worlds[3] of both children and care workers. Basically, the actor-oriented approach seeks to clarify how actors attempt to create space for themselves amidst interventions in their lives and 'to determine which elements contribute to or impede the successful creation of such space for manoeuvre' (Leeuwis, Long and Villarreal 1990:19).

Research Methods

This ethnographic study took place between August 2009 and February 2010. It focused on one international agency and one faith-based organization. The research sample of twenty was selected by both snowballing techniques, which depended on children's social networks, and the purposive selection of the children. The selection of boys for interviews stopped at 20 as it had reached a point of sample redundancy. I did not participate directly in all the money-making activities of children. I did profit by being partially embedded in the work of the selected service providers and this enabled me to get an insight into their experiences.

Data from care workers was collected through situational interviews, in-depth interviews, and participant observation. Then the three data collection techniques together with focus group discussions (FGDs) and vignettes were used to collect data from children. These are 'short stories about hypothetical characters in specified circumstances, to whose situation the interviewee is invited to respond' (Finch 1987:105 cited in Barter and Renold 1999). Since expressing an opinion on a hypothetical story is less personal and intimidating than talking about direct experience, vignettes can assist in exploring potentially sensitive topics that participants might be uncomfortable to discuss openly (Barter and Renold 1999).

Interviews with children and some care workers were conducted in Shona, and for the purposes of this chapter their responses have been translated by the author.

Ethical Considerations

Ethical principles of informed consent, costs and benefits of participation, anonymity, confidentiality and rights of withdrawal were shared with research participants, including children (see Hopkins 2008; Greene and Hogan 2005).

One of the established practices for a research with children to be ethically compliant is getting consent from parents or those '*in loco parentis*'. However, it is impossible to obtain parental consent on behalf of unaccompanied children (see Hopkins 2008:40). There were few social workers in Musina, so I obtained consent instead from care workers who were looking after children in their shelters (see Hopins, 2008: 41), who insisted that I do so.

Children who needed assistance or were in perilous situations were referred to service providers, but only after obtaining their consent. Children partaking in illegal activities such as living in South Africa without valid documents were not reported to authorities.

Study Results and Discussion

Children's Work and their Relations with the Social Environment

The unaccompanied migrant children's work and their relations with the social environment shaped the way these children represented themselves and were represented by others. The common factors pushing these Zimbabwean children to migrate to South Africa were poverty, hunger, lack of access to education, abuse at home, and limited employment opportunities (see Palmary 2009; Hillier 2007). Some pursued adventure while others wanted to reunite with family members.

The majority of migrant boys in Musina lived in a shelter or transit centre then co-managed by the two service providers. The second biggest group were living on the streets and at the border post. Very few children were renting places to stay in informal shelters.

The boys in the formal shelters complained of lack of freedom of movement to look for work. They were only allowed to be out between 7.00 and 19:30 hours. Consequently, many children used to sneak back into shelters after hours.

One of the boys, aged 15, argued: 'We didn't come to South Africa to eat and sleep. We crossed the border to work.' Many left the shelter in the early hours in the morning to work. This behaviour led some care workers to describe them as lacking discipline. The majority of children living on the streets did not want to live at the centre. Their major complaints were fear of being physically abused by other children, overcrowding, and theft of their personal possessions like clothes.

Musina town (including the Beit Bridge border post), with an approximate total population of 40,000 people, was characterized by poverty and violent crime. Some children gave care workers and trusted adult women their goods including clothes, groceries for safe keeping.

Although most children were holders of provisional asylums permits, which only allowed them to study in South Africa, they were working. In fact most Zimbabwean applications for asylum were from economic migrants and not refugees as defined by the Refugee Act (1998). Most children were experiencing the same social pressures that adult migrants have of supporting their families in the country of origin (see Kankonde 2010).

The majority of children, including those attending primary and secondary school, were doing menial jobs. Their common working areas were streets, the high density area, and the environs of the border post. They worked as porters, collectors and sellers of shopping receipts with value added tax (VAT, which could be claimed by non-resident travellers when they leave South Africa), human smugglers, vendors (including selling pornographic DVDs), collectors and sellers of firewood, domestic workers, and car and truck washers.

A few boys also worked as informal pimps for truck drivers and sex workers. Some guarded business premises and vendors' stalls at the border post in return for a sleeping place. Children were perceived by care workers as not calculative in taking this dangerous and exploitative work. However, children said this arrangement solved their monetary and homelessness problems.

Working migrant children were exposed to crime and some were being initiated into crime. Pressure to survive forced some of them to engage in criminal activities. For example, some children were moving with razors and using them to forge shopping receipts. This practice was introduced to them by an adult migrant man. In a mocking but advisory manner, he had asked the boys, 'You do not have a razor? Why do you move without your work tools? If you do not know your work you must resign.'

Generally, a spirit of camaraderie prevailed amongst migrant children. In most cases this was regardless of where they stayed, their ethnicity, ages, etc. The rallying point was the shared vulnerability to hunger, abuse and exploitation. They shared food to save money and to help those who had no money. As a protection strategy they usually moved around in a group.

However, there were also individual and group rivalries around territorial claims. For example, those who lived at the centre said, 'Generally we do not touch a rubbish bin [in the centre of Musina town].' There was an unwritten understanding between them and street children that rubbish bins belonged to the later. Violators of this 'rule' risked being beaten by street children.

Despite efforts by adults to marginalize and exclude unaccompanied minors from South Africa, and through 'regular harassment, fabrications that we committed crimes, beatings, detentions and deportations by the South African police' as Thabani described, all these efforts proved fruitless. Children at a great cost to their physical and emotional well being, weathered the police's heavy-handed blitzes against child work. They mastered the art of evading arrest and deportation. Melusi (aged 15) explained:

> We are used to these raids which often happen either when a new group of police officers which is not child friendly arrive to police the border or when they receive directives to weed out migrant children. We have several 'gate-ways' or escape routes, and hideouts like trees and rooftops.

The adults who harassed children included South Africans and Zimbabweans, criminals and non-criminals.

One of the strategies used by children working at the border to either curry favour with the police or hit back at the *magumaguma*[4] was supplying the police with intelligence information about their identity and operations. Then some, like those who begged for shopping receipts, periodically thwarted efforts by thieves to steal in return for being 'allowed' by security guards to work at shop entrances. Some of them clandestinely collaborated with children by collecting and giving them receipts to sell in return for a commission.

Partially due to children's contribution to efforts against crime, some law enforcement agents did not arrest or beat them. 'When police are told to arrest all the children from Zimbabwe some of them warn us of the impending raids and on that day they don't find us,' claimed Melusi.

Foreigners, including children, periodically experience xenophobic attacks in South Africa (see Livesay 2006). Soon after arrival in South Africa children make concerted efforts to speak local languages fluently. Many tried to dress like local people. These strategies helped to mask their Zimbabwean identity and reduce hostilities between them and locals. In addition, speaking the local languages helped foreign children to negotiate in business transactions and to ward off accusations of being criminals as they could express themselves clearly. For example, Mandla (aged 16) worked as a vendor and spoke Ndebele, Shona, English, Zulu, Venda and Shangani: he said he sold more cigarettes than his friend who only spoke the first three languages.

The area is a melting pot of many ethnic groups but the dominant one is Venda. Ethnic undercurrents simmer amongst people. Some children from the Shona ethnic group masquerade as Ndebeles in order to get protection from the Ndebele and Zulu transport operators at the border post.[5]

Dominant Thinking of Care Workers Towards Working Migrant Children

Generally, care workers portrayed working migrant children as a vulnerable and exploited group in urgent need of care and protection. They often sensitized children about exploitation and tried to dissuade them from working. Instead they wanted children to attend school in Musina or re-unite with their parents or guardians.

Common perceptions amongst care workers were also that these children were well behaved, trustworthy, intelligent, hard-working and resilient. Care workers regarded the children as coming from resource-poor households. This led many of them to think that these children were prepared to accept any kind of work. However, this was not always the case. Despite shortage of money, some remained selective in the type of work they did. For example, they refused strenuous work associated with poor rural people like fetching firewood for sale, or dangerous work like hunting.

In response to reports of children being exploited, care workers often lobbied the South African Police Services (SAPS) to intervene. SAPS frequently conducted operations to stop child work. However, children complained that SAPS physically and verbally abused them during these operations. Ironically, children also accused care workers of covertly working with SAPS since they had a common agenda of stopping child work. Despite this mistrust, children appreciated care workers' intervention to stop police from beating, detaining and deporting children.

Care workers widely accused children of falsifying their biographical information, particularly names and ages. 'They drop or pick up some years and names when they cross the Limpopo River into South Africa,' said one care worker. Children used fake names to disguise their identity from parents and guardians looking for them. It was also a strategy of hiding their true identity from ordinary people who fabricated stories of theft.

Realizing that most migrants from Zimbabwe were economic migrants instead of political victims; the South African government in 2009 changed its policies of treating irregular migrants from Zimbabwe. Adult Zimbabweans with asylum papers were allowed to work in South Africa. Zimbabwean children with the assistance of care workers and social workers were also getting asylum permits, which only allowed them to study. To overcome the challenge of being barred from working, some children lied that they were over 17 years. At the shelter these boys claimed to be less than 18 years to access services meant for children.

The inflation of ages was part of a strategy of undermining the 'care and protection' system as it obstructed them from realizing their aspirations. Desperation forced them to focus on pressing challenges like getting money to buy food for themselves and their starving families in Zimbabwe. Fear of dying in foreign lands and not being identified remained remote.

Consequently, care workers described these children as money-centred and having a negative attitude towards education. Care workers said whilst the majority of unaccompanied minors wanted to continue with schooling, a significant proportion of them did not. In 2009, a number of those who enrolled in local schools dropped out. However, in 2010 there was an increase in the number studying, including some who had dropped out in 2009 and who expressed interest to go to school. Some children felt under pressure from their benefactors, both care workers and ordinary people (including employers), to attend school. 'Saying you attend school results in less verbal abuse against you by every adult. Every day we are told about the importance of education,' observed a 14-year-old boy.

Some children were also accused of spreading falsehoods that they were victims of political violence.[6] This claim elicited sympathy from community members who responded by giving them money, shopping receipts, and menial jobs, and led care workers to view the children as manipulative.

According to care workers another familiar lie peddled by migrant children was that they were orphans. 'I really don't know where they get this idea from that if you say I am an orphan you quickly get assistance or a job,' said one care worker. Several children were often unmasked as non-orphans.

Some boys, particularly those living on the streets, were characterized as sexually decadent. Children indulged in high-risk sex with adult women, particularly sex workers on both sides of the border. These boys often had sex with fellow girls who lived with them to have 'fun, just to help each other with sex, for protecting and giving them food', said a boy aged 13. Despite criticising children's behaviour, care workers said these children needed protection from unscrupulous adults including those who employed them to sell illegal pornographic DVDs. In the evening these children found amusement from viewing these DVDs.

Although all migrant children were supposed to be fairly assisted, care workers tended to either resign or have a lethargic response towards those who lived and worked on the streets. Despite recognising their resilience and ingenuity in developing survival strategies, care workers described them as uncouth, delinquent liars, naughty, criminals and drug consumers. 'Their parents and other aid organizations failed to take them away from the street. They do not appreciate help,' said one care worker. Street children were viewed as delinquents who were beyond rehabilitation.

Care Workers' Inconsistent and Varied Responses to Working Children

Care workers were inconsistent and had varied responses to working children. They often held out some sympathy for them. They accepted children's argument that they had to work to alleviate poverty in their Zimbabwean households. Some care workers questioned the utility of efforts to stop migrant children from working, since the major push factor was poverty which service providers did not have resources to address.

Care workers tacitly supported children through allowing and encouraging them to work, helping them find work and get paid, and keeping their money and groceries. One care worker remarked, 'I am impressed by their ability to save money and their unselfishness to use their money to buy basics for their siblings, parents and even grandparents.'

However, care workers' attitudes towards working children were often contradictory, depending on their audience. To management, people, or organizations that were opposed to child work, they projected an image of sharing those sentiments. When care workers were with children, they encouraged them, particularly those who used their money 'wisely'. For example, a female care worker publicly praised a 14-year-boy for behaving 'like a father' as he periodically remitted groceries to his family.

In a further endorsement of child work, care workers often accepted goods bought by children like soft drinks. This invited accusations by some children that they favoured working children who gave them something. Children complained that care workers considered these children to be well behaved.

The conflicting attitudes towards child work confused children. Children either ignored or did not take seriously care workers' messages against child work.

Some care workers argued that their inability to provide children with all their needs like clothing, school uniforms, pocket money, a varied diet, and material support for their families in Zimbabwe had a debilitating effect on their campaigns against harmful and exploitative child work. 'When we try to stop children from working, they accuse us of wanting to make them vulnerable and for frustrating their efforts to help themselves and their families,' said one care worker.

Some care workers viewed children as immature and incapable of defending themselves against exploitation, and opposed child work. One Zimbabwean care worker who also fled from the economic meltdown in Zimbabwe said, 'Migrant children must go back home [Zimbabwe]. Children rejected this appropriation of migration by adults, arguing that they could not live in an environment where adults failed to live.

Unaccompanied minors including those with asylum permits faced a great challenge in saving money, since they could not open bank accounts. To overcome this challenge, some children negotiated with care workers and people they trusted to keep their money. These adults often either abused or used the money they held in trust. Children were often forced to change their plans, for example, postponing going to Zimbabwe with groceries to help their poor siblings and relatives since they failed to collect adequate funds. Children expressed hopelessness, powerlessness, and fear of being victimized if they tried to claim back their money.

Children's Reality and Self-perception

Contrary to their portrayal as people who had 'self-destructive agency' (Gigengack 2008:216), had no capacity to make rational decisions, and succumbed to peer pressure, some children behaved otherwise. For example, 16-year-old Thabani was teased by other children and adults for working as a herd boy. One *magumaguma* mocked Thabani by asking him, 'How can you come to South Africa to herd goats?' He countered his critics by saying, 'Money earned from working as a herd boy or fetching firewood for sale is still money.' He further said the most important thing was earning an honest living, extricating himself and his family from poverty.

A serious argument also brewed between children and care workers on whether children should work or attend school. Many children called for the latter to let them freely make that decision. Children argued that making them go to school was a sheer waste of money and resources as most of them soon dropped out. Moses, aged 15, declared, ' I did not come to South Africa to attend school or to be idle at the shelter like a chicken on a feeding scheme. I am here to work.'

Since agencies did not provide most of the things they needed, children dismissed their efforts to make them focus on education alone. For example, 12-year-old Farai argued, 'Not working is as good as going back home [to Zimbabwe]. Attending school is good, but my family and I cannot live on education alone.'

A number of children had great admiration for migrants, including children, who periodically visited Zimbabwe and sent remittances and groceries to their families. However, others vowed to return only after having realized their dreams like buying large amounts of groceries, nice clothes, and owning an expensive car. For example, Daniel aged 16 said, 'I have to present myself as a person who has been working in South Africa.' Pressure to succeed amongst children was very high.

A number of children felt that some care workers did not respect their decision to work. John, aged 14, reported that care workers usually described them as 'people who like money too much and hate school, which is not the case'. Children preferred combining work and school, arguing that this would be an effective short- and long-term strategy against poverty.

Despite children's concerted efforts to meet their needs, some care workers at the temporary shelters infantilized their spending ways. They said children tended to buy 'childish stuff like radios, food, and sweet things'. These sentiments were echoed by some children.

However, many children challenged this view that they were immature and wasteful. They argued that buying their own food was imperative as the food which was served in shelters was 'monotonous and distasteful'. As for buying 'sweet things', a 14-year-old said, 'Care workers forget we are children. We also want to eat those things their children are eating. They expect us to use every cent we get to buy serious staff like cooking oil, flour etc for our families.' Another boy argued that since his move to South Africa to work, he was well nourished but not as a result of eating food provided at the shelter. He claimed that his grandmother in Zimbabwe took this as a cue that he was living well in South Africa and should continue working.

In addition, several boys periodically bought groceries, clothes and blankets which they gave to friendly adult community women for safe keeping. Generally men were not trusted, nor were those who talked of visiting Zimbabwe in the near future. Children knew that these people were under pressure to buy goods to take to Zimbabwe and often left with people's money or goods.

Children felt disrespected by some care workers who sometimes called them *magumaguma*. This label was usually used when children fought each other. Tindo, aged 15 years feared, 'If people associate us with those beasts, we will end up consciously or unconsciously imitating their behaviour.'

In response to their criminalization, some children felt compelled to engage in crime. For example, Tindo revealed that if he saw an opportunity to steal, he would do so, since it would be pointless to refrain. He and other children would still be accused of stealing that thing and then be beaten thoroughly. 'It's better to be accused and punished for something you have done,' he argued. However, the majority of boys claimed to be law-abiding migrants.

Children viewed themselves as victims of crime. They often experienced violence and robbery. Some children, particularly the older ones and those who had stayed at the border for a long time, warded off the *magumaguma* by threatening to expose their whereabouts to the police. Some boys claimed that the *magumaguma*, to some extent, feared them as they held vital information about their identity, operations, escape routes, and at times their sleeping places. Timothy, aged 14, for example, managed to stop being harassed by one *magumaguma* after he threatened to pour petrol over his body and burn him when he was drunk and asleep at his hideout.

Thus children were not as powerless as often portrayed in literature. They were knowledgeable about the vulnerabilities of the feared *magumaguma* and 'the rules of engagement' in their dangerous work environment, like lying about their identity, using blackmail and intimidation, and seduction (see below) as survival strategies. However, outsiders like care workers condemned these tactics.

Children who worked as human smugglers resisted to be marginalized and excluded by *magumaguma* and other adults from this lucrative but dangerous work. They tried to capitalize on their young ages and assumed innocence to lure illegal migrants from adult smugglers who were widely regarded as the *magumaguma*.

However, children revealed that when smuggling migrants, they sometimes resorted to using tactics used by *magumaguma* 'just to threaten those who would be refusing to pay us', explained a boy aged 13. Children complained of being abused by SAPS soon after a case of an illegal migrant being robbed was reported.

Children portrayed themselves as people who tried to tackle their everyday challenges. A 14-year-boy stressed, 'We are on our own.' Most boys did not have confidence in the commitment of care workers to help them since they were against child work. They observed that most care workers seemed only concerned about reporting for duty in order to earn money. For example, 13-year-old Thabo reported that a few weeks after police launched a heavy clampdown against cross-border people who were engaging children as porters, he together with two other boys appealed to the police to allow children to work. They told the police that they no longer had viable sources of livelihoods. They also stressed that the continuation of this operation would drive children into engaging in crime thus making them vulnerable.

Within a few days of this operation, police relented and turned a blind eye on working children. Although Thabo claimed that the police listened to their calls, Melusi aged 15 attributed the police's waning response to fatigue of dealing with the multitudes of migrant children from Zimbabwe, many of whom had been arrested and deported several times but continued to come back.

Exploitation, Fear of Exploitation, and Children's Responses

Cases of children being grossly underpaid, not paid at all and working under very difficult conditions like long hours without eating were common. Most cases were not reported to the care workers, police or responsible government labour officers. There was consensus amongst children that reporting was useless as they claimed not having anyone who could represent them. Children said a common saying amongst care workers to them was, 'Leave the responsibility of working to adults. What do you want to do when you grow up?'

To minimize chances of being exploited, if the employer insisted that they 'first work and discuss payment later or that we will be paid later' some children refused to work. Such employers usually did not honour these agreements. Children also shared information of the names of people who exploited children. However, desperation for money often undermined their negotiations for a fair deal.

Children who collected shopping receipts complained that buyers used a sharing formula which underpaid them. Despite being aware of this exploitation, children could not do much to correct the situation. Children could not claim money directly since they did not have valid passports, were too young, and were perceived to be too poor to buy goods.

Buyers usually refused to buy shopping receipts with small amounts of VAT saying they were often rejected at the border post. To overcome this problem, children sold a receipt with a big value of VAT together with receipts with small amounts. If buyers refused then they would not have the prized one. Buyers usually agreed. The boys also tried to sell receipts to the highest bidders, but this strategy was not effective as buyers often had a uniform buying rate.

Some children forged shopping receipts by erasing that part which showed that they were copies of the originals. Children sold these receipts to buyers not known to them so that if these receipts were rejected they would not find them.

Then the children who worked as informal pimps called sex workers cheats. Sex workers often reneged on their promise to pay children who referred clients to them claiming that they had been underpaid. To avoid being exploited, the boys demanded advance payment from the sex workers.

Children, particularly those who lived on the street, were seen as vulnerable to sexual exploitation. Boys reported that some adult women, particularly vendors, paid them for sex. 'Unlike adult men, we easily tire when having sex so we do not overwork these women,' explained a 13-year-old boy. Children said most of these local women did not want them to use condoms. Children, fearing being denied sex accepted that condition. Some boys did not care about using protection, exemplified by a 14-year-old who declared, 'Using a condom is outdated.' Consequently, many boys periodically suffered from sexually transmitted infections.

As a strategy of avoiding paying for sex or paying these women and girls whom they accused of being after their money, the boys would take the hard earned money away for safe keeping from the boy who planned to have sex. They were aware of their weakness to part with money after sex.

Some boys were not just victims of sexual exploitation but also perpetrators. They adopted a strategy of getting free sex and having fun through sex. They seduced women, regardless of their age, by stealthily putting aphrodisiac pills into their soft drinks. Musina is an arid area and some women could not resist the offer of a soft drink to quench their thirst, particularly coming from an innocent looking boy. This strategy was introduced to the boys by a local adult man. Then later on women would periodically give the boys some free food and accommodation as they were their secret 'lovers'.

Working Children's Self-image

Respectful, honest, well cultured, vulnerable, but hard-working were some of the attributes that working migrant children claimed to have. These characteristics were used as social capital to get jobs, protection, to be allowed to work, for example, as porters who crossed the border illegally many times a day.

Children also considered themselves clever. For example, those working as human smugglers viewed illegal migrants as fools. They teased illegal migrants who looked down upon them and often ignored their advice when using illegal entry points, but also felt pity for them. 'We might be children but we live at this border. We know how to survive here,' explained a 13-year-old boy. Often illegal migrants who ignored children's advice at their own peril were violently robbed, raped, and even killed by *magumaguma*.

However, some children admitted engaging in petty crime as a survival strategy, like stealing shopping receipts from the shopping bags and shop lifting. 'We are not criminals. That is why SAPS usually do not take us to court but just beat and release us,' Thabani insisted.

Children who did not live on the streets shared the sentiments of care workers who criticized the glue-sniffing behaviour of children who lived and worked on the streets. This practice was not condoned at the border post. 'We did not cross the border to sniff glue but improve our lives,' explained one 15-year-old.

Although children accepted that they engaged in illegal activities and had pre-marital sex, they also had some moral standards. For example, Emmanuel said, 'When passing through the bush with illegal migrants... *magumaguma* can rob or rape illegal migrants but not my relatives.' In another example, three boys aborted a plan to have sex for fun with a woman aged approximately 45 who flirted with one of them. They wanted to seduce her by secretly putting an aphrodisiac pill in her soft drink. Although these boys have seduced adult women before, they decided to respect her after considering that she was a mother of three grown up children.

Children had a love and hate relationship with sex workers. 'These women are like our mothers but they are shaming us by having sex with us. They say, my son if you have money to pay for sex you can have it with me,' said Daniel. Most boys claimed sexual innocence and regarded having sex with adult women as against their culture.

The children felt that their portrayal as people who had a negative attitude towards education was unfair, misinformed and an over-generalization. Many of them were attending school in Musina. Poverty, erratic opening of schools in Zimbabwe and abuse at home forced many of them to quit school.

Children also argued that working was a pragmatic move. Timothy (13 years) commented, 'After the 2010 Soccer World Cup, the South Africans will be at it again, attacking foreigners and chasing them from this country. When that happens I don't want to go back to Zimbabwe without even a pair of underpants. If I do that people will laugh at me.'

Instead of fully blaming people who exploited and abused them, many children often blamed evil spirits. These forces were blamed for constraining their opportunities to negotiate successfully for livelihoods. For example, Daniel said, 'I am struggling to get casual work and get paid. When I get paid, I quickly lose the money. My relatives must be complaining in Zimbabwe. Every time they complain they invite evil spirits to wreak havoc in my life.'

To resist these forces, and instead receive blessings from their parents and ancestors, some boys attended church services and periodically used the little money they had to call their family and to remit groceries. Some care workers even advised those boys who were struggling to earn a living to temporarily visit their homes and appease these spirits. This information buttresses one of Kankonde's (2010) arguments that migrants remit primarily to foster familial belonging.

Conclusion

Care workers' representations of unaccompanied working children were situational and inconsistent. Children were portrayed as vulnerable and generally indomitable, as innocent victims and perpetrators of social ills including crime, as responsible social beings and irresponsible beings, as manipulators and manipulated, and as cultured children and uncouth children. These representations were a reflection of children 'shaping and being shaped by their social world' (Honwana and Boeck 2005: ix): unaccompanied minors were like child soldiers who 'find themselves in a luminal position which breaks down established dichotomies between...victim and perpetrator, initiate and initiated, protected and protector, maker and breaker' (Honwana 2005:32).

These contradictory representations were related to care workers' inconsistent approach towards child work. There were also mixed and conflicting responses by care workers to the ACRWC (1990) recognition of the responsibility of children to assist their families in case of need (Article 31a). Most care workers formally endorsed the UNCRC's position as their careers were anchored on such discourse (see Bourdillon 2003): they did not want to see minors doing work which was either dangerous or affected their development. However, some of them were against all forms of child work, although even these sometimes sympathised with and supported working children.

The ambivalence of care workers towards child work made children hesitant to seek care and support. They did not have confidence in care workers, and were aware of the prevalence of sentiments against child work which fuelled concerted efforts by both the care workers and adult community members to marginalize them and exclude them from working. Consequently, they did not always report cases of abuse and exploitation, and relied instead on a spirit of camaraderie amongst themselves.

Although care workers 'officially' believed that they were saving children's lives, the intended beneficiaries often expressed frustration over their protectionist and paternalistic tendencies. Care workers' actions neither promoted their personhood nor addressed most of the push factors to migrate. Aid agencies' failure to provide children with basic things like clothing, good diet and security made a mockery of their efforts to help them. Instead of depending on adult guidance, nurture and protection, as expected in modern society, this study showed that children assumed many responsibilities, including that of protecting themselves against abuse and exploitation.

Although care workers accepted that the Zimbabwean crisis had wreaked havoc in many households, some regarded children as too weak and immature to make a contribution. The general competence of children was underestimated, illustrated by a lack of respect for their prioritization of how to spend money. Instead of children's efforts being complemented through, for example, adequately protecting them from abuse and exploitation, some care workers pathologized children's efforts.

The power relationship between unaccompanied minors and adults, which is usually characterized as adults' dominance and children's submission, is not unidirectional and static. Children often used their knowledge of the environment and its rules of engagement to enjoy themselves, make a living, and protect themselves from ordinary people, employers, criminals and law enforcement agencies. Children, like women, could 'negotiate and renegotiate strategies and alternatives within abusive relationships in order to cope within their immediate constraints' (Boonzaier 2006:146). Although children's agency and resistance in abusive relationships or encounters should be acknowledged, this should not excuse adults from adequately protecting children. Children acknowledged that their agency was limited, for example, when they interfaced with repressive state apparatus. In a case of the end justifying the means, children employed crude tactics like working as human smugglers, coercing illegal migrants to honour their agreements to pay them, forging shopping receipts, seducing women to enjoy themselves. What is needed is a safe working environment for children, a reduction in factors which precipitate them to leave their homes, not prioritize education, adopt delinquent and criminal behaviour.

Child agency appears in unpredictable ways, it sometimes forces adults to re-think the way they view children (Bourdillon 2008a:1). Adults should understand how children exercise their agency and support their efforts to control their lives. However, Nieuwenhuys (1997 cited in Bourdillon 2008b:270) warns that an emphasis on the agency and competence of children can be used to justify the withdrawal of institutions from responsibility toward vulnerable children. Thus interventions should be scaled up but with focus also on supporting children's efforts in a way which respects their rights, choices and their life world.

Aid agencies should also understand the pressures on these children that can constrain their negotiations for livelihoods, including pressure from their belief system. These are beliefs and other social pressures like the need to send remittances, shape their meanings and responses to abuse and exploitation.

In addition, an acknowledgement of children's sense of responsibility to support their families might result in agencies developing and implementing educational programmes which will not be in conflict with children's aspirations. Generally, unaccompanied minors appreciated education but the policies against child work, with their focus on school attendance and repatriation, were not appealing to children. When their negotiations for livelihoods are restricted, children as actors always seek room for manoeuvre (see Long 1992:20) and this includes consciously undermining interventions which are supposed to care and support them. For example, through manipulating vulnerability indicators used in aid discourse like being under-age, orphanhood status and political persecution.

Acknowledgements

The author acknowledges award of a Zeit-Stiftung Ebelin und Gerd Bucerius 'Settling into Motion' PhD scholarship and funds from the Atlantic Philanthropies that enabled the research to be conducted. He is grateful for the support of the University of the Witwatersrand's African Centre for Migration and Society (formerly called Forced Migration Studies Programme) and the unwavering guidance he received from his study supervisor Professor Ingrid Palmary while carrying out the study. He would like to also thank Professor Michael Bourdillon for comments and suggestions on the study proposal and drafts of this chapter. Gratitude is also extended to unaccompanied migrant children and humanitarian workers in Musina, South Africa for sharing their experiences with me. Of course, any shortcomings in the chapter are solely the author's responsibility, and in no way should they be attributed to anyone.

Notes

1. Unaccompanied children (also called minors) are under 18 years. They have been separated from both parents and other relatives and are not being cared for by an adult who by law and custom is responsible for doing so (Inter-agency Guiding Principles on unaccompanied and separated children - International Committee of the Red Cross, 2004).
2. United Nations Convention on the Rights of the Child (1989) and the 1990 African Charter for the Rights and Welfare of Children.
3. Magadlela defines the concept of life-world as "the way actors view their situation in a particular place, together with the constraining and enabling factors around them, in their world" (2000:15).
4. An umbrella term for non-state actors responsible for various forms of abuse, exploitation, and extortion along the border (Araia and Monson 2009:68).

5. Shona is the dominant ethnic group in Zimbabwe, followed by Ndebele. Zulu, which is close to Ndebele, is one of the dominant ethnic groups in South Africa.
6. Since 2000 Zimbabwe has experienced political and economic instability.

References

Araia, Tesfalem and Monson Tamlyn, 2009, 'South Africa's Smugglers' Borderland', *Forced Migration Review*, Issue 33, September, Refugee Studies Centre, Oxford: Oxford University.

Barter, Christine and Renold, Emma, 1999, 'The Use of Vignettes in Qualitative Research', *Social Research Update*, Issue 25, Guildford: University of Surrey, http://sru.soc.surrey.ac.uk/SRU25.html (Date of access: 16 February 2009).

Boonzaier, Floretta, 2006, 'A gendered analysis of woman abuse', in Tamara Shefer, Floretta Boonzaier and Peace Kiguwa, eds., *The Gender of Psychology*, Cape Town: UCT Press, pp. 135-150.

Bourdillon, Michael, 2008a, 'Children's agency and adult intervention: dealing with children's work', Seminar in the Department of Anthropology, University of Leiden, 25 February.

Bourdillon, Michael, 2008b, 'Children and supporting adults in child-led organisations: experiences in southern Africa', in Erdmute Alber, Sjaak van der Geest and Susan Reynolds Whyte, eds, *Generations in Africa: Connections and Conflicts*, Beyruth: LIT Verlag. pp. 323-347.

Bourdillon, Michael, 2003, 'Author Response to the Review of Earning a Life', *Children, Youth and Environments*, Vol.13, No.1, Spring, http://www.colorado.edu/journals/cye/13_2/responses/BourdillonResponse.htm (Date of access: 16 February 2009).

Burman, Erica, 2008, *Developments: Child, Image, Nation*, London and New York: Routledge.

Burman, Erica, 1995, 'Developing Differences: Gender, Childhood and Economic Development', *Children and Society*, Vol.9, No.3, pp. 121-142.

Burr, Rachel, 2006, *Vietnam's Children in a Changing World*, London: Rutgers University Press.

Finch, Janet, 1987, 'The Vignette Technique in Survey Research', *Sociology*, Vol.21, pp.105-14

Gigengack, Roy, 2008, 'Critical Omissions: How Street Children Studies can Address Self-Destructive Agency', in Pia Christensen and Allison James, eds, *Research with Children*, Second Edition. New York: Routledge, pp. 205-219.

Greene, Sheila and Hogan, Diane, eds, 2005, *Researching Children's Experience: Approaches and Methods*, London: Sage Publications.

Hillier, Lucy, 2007, *Children on the move: Protecting Unaccompanied Migrant children in South Africa and the Region*, Pretoria: Save the Children UK.

Honwana, Alcinda, and De Boeck, Filip, 2005, 'Children & Youth in Africa: Agency, Identity & Place', in Alcinda Honwana and Filip De Boeck, eds, *Makers & Breakers: Children & Youth in Postcolonial Africa*, Oxford: James Currey, pp. 1-18.

Honwana, Alcinda, and De Boeck, Filip, 2005, 'Preface', in Alcinda Honwana and Filip De Boeck, eds, *Makers and Breakers: Children and Youth in Postcolonial Africa*, Oxford: James Currey, pp. ix-xii.

Hopkins, Peter, 2008, 'Ethical issues in research with unaccompanied asylum-seeking children', *Children's Geographies*, Vol.6, No.1, pp.37-48.

Kankonde, Bukasa Peter, 2010 'Transnational Family Ties, Remittance Motives, and Social Death Among Congolese Migrants: A Socio-Anthropological Analysis', *Journal of Comparative Family Studies*, Vol. 42, No. 2.

Kitzinger, Jenny, 1990, 'Who Are You Kidding? Children, Power, and the Struggle Against Sexual Abuse', in Allison James and Alan Prout, eds, *Constructing and Reconstructing Childhood: Contemporary Issues in the Sociological Study of Childhood*, London: The Falmer Press, pp157-183.

Leeuwis, Cees, Long, Norman and Villarreal, Magdalena 1990, 'Equivocations on knowledge systems theory: An actor-oriented critique', *Knowledge, Technology & Policy*, Vol. 3, No. 3, pp. 19-27. http://www.springerlink.com/content/b283553hh8w110g6/ (Date of access: 28 March 2009).

Livesay, Tracy Kay, 2006, *A Survey on the Extent of Xenophobia Towards Refugee Children*, Master of Diaconiology, Unpublished Thesis, Pretoria: University of South Africa.

Long, Norman, 1992, *Battlefields of Knowledge: The Interlocking of Theory and Practice in Social Research and Development*, London: Routledge.

Magadlela, Dumisani, 2000, *Irrigating Lives: Development Intervention and dynamics of social relationships in an irrigation project*, Published Thesis, Wageningen: Wageningen University.

Nieuwenhuys, Olga, 1997, 'The Paradox of the Competent Child and the Global Childhood Agenda', in Richard Fardon, Wim van Binsbergen and Rijk van Dijk, ed., *Modernity on a Shoestring*, Leiden and London: EIDOS, pp. 33-48.

Palmary, Ingrid, 2009, *For Better Implementation of Migrant Children's Rights in South Africa*, Pretoria: UNICEF.

Patton, Michael Quinn, 2002, *Qualitative Evaluation and Research Methods Enhancing*, Third Edition, London: Sage Publications.

Rutherford Blair, 2008, 'Zimbabweans living in the South African Border-Zone: Negotiating, Suffering, and Surviving', *Concerned Africa Scholars, ACAS Bulletin* 80: Special Isuue on Zimbabwe 2.

Twum-Danso, Afua, 2004, 'Africa: A Hostile Environment for Child Participation?' *ECPAT International Monitoring the Agenda for Action Report*, Bangkok: ECPAT International.

Walkerdine, Valerie, 2001, 'Safety and Danger: Childhood, Sexuality, and Space at the End of the Millennium', in Kenneth Hultqvist and Gunilla Dahlberg, eds, *Governing the Child in the New Millennium*, London: Routledge Falmer, pp. 15-34.

Woodhead, Martin, 2007, 'Harmed by Work or Developing Through Work?', in Beatrice Hungerland, Manfred Liebel, Brian Milne and Anne Wihstutz, ed., *Working to be Someone: Child Focused Research and Practice with Working Children*, London: Jessica Kingsley Publishers. pp. 31-43.

6

Scavenging by Minors at Huruma Garbage Dumpsite: The Children's Story

Josephine Atieno Ochieng'

Introduction

Children and youth have been the subject of much debate, ranging from issues concerning their rights, poverty, homelessness, and in particular their work. Certain forms of child work have been found to be more beneficial than detrimental to children's well-being. These benefits could range from a higher sense of responsibility, self-worth, a sense of satisfaction, and an ability to meet certain basic needs. Nevertheless, certain work that children and youth get involved in may be hazardous and dangerous to their lives, and strenuous. The subjects of this study are involved in such kind of work and I sought to find out the children's reasons for engaging in seemingly unsafe work. Certain observations accruing from this study will be useful in modifying the way society thinks about children's work.

The study was carried out at Eldoret's major garbage dumping site in Huruma. Eldoret is a cosmopolitan town that lies in the western region of Kenya. It is a major transit point for long-distance trucks that ferry goods to neighbouring countries such as Uganda, Rwanda, Burundi, and the Democratic Republic of Congo. The city is served by an international airport.

Huruma garbage dump is the central place where all the garbage collected in the city ends up. It is also the place that hosts the main sewage dump for the whole city which is home to several factories, business premises and a population of about one million. The dump swarms with youngsters, and some older people, whose main occupation is to sift through the garbage in search of valuables they can use or sell. These are boys and girls of ages ranging from as young as four to young adults of twenty-two. There are about forty to fifty youngsters at the site. These collectors use the water from the stream flowing near the dumping site to bathe in the open.

Rationale

Many African cities have seen an influx of large populations in search of livelihoods. The UN-Habitat's then Executive Director, Dr. Anna Tibaijuka, on 30 June 2009 told a conference on Peace, Justice, and Reconciliation in Africa that in 2008, the number of people living in urban areas exceeded those in rural areas, with Africa being the fastest urbanizing region. According to her, six out of ten urban residents in Africa are slum-dwellers, forced to live in deprivation with chronic lack of access to safe water, sanitation, sufficient housing, and security of tenure. The unfolding trend is referred to as 'the urbanization of poverty'. Employment opportunities and livelihood options are few and far between.

Children have also joined the older generation in this pattern of migration. However, they cannot get proper employment and have limited opportunities to create self-employment due to their limited education, experience, ability, and maturity. Consequently, they look for other means of survival, chief among them being street life, engagement in the informal labour sector, petty trade, begging, stealing, etc, in order to supplement family incomes. Some of the children have opted to go and live in major garbage dumping sites where they scavenge for discarded items for sale to be recycled or used for other purposes.

There have been some studies on scavengers outside Africa. Barboza (2003) mentions minor scavenging activities in Nigeria, Brazil, Argentina, the Dominican Republic, and Cambodia. He describes children working barefoot and shirtless, and in circumstances where it is survival of the fittest, on dumpsites in Vietnam. The children had to make sure that they got to the dumpsite before the trucks started arriving. Some of the scavengers arrived as early as three o'clock in the morning and stayed until after seven in the evening. They foraged in the dump despite the extremely high temperatures. He mentions children as young as five racing after garbage trucks. Another study in Vietnam showed that children working all night on rubbish dumps were among the happiest, despite the dangers and dirt involved. They had good income, and worked within flexible hours among themselves. The children were as young as six and they worked without adult supervision (Theis 2001:103, cited in Bourdillon et al., 2010). Another study argued that children scavenging on rubbish heaps in the Philippines valued and enjoyed their work for its excitement and the companionship they found there, to the extent that it proved difficult to entice them to leave it (Gunn and Ostos, 1992 cited in Bourdillon et al., 2010). As yet, there have been no major studies on child scavenging in Africa and this is a beginning.

The Huruma garbage dumping ground in Eldoret, Kenya, receives tens of truckloads of garbage of all kinds on a daily basis. The contents of these trucks include recyclable and unrecyclable items such as glass materials, plastics, paper, polythene, pieces of metal, boxes, and food items. The scavengers, who will sometimes be referred to as collectors, have cut out a niche for themselves at the dumpsite.

The collectors are faced with several difficulties in their daily activities at the site. Eldoret is a high altitude area with extremely cold temperatures that can go as low as 12 degrees Celsius during the months of April through August, with the coldest being July. The children are also subjected to harassment from the residents of the neighbouring Huruma estate, especially if they stray into this neighbourhood. Yet, despite these squalid and harsh conditions, they continue working here – something that confounds observers who think it would be better for them to find more 'decent' livelihoods. Some have been said to run away from their homes, internally displaced persons' camps, and even centres specifically set up for them to come and scavenge here.

With the introduction of free primary education in the year 2003, it was expected that many out-of-school children – including those who were homeless – would go back to school. Indeed, in the first few years of implementing the policy, there was a reduction in the numbers of these children on streets in Kenyan towns as a result of frequent swoops conducted by law enforcement agencies. However, with time the enthusiasm of the enforcement authorities started waning, and many urban centres are now teeming with homeless and/or out-of-school children.

I approached the subject of children's work from their own point of view because of the emerging concern about the need to understand children in their own right. Ansell (2005:21) reiterates two important issues: first, that children should be studied independent of adult concerns; and second, that they are actually involved in constructing their own livelihoods. The ethnographic methods I employed allow children's voices to be heard. There have been concerns that children's voices are seldom heard, but that it is their photographs that are common (Ansell 2005:28). This chapter gives a voice to the children's choice. At the same time, Woodhead (2007:34, 40) argues that children are social actors in the business of trying to make sense of their experiences, beginning at an early age to develop an appreciation of their and their families' circumstances. He continues to state that consulting them is respectful of their participatory rights. Bourdillon (2004:101-102) reiterates the fact that most studies present only adult perspectives while paying very little attention to children's views and agency in shaping their lives. He argues that scholars need to pay more attention to children's potential and actual roles in development. Finally, it is mentioned by Rogers (2009:155-156) that when evaluating the quality of life, it is important to consider the views of those whose well-being is sought. Children are key stakeholders in the services and care provided for them, and so their priorities and concerns are of paramount importance given that these may not necessarily be the same as those of their parents. I also intended to ascertain the role played by families in encouraging their children's scavenger activities. While many families in Eldoret live in poverty, not all of them produce scavenger children. Thus the study aimed to shed light on the production of collectors.

Methods Used

There were three categories of respondents for this study. The main category was that of the collectors who worked at the Huruma dumping site. These were purposively sampled to enable more meaningful data collection, targeting those who had been at the site longest. I used three methods to collect data from the scavengers, namely, participant observation, intensive interviewing, and focus group discussions. I chose these three methods because they emphasized observations of natural behaviour and captured social life as it was experienced by the participants. These methods also allowed me to get a richer, more intimate view of the social world of the scavengers than I could have achieved using structured methods (Schutt 2006:320). During the interviews and group discussions, I used a guiding questionnaire. Data were collected over a period of two months.

Partnerships were built by establishing rapport in the initial stages of contact. Rapport was useful in ensuring that the respondents spoke as honestly and as freely as possible. Catherine, my research assistant, and I first visited the site on a Sunday. We found several collectors idling about. Some of them were rummaging through the rubbish trying to find anything valuable. They became a little hostile to us and started asking which media house we were from. We told them that we were not news reporters and one of them informed us that, one time, a visitor came to the site and took a photograph of him. The next day, the photograph was published in a local newspaper and this caused some conflict with his family to whom he had not revealed that he was involved in scavenging. Catherine then told them that she worked at the local government hospital and, indeed, one of the collectors recognized her. He came over to us and reminded Catherine of their meeting at the hospital. She was also able to recall Maina and so our friendship with him began. He said that many of them had been cheated into believing that they were talking to donors who would bring them money; thus the hostility from the other collectors. We explained to him that we were on a research mission. He sent away the other scavengers and told them that we were his friends and that anyone who needed help at the hospital in future should not accost us. Maina then became our guide and informer and he provided us with much-needed protection. He took us round the approximately one-hectare dumpsite, showing us garbage in various stages of decomposition. Light and heavy clouds of smoke billowed from different sections of the garbage dump while a pack of swine and goats rummaged through the heaps. Maina discreetly showed us his store, a place where he kept his collections. He then informed us that this day he was not dressed for work. On noticing our surprise, he offered to go and put on his work clothes. He disappeared into the bushes behind the dump and came back a few minutes later, dressed in the clothes. However, he told us that he could not show us his work tool, a metal prong with which he scratched through the garbage because the other collectors would see him retrieving it from its secret place. We spent around two hours at Huruma acquainting ourselves with the place and chatting with the few collectors who were present that day. Maina then said that it was getting late and that he wanted to go home to prepare for his favourite football show in the evening. He therefore took us on a brief tour of the slum area around the dumpsite and even showed us his house. His mother lived a few metres from there and he told us that she was not at home at that time, so there was no need to pass by her house. We agreed to meet the following Thursday to start our interviews with the other collectors, and he promised to convince his colleagues to cooperate with us.

On the Thursday, I arrived at the Municipal Council Department at six o'clock in the morning. The Clerk-in-Charge assigned me a truck whose driver I shall henceforth refer to as Gilbert. Gilbert proved to be a very key informant for this study. As we rode around town loading the truck with garbage I noticed three collectors in the back. They assisted in loading the garbage onto it while they ran errands for the municipal loaders. They seemed to have good rapport with Gilbert and his colleagues and he informed me that they were scavengers whom he allowed to ride in the truck. These 'privileged' collectors started the process of scavenging for valuables in the truck before we got to Huruma. At one point, they showed me a half a sack of charcoal that they had found in the dustbin in one of the town restaurants. One of them, Tom, told me that this charcoal could fetch about sixty Kenya shillings (US$ 1 was at the time equivalent to approximately Ksh. 75). As the garbage heap grew in the truck, all the collectors and loaders in the back would alight and Gilbert would engage the compressor to push the garbage to the back to make space for more garbage to be loaded. When the truck was full, we headed for Huruma. As we neared the dumpsite, he stopped the truck and all the scavengers alighted with their collections for the day. Gilbert explained to me that the Huruma scavengers were not happy that he gave privilege to some collectors to start scavenging in the truck before arrival at the site. And as if in confirmation, during my interview that day with the collectors, some of them reported to me that Gilbert and his fellow drivers gave priority to other collectors from town and that, in fact, some of the valuables they collected were given to the municipal council workers. A twenty-year-old collector told me in no uncertain terms to tell Gilbert and his colleagues to stop subjecting them to unfair competition while they were in paid employment.

As soon as I alighted from the truck and tried to approach the collectors, the younger ones scurried off. Gilbert told me it was because they feared me. The older ones, on the other hand, were curious to know the purpose of my assignment. We told them that I was a teacher and that I had come to learn about their problems. They asked me to explain to them what I needed to know and how they would gain from my mission there. Gilbert helped me to organise them and to seek their permission to record our discussions. The children started opening up gradually and I realized that Maina had told them of my impending visit.

During subsequent visits, I requested that we sit in a circle. The purpose of this sitting arrangement was to reduce the distance between us and to minimise any barriers that would interfere with the free flow of information. During the whole period that I visited Huruma, I dressed casually.

Second, neighbourhood residents were conveniently drawn from the estate immediately surrounding the dumping site for discussion of their perceptions of the collectors' activities. This depended on their availability, willingness, and ability to communicate in a common language. These included three government administrators (the chief of the location, the assistant chief, and the village elder), business owners and the residents. There was one group of five business owners and another group of seven residents. I did not put them together in one group because I wanted them to have uniformity of perspectives.

Third, the municipal council workers who delivered garbage at the site everyday were interviewed on how they perceived child scavengers. All focus group discussions were carried out in unstructured interviews.

We faced some challenges in carrying out this study. At first, the municipal authorities, especially some of the administrators, suspected that their work was under investigation. I had to explain to them the exact nature of the study and how the information would be used. When I first went to them, they said I was not authorized to ride in their trucks. Second, they were worried that I was going to report any anomalies I would notice at the department. When I gave them a letter of introduction from my employing organization, the Clerk-in-Charge agreed that I could go along in one of the trucks. However, some of the staff were still reluctant to have me around them as they went about their work. For instance, the driver of the first truck I boarded seemed uncomfortable with me. I had been assigned this truck and I got onto it but as soon as the driver arrived, he grew cold feet. He put me through a 'grilling' session on what my agenda was with collectors. He pointed out that he feared liability in case I got injured by the scavengers when we got to Huruma. The loader riding with him reiterated that the scavengers were quite unruly and that they could even snatch my camera. I therefore alighted and waited for ten minutes until Gilbert came in 'his' truck.

It is an important aspect in every research study to explain to participants what the information sought from them will be used for. This became apparent when the Municipal Council workers wanted an explanation of why I was interested in garbage collectors. To them, scavengers were not important people in society and I realized that there was a need for public sensitization. A common name given to scavengers in Eldoret is *chokora*, a derogatory term which, according to Davies (2008:314), denotes homeless children who do not attend school, and who only beg, steal, sniff glue, work for their food, and are always dirty and unclean.

Some of the Municipal Council workers I interviewed also requested to have a copy of the tape I used in recording our discussion made available to them. I therefore had to incur extra costs to facilitate this.

The collectors were in the business of making a living and so my data collection was an intrusion into their programme. In fact, on the day I was with Gilbert, most of the collectors participated in the interview while scratching through the garbage. Nonetheless, this had the benefit of yielding more accurate information as naturally as possible. I even spotted Maina and I asked him whether he remembered me. He responded in the affirmative but he seemed quite absorbed in his work. Some of the collectors expected hand-outs from me for accepting to suspend their work in order to give me attention. Others were suspicious of my intentions especially during initial contact. This was especially so with the younger children at the site. However, being a helping professional, I was able to find ways to go about it. This is described in the next section.

Fig. 1. Collectors busy at work at Huruma

The Children

The majority of the collectors came from low socio-economic backgrounds as they indicated that they lived in the slum area just next to the dumpsite. Many of them came from broken homes while some of them were orphaned. During the interviews, it emerged that many that many of them lacked food and proper shelter while others faced abuse and neglect. One of the respondents, Kimaru, said that his father had abandoned his mother before he was born and that his mother had died soon after his birth, leaving him in the care his grandmother, who also died when he was only five. He was eighteen at the time of the interview and had been at various dumpsites for close to twelve years. According to the others, Kimaru had been at the site longest.

Those whose families were intact complained of idleness and need for money and food. They said that most of them attended school during business hours and only came to the site in the afternoons. These children mostly comprised younger boys and girls who claimed that they were bored at home because their parents, especially their mothers, worked all day. Ennew (1996:207) agrees that in urban settings, working mothers of children in difficult circumstances lacked child care, a significant recipe for what she calls 'streetism'. The collectors also supposed that they did not get enough food at home and that the dumpsite provided an alternative source of food. This is alluded to by Evans (2004:70) who states that children encountered a 'greater variety of food to be gained from the street'. According to Ansell (2005:47), many poor families were becoming increasingly unable to secure adequate food and their children were vulnerable to inadequate diets. One respondent showed me a polythene bag in which he had put all kinds of food items picked from the site. He said that younger ones fought for food with swine. The foodstuffs included *ugali* (a local staple made from maize flour), pieces of beef and chicken bones, bread, rice and *chapati* (a local delicacy made from wheat flour), decaying fruits such as mangoes, oranges, bananas, and lots of tomatoes. From interviews with Gilbert, such foodstuffs were often collected from restaurants while the fruits were found in the municipal market. For the children, this provided a balanced diet comprising starch, protein, and vitamins.

The collectors had very low levels of education with the most highly educated having dropped out at standard five (in Kenya, children join primary school in standard one at around age six, and complete their primary education in standard eight). There were three categories of collectors: those who were engaged at Huruma full-time, those who came in the afternoons after school, and those who came to do some collecting during the school holidays only. Most of those who did not attend school indicated that despite the promises of free primary education, they still needed money to buy school uniforms, food, and other necessities. Ansell (2005:47) asserts that one reason children drop out of school is to be able to contribute to household survival; while Bourdillon (2009:23-24) argues that schools in Africa may sometimes be unwelcoming, demeaning and grim, and may lack essential resources such as books, desks and even classrooms. One boy, Kodwaran, who had run away from home, reported that his father was too harsh and that he gave Kodwaran too much work to do. He also said that his father used to force him to go school yet he felt too old for that.

Seemingly, with no proper source of income, some of these children were unable to meet their needs. To them, as indicated by Abraham Maslow in his hierarchy of needs, physiological needs such as food and clothing were more important than education. With low levels of education, most of the collectors could not find meaningful occupations in town because most of their competitors were better educated and consequently preferred by employers. Many of the collectors could barely write their names. Because most of the scavengers came from poor families, where other members most likely had minimal schooling, the parents might have been oblivious or even indifferent to the engagements of their children. Alternatively, because of their low levels of education and consequent low income, the parents allowed their children to work at Huruma provided they brought home some money. Indeed, as Lopez-Calva (2002) points out, the poverty status of the household and the education of the household head are the most robust determinants of child labour. According to him, under certain circumstances, a parent would rather send a child to work instead of sending him or her to school. However, this should not be used to conclude that parents are not altruistic toward their children.

Many of those interviewed had running themes of broken homes and female-headed households. Most of them talked of having only a mother or no parent at all; but hardly any of them mentioned a father. In fact, fifteen out of twenty-three said they did not know about their fathers. Evans (2004:80) notes one positive aspect of female-headed households as the greater freedom to engage in paid work. On the other hand, these households may face greater difficulties in gaining access to labour markets, credit, housing, and basic services. She enumerates part-time, informal jobs with low earnings, which are favoured by these females as beer-brewing, gardening, poultry-keeping, pig-keeping, and petty trading in foodstuffs and charcoal. These households are thus more vulnerable to impoverishment and insecurity, with negative consequences for the children.

However, one of the collectors, James, said that he did not know about his father but later, a key informant confided that James actually had a responsible businessman father. According to the informant, James had decided to rebel against his father because he was unhappy with the latter's choice of James' brother as overseer of his transport truck. When I confronted James another day about this, he just laughed it off and said it was not true. However, the manner in which he said it, with a naughty smile on his face, was not convincing.

Some of the collectors lived alone in rented rooms while others lived with their families; but all of them lived in the slum area next to the dumpsite. Most of the housing there was temporary, with cracked mud walls and iron sheets and only large enough for a bed and a kitchen area. The windows and doors were made of wood. Many of the collectors without families shared these rooms. Some of them such as Kevin did not have rooms of their own. Kevin mostly engaged in scavenging for foodstuffs which he sold to swine breeders at thirty Kenyan shillings per sack. He then paid twenty shillings to someone for accommodation each night. He fed on the pig food he collected. Kevin did not know his parents and he scavenged along with his twin brother who was not at the site the days I visited. The participants informed me that he was not mentally alright and that was why he did not even own a prong with which to scratch. When I asked him about using his bare hands in the garbage, he did bother to respond and instead asked me for money to buy lunch.

From the children's point of view, they engaged in collecting due to several factors including helplessness, the need to fill their leisure time, irresponsible parenthood, frustration, poverty, and general family dysfunction. Thus, as has been discussed, the dumpsite provided a sure and precise way to get around their situation while it helped to fill the gaps in their lives.

The Children's Work

The collectors arrive at the site in the morning hours to await the delivery trucks. As a truck approaches, they all follow it to be in the best position to start sifting through the garbage.

Many of the collectors did not like what they did, but said that there was no other way for them to get money. Others did not mind the work provided it brought them money. One of the collectors, Peter, was concerned that some of the garbage came with used syringes and needles which as stated by him, posed a threat to the younger children in this era of HIV. One thing that these children enjoyed was the autonomy with which they engaged in their activities.

Gilbert, Catherine, and the municipal council clerk all informed me that there was a destitute children's home in the town where needy children could go to be taken care of. On broaching this subject with the collectors, they all responded negatively. This made me wonder about their unanimous response to the subject. Then one of them said that the conditions at the home were not conducive for them. He said, 'How can I be told to cut grass around the compound before I am given food to eat? Even my late father did not ask me to do that when he was alive!' On saying this, all the others burst into laughter.

Seemingly, these children did not like to be told what to do or to be supervised as they worked. I had got to know that the local Department of Social Services provided food for needy children every day around lunchtime. On enquiring about this too, all the participants chuckled. They said that walking to the social hall to get food was a waste of the time they would rather spend collecting valuables for sale. The collectors thus appeared to feel a sense of pride in being able to earn some money for food rather than to be provided with free hand-outs. This seemed good for their self-esteem and sense of self-worth and it may provide fertile ground for further research into children's work.

The conditions at the dumpsite are very hard on the children. As we approached the dumpsite in the truck, scores of children and youth started running after the truck(s) and directing the driver(s) as to the best location to empty the garbage. Some of them started pulling out items even before the trucks come to a complete stop. This struggle assures them of a vantage point from which to embark on their work. Each of the scavengers was armed with a metal prong with which he or she sifted through the 'fresh' garbage. And as if that was not difficult enough, a herd of swine joined in rummaging through the garbage. Consequently, the scavengers had to fight off the swine while, at the same time, making sure they continued searching.

Ansell (2005:171) has supposed that opposition to children's work has centred on the potential hazards it poses. He writes that children are more liable than adults to suffer occupational injuries due to inattention, fatigue, poor judgement, and insufficient knowledge. At Huruma, the competition for the garbage is so intense that the children sometimes throw caution to the wind in a bid to survive. One participant in the study showed me a large scar on his right thigh that has remained as a constant reminder of his difficult life. Julian was going about his collecting business as usual one day when a truckload of garbage arrived at the site. Together with his colleagues, he chased after it as usual. Julian decided to climb onto the moving truck but accidentally, he slipped and fell and the truck ran over his leg. He was seriously injured and after offloading the truck, the driver together with some of Gilbert's friends took him to hospital. He remained there for close to three months and he had to undergo major reconstructive surgery. I was saddened by the account, yet Julian and his colleagues laughed as they narrated it to me. It seemed as if the ordeal was only a temporary setback as they stated that Julian was back at Huruma soon after his release from hospital. In fact, whenever he omitted any part of his narrative, his colleagues would gladly fill in the missing facts.

Julian's story made me wonder how the collectors managed to pay their medical bills. It was encouraging to hear that the local government hospital provided free medical care for them. However, they indicated that whenever they visited the hospital, they had to dress in a certain way in order to pass as needy citizens. This was a very good example of how these children manage to negotiate their livelihoods in difficult circumstances.

Along with these, other hardships included being roughed up by the municipal council guards, aggression from passers-by and estate residents, and harassment from the police and the public whenever a crime was committed in the neighbourhood. Despite all this, the collectors continued their businesses here with determination.

The collectors indicated that most of them suffered respiratory-related complications and my research assistant confirmed this form her observation at the hospital. They told me that their work exposed them to risks of respiratory infections because of prolonged exposure to the smoke and stench at the dump. Gilbert told me that part of the garbage delivery teams' work was to set the garbage on fire in order to create space for yet more garbage. A study at the Stung Meanchey Municipal Waste Dump in Cambodia found dangerously high levels of dioxin in the soil and large amounts of heavy metals in the metabolism of children working there. These children sought treatment for rashes, infections, cuts and bruises (Barboza 2003:A4). Other illnesses that the children suffered were related to the occasional low temperatures.

Social Networks

There were strong social networks and a sense of comradeship among the collectors, together with a feeling of responsibility for each other. This was attested to by most of the collector respondents who intimated that whenever any of them became too ill, it was the responsibility of the others to help him or her get to hospital and to ensure that they got treatment. Veale et al in Evans (2004:70) affirms that some of the gains of street-life were the development of strong friendships and the satisfaction of being able to manage their lives. Davies (2008:319) found out that, indeed, scavenging and eating leftovers united (both males and females) in a common bond; other children did not engage in such activities. Another social benefit of living off the dumpsite was that the collectors were well treated by the staff of the Moi Teaching and Referral Hospital where they received free medical treatment.

As children approach adolescence, peer influence increases while parental influence diminishes (Myers 2008:121). This may help explain why the bond these children have developed at the garbage dumpsite is very strong. At Huruma, they can interact with peers, learn from them, and provide each other with a safe haven from which to explore. On the Sunday Catherine and I first visited the site, we found several collectors sitting around and chatting casually. One of them had a radio on which he was listening to music. This was an indication that they had a sense of belonging to the dumpsite and that they felt at home in Huruma. Thus, as every human being needs a sense of identity, so the collectors have found that identity at the dumpsite, thereby passing time even on days when trucks do not bring in any garbage. In fact, one study of street children who lived in a dirty polluted territory with open sewers and mud in Makutano in Kenya, revealed that they were actually relaxed and that they played without the threat of harassment. They were powerful in this territory and were considered dangerous and threatening. The children paradoxically reinforced notions of pollution and danger to create a safe and empowering world around them, and this was referred to by Beazley as 'winning of space' (cited in Davies 2008:321).

During the interviews, some of those who were not participating were busy playing after keeping their valuables in their 'stores'. Each of the scavengers had a 'store' that was well known and respected by others. On asking how safe their belongings were in the open 'stores', they told me that nobody dared touch another person's belongings. I was impressed with this sense of morality and respect for each other's rights. There was a high degree of organization at the dumpsite and the collectors seemed to have developed a sense of maturity not common among other children their age. As they played, I could perceive fairness, teamwork, and advocacy in their dealings; all these without any supervision from an adult. This concurred with Woodhead's observation that one function of work was that it provided an opportunity for children to learn skills like responsibility, communication, and teamwork (Woodhead, 2007:41).

The garbage site seemingly provided an escape from adverse conditions at home. According to Hungerland (2007:172), when children engage in activities that are unsupervised by adults and have their own money, it gives them a sense of autonomy they can scarcely find elsewhere.

Earnings

According to the children, they could not sell their wares directly in the market as they had no links with the recyclers. They depended on middlemen to buy the assorted items from them for onward sale to recycling plants. The collectors scavenged for assorted items such as tin, glass, plastic, paper, cloth, sacking, food, and many other valuables. They sold plastic for Ksh. 4 per kilogramme and paper for Ksh. 2. Pig food was sold to estate residents for Ksh. 30 per sack. On average, each scavenger made about Ksh. 100 a day, but this depended on how hard one worked and how keen one was in following the trucks. On a less fruitful day, each made only around fifty shillings. The scavengers complained that they were exploited by the middlemen who paid very little for the scavenged items. For instance, they (middlemen) sold a kilogramme of plastic for Ksh. 16, and sometimes even Ksh. 18, which was way above the buying price. I did not get a chance to verify this from the middlemen.

So how did they spend the small amounts of money they earned? Some of the younger children said that their parents were aware of their coming to scavenge and that they even contributed to the upkeep of their families. Others said that they used the money for needs such as food, clothing, and to pay for video shows including European football. Some of them complained that the money they earned was so little that they had to share accommodation to cut on costs.

Those who came after attending school were mostly interested in foodstuffs. These were younger boys and girls who occasionally stumbled upon valuables such as tins or bottles which they exchanged with the older collectors already linked to middlemen. They in turn received favours in cash and/or kind – including protection from bullies – or for as little as two shillings. They were also too young to fight with the older ones for garbage and to negotiate fair prices for their goods.

Views of Residents and Municipal Workers

The views of neighbourhood residents differed sharply from those of the collectors. Residents were of the opinion that the garbage dump was a menace to them, given the stench that it produced during the rainy season. Second, according to them, it had led to cases of indiscipline among children who preferred to go and scavenge rather than stay at home to work. The dump made the children to want to get money at a tender age when they were supposed to concentrate on their childhood and education. Residents also insinuated that their own children liked to go and pick food items from the garbage. They thought that the dump attracted all kinds of children, some of whom were in the habit of stealing from them. They were concerned that whenever they reported these incidences to the police, they fell victim to acts of revenge. They were unhappy that the dump site exposed them such insecurity. As a result, they suggested that the site be relocated to another part of the municipality and that the government improves on its responsibility to protect its citizens. However, this would only be a relocation of the problem. It should be clear that the residents said nothing positive about the collector activities at Huruma. This is supported by Tagliaventi (2007:166) who confirms that children's views of their work differ a great deal from those of adults.

The municipal council workers were sympathetic to the collectors. As mentioned earlier, some of them allowed collectors to scavenge on the trucks. Their argument was that there was no point disposing of items that could be of use to collectors and that the garbage was a major source of livelihood for the children. They provided an example of a time when the municipal workers went on strike to protest against low salaries. The collectors held a demonstration in town demanding that the workers' grievances be addressed so that they could return to work and restore their (scavengers) lifeline.

On the issue of persistence of collectors, they suggested four main factors responsible for this problem. These included very large families, poverty, broken homes, and indiscipline in society. They thought that the public played a role in encouraging scavenging because they bought goods from collectors and also gave them handouts. Another point that emerged from my discussions with the municipal workers was that the collectors did not like to take on paid employment and that they liked the 'easy' money they got after scavenging. They gave an example of a collector who got a job as a herd-boy, but failed to keep it and ran away after one week. In fact, Tagliaventi (2007:165) acknowledges the immediate and tangible satisfaction children derive from their work; and they are aware of discerning both its positive and negative aspects. The municipal workers explained that the collectors were uncomfortable with a programmed life such as is found in needy children's homes probably because of the discipline involved. They indicated that the majority of those who were taken to these centres later ran away. Hungerland (2007:171) suggests that children find tasks assigned them by parents [and other adults] undesirable, natural, unpleasant and boring. One important finding though, was that most of the adult respondents believed that irresponsible parenthood was the main cause of minor scavenging. They supposed that most of the children at the site came from broken or unstable homes that were mostly female-headed. This fact was confirmed in the discussions with the children themselves. As Evans (2004:86) notes, increasing numbers of children from households that had dispersed are turning to the informal sector to support themselves as families and communities are unable or unwilling to support them.

Conclusion

This chapter is partly a revelation of the value of children's work. Children use work to fill up their free time while they contribute to their upkeep. Not all children place a high premium on education, perhaps because the dividends are not readily realised. Children's work is not all negative as it may help them to develop a sense of responsibility and maturity in them. It also assists children's sense of autonomy while providing a positive way of avoiding 'adult domination'. This therefore should provoke society to rethink their attitudes about children's autonomy and independence. Invernizzi (2007:141) avers that when work allows greater control over the environment, the result is self-esteem and confidence. Children are creative beings with a certain capacity to negotiate their livelihoods. They are not merely empty vessels waiting to be filled with adult ideas. They should be given an ear; their opinions ought to be valued and incorporated in programmes targeting them.

Nevertheless, a certain degree of adult responsibility is still wanting. For instance, society should be ready to protect children in whatever they choose to engage in. This is in relation to providing and facilitating a safe environment for all children's activities. In the case of Huruma, for instance, medical and other establishments should be responsible enough to follow safety precautions especially when discarding used apparatus. The government should ensure that children and minors are not exploited nor taken advantage of. All members of society need to respect children's rights. They should provide good role models for all children.

From this study, I found out that most children enjoyed what they did in terms of work. The connotation of child labour may not be so for the children themselves. This is because children's work may provide a safety valve for pent-up struggles, frustrations, and emotions. According to the frustration-aggression principle, an individual's frustration can generate aggression when they do not get a safety valve for venting the negative energies that may result (Myers, 2008:553). They may therefore turn to destructive behaviours such as delinquency and violence. The minor scavengers at Huruma faced several challenges in their lives, and despite the frustrations they may have faced, they decided to channel their energies into a relatively positive pursuit. This pursuit was helpful to society in the recycling process and in the prevention of delinquent behaviour.

An important suggestion is that children who are involved in the informal labour sector could be provided with formal schooling outside their working hours. They could also be registered by the government so that they get protection and be provided with care where need be. The psychological benefits of paid work for these children could be investigated. Ways of making the work safer for them should be explored since working in the garbage dumps is hazardous in nature.

References

Ansell, Nicola, 2005, *Children, Youth and Development,* New York: Routledge/Taylor & Francis Group.

Barboza, David, 2003, 'Children Scavenge a Life, of Sorts, in the Garbage', *Phnom Penh Journal.* Reproduced by the *New York Times,* available at www.nytimes.com. Accessed 20 January 2010.

Bourdillon, Michael, 2004, 'Children in Development', *Progress in Development Studies,* Vol 4, No.2, pp. 99-113.

Bourdillon, Michael, 2009, 'Children's Work in Southern Africa', *Werkwinkel,* Vol 4, No.1, pp. 103-122.

Bourdillon, M., Levison, D., Myers, W., and White, B., 2010, *Rights and Wrongs of Children's Work,* New Brunswick, etc.: Rutgers University Press.

Davies, Matthew, 2008, 'A Childish Culture? Shared Understandings, Agency and Intervention: An Anthropological Study of Street Children in Northwest Kenya', *Childhood: A Journal of Global Child Research,* Vol. 15, No.3, pp. 309-330.

Ennew, Judith, 1996, 'Difficult Circumstances: Some Reflections on "Street Children" in Africa', *Africa Insight,* Vol. 26, No.3, pp. 203-210.

Evans, Ruth M.C., 2004, 'Tanzanian Childhoods: Street Children's Narratives of "Home"', *Journal of Contemporary African Studies,* Vol. 22, No. 1, pp.69-92.

Gunn, S.E. and Ostos, Z., 1992, 'Dilemmas in Tackling Child Labour: The Case of Scavenger Children in the Philippines', *International Labour Review, Vol.*131, pp.629-646.

Hungerland, Beatrice, 2007, 'Work - A Way to Participative Autonomy for Children', in B. Hungerland, M. Liebel, B. Milne, and A. Wihstutz, eds, *Working to Be Someone. Child Focused Research and Practice with Working Children,* London: Jessica Kingsley, pp.167-175.

Invernizzi, Antonella, 2007, 'Children's Work as "Participation": Thoughts on Ethnographic Data in Lima and the Algarve', in B. Hungerland, M. Liebel, B. Milne, and A. Wihstutz, eds, *Working to Be Someone: Child Focused Research and Practice with Working Children*, London: Jessica Kingsley. pp. 135-144.

Lopez-Calva, Luis F., 2001, 'Child Labor: Myths, Theories and Facts', *Journal of International Affairs*, Vol. 55, No.1. Available at www.questia.com.

Myers, David G., 2008, *Exploring Psychology*, 7th Ed, New York: Worth Publishers.

Rogers, Wendy Stainton, 2009, 'Promoting Better Childhoods. Constructions of Child Concern', in M. J. Kehily, ed., *An Introduction to Childhood Studies*, 2nd Edition, Berkshire: Open University Press, pp.141-160.

Schutt, Russell K, 2006, *Investigating the Social World. The Process and Practice of Research*, 5th Edition, Thousand Oaks: SAGE Publications.

Tagliaventi, MariaTeresa, 2007, 'Child Work and Child Labour in Italy: The Point of View of the Children', in B. Hungerland, M. Liebel, B. Milne, and A. Wihstutz, eds., *Working to Be Someone: Child Focused Research and Practice with Working Children*, London: Jessica Kingsley, pp.161-166.

Theis, Joachim, 2001, 'Participatory Research with Children in Vietnam,' in Schwartzman, H. B., ed., *Children and Anthropology: Perspectives for the 21st Century*, London, etc.: Bergin and Garvey, pp.99-109.

Tibaijuka, Anna, 2009, Keynote Address for the Association of Catholic Universities and Higher Institutes in Africa and Madagascar Conference on Justice and Peace at the Catholic University of Eastern Africa, Nairobi, 30 June 2009.

Woodhead, Martin, 2007, 'Harmed by Work or Developing Through Work?: Issues in the Study of Psychosocial Impacts', in B. Hungerland, M. Liebel, B. Milne, and A. Wihstutz, eds, *Working to Be Someone: Child Focused Research and Practice with Working Children*, London: Jessica Kingsley, pp. 31-42.

7

Les jeunes commerçants handicapés moteurs dans la négociation de la vie entre Brazzaville et Kinshasa (1970-2009)

Jean Félix Yekoka

Introduction

Nées majoritairement de la volonté coloniale, les villes africaines sont depuis engagées dans une dynamique des échanges multiformes. Brazzaville et Kinshasa, deux « villes miroirs[1]», semblent être l'archétype de ces échanges trans-urbains en Afrique centrale. Le rythme de ces échanges peut amener à croire qu'on est en présence de deux sociétés urbaines où le niveau de vie des populations demeure élevé. Pourtant, la réalité que l'on observe de ces deux métropoles prouve plutôt le contraire : pauvreté, crise des valeurs, chômage, illettrisme, misère et précarité impriment chez nombre d'individus le sceau du désespoir. Cette situation a considérablement modifié la nature des relations entre les individus à l'intérieur de la société ; appelant ainsi à certaines considérations culturelles qui renvoient à la sphère marginale une catégorie de personnes. À première vue, les personnes handicapées semblent être les premières victimes des « relations conflictuelles» qui empestent l'harmonie sociale entre individus.

Selon des stéréotypes socialement construits à l'intérieur de l'espace urbain, les personnes handicapées sont des éternelles mendiantes, des demandeuses d'aumônes, des parasites sociaux, des déchets humains qui encombrent abusivement les places publiques. Cette façon de comprendre et de justifier l'état de ces hommes s'apparente à un procès sévère qu'il faut relativiser, dans la mesure où plusieurs handicapés prennent leur destin en main, par la réalisation de diverses activités comme la coiffure et le commerce.

En effet, depuis plus de quatre décennies, les échanges commerciaux se sont intensifiés entre Brazzaville et Kinshasa ; et beaucoup de gens dont les jeunes handicapés moteurs ont trouvé dans ces échanges l'opportunité de négocier leur vie, en trafiquant entre les deux métropoles. La négociation de la vie renvoie à la quête quotidienne du bien-être à travers quelques activités économiques loin du cadre familial. Dans un contexte de crise et de pauvreté, le goût du risque reste avant tout l'option ultime qui oriente vers des tentatives de mise en œuvre des stratégies de lutte contre la pauvreté. En posant ainsi l'hypothèse, les jeunes handicapés moteurs qui s'adonnent au commerce entre Brazzaville et Kinshasa ont-ils réussi à modifier positivement leur condition sociale ? Comment identifier des indicateurs socio-économiques qui puissent permettre d'apprécier le niveau et la qualité de leurs activités ? Comment encadrer ces jeunes pour que l'impact de leurs activités soit socialement plus visible ? Répondre à ces questions signifie faire une analyse critique de l'activité marchande de ces jeunes.

Les personnes handicapées ont fait l'objet de quelques études qui répondent à des préoccupations propres aux institutions internationales et gouvernementales. La production littéraire à leur sujet, qui n'est pas sans valeur, est cependant orientée jusqu'ici vers des possibilités de leur accès aux technologies et aux services de l'information et de la communication,[2] à la valorisation de leur savoir-faire artistique[3] et à l'émancipation de la femme handicapée.[4] Outre ces dimensions, il faut aussi noter celle qui est orientée vers les personnes handicapées du troisième âge vivant en milieu rural.[5] Ces réflexions répondent à des motivations d'ordre sociopolitique plutôt que scientifique. La production relevant de la société savante concernant les personnes handicapées, à notre connaissance, est celle de Miankenda (2001:4). Dans cette rcherche, l'auteur oriente sa pensée vers l'inaccessibilité des personnes handicapées aux services sociaux de base.

La présente contribution se distingue donc des autres études inventoriées de ce qu'elle tente d'analyser les possibilités et les modalités d'autoprise en charge juvénile des personnes handicapées motrices, entre 1970 et 2009. Le *terminus ad quo* (1970) correspond à la période où s'amorce, dans les deux Congo, la crise d'ajustement structurel et la période du redressement économique. Cette crise a eu des effets négatifs sur l'ensemble de la population, et en particulier sur les personnes handicapées. Pour essayer d'aider cette frange vulnérable, les présidents Mobutu du Zaïre (RDC) et Marien Ngouabi du Congo-Brazzaville signèrent, entre 1971 et 1973,[6] un accord qui exemptait les commerçants handicapés de toutes taxes douanières entre les deux rives du fleuve. Quant au *terminus ad quem* (2009), il correspond à la période où une série d'enquêtes assidues ont été menées sur la problématique des jeunes commerçants handicapés moteurs de Kinshasa et Brazzaville. Ces enquêtes viennent compléter celles réalisées en 2005 et 2007, sur les migrations pendulaires entre Kinshasa et Brazzaville, mobilités consécutives aux activités commerçantes entre les deux métropoles.

À cause de l'inexistence des études sur la question, nous avons privilégié les enquêtes de terrain. Celles-ci ont été qualitative et ont été menées à Brazzaville en 2009. Elles ont concerné 100 jeunes des deux Congo, d'âge variant entre 18 et 28 ans que nous avons choisis au hasard, sans discrimination de genre, d'origine, de religion et statut matrimonial. Nous avons mené des entretiens libres et semi directifs selon la méthode inspirée par Alain Blanchet *et al.* (1985), Jean Pierre Doury (1992) et Jean Copans (1999). Les informations ont été enregistrées avec un dictaphone. Selon la préférence des sujets enquêtés, les entretiens ont été menés en lingala et en kituba, deux langues officielles des deux Congo. Précisons que sur l'ensemble des périodes ayant couvert l'enquête, 22 Brazzavillois ont été interrogés dont 11 hommes et 5 femmes handicapés, 6 hommes valides, contre 78 Kinois, soit 43 hommes et 19 femmes handicapés, 16 personnes valides. La question centrale adressée à tous ces jeunes handicapés moteurs était celle de savoir les raisons de leur choix du commerce entre Brazzaville et Kinshasa, et si ce commerce répond bien à leurs attentes.

Cette étude sera menée dans une perspective pluridisciplinaire, en convoquant notamment l'histoire et la sociologie. Reste à préciser ses différentes articulations. De manière générale, on distinguera trois grandes phases : celle qui apprécie la vie et les rapports des jeunes handicapés par rapport à la société globale, celle qui rend compte de leur engagement dans le commerce transnational et enfin celle qui analyse leur niveau de vie actuel et interroge leurs perspectives avenirs.

Les facteurs explicatifs de l'engagement des jeunes handicapés dans le commerce entre Brazzaville et Kinshasa

Deux facteurs essentiels tentent d'expliquer le dynamisme des jeunes handicapés moteurs quant à leur engagement dans le commerce entre Brazzaville et Kinshasa. Ces facteurs, qui ne sont pas interposables, renvoient d'abord à l'environnement socio-économique précaire des deux pays depuis la fin de la décennie 60 ; ensuite aux productions culturelles qui, en milieu urbain, tentent de renvoyer les personnes handicapées à la sphère de la marginalité, selon l'approche conceptuelle de Morelle. Récusant la position des géographes qui voient en la marginalité un concept purement spatial fondé sur l'opposition centre-périphérie, Morelle (2007 : 23) souligne :

> Un individu ou un phénomène marginal peut se localiser en un point central d'une organisation spatiale, introduisant nécessairement l'idée d'une éventuelle proximité spatiale pourtant en contradiction avec une distance sociale.

La précarité vitale consécutive au marasme socio-économique

La débrouillardise dans l'espace urbain des jeunes africains est intimement liée en partie à l'état de pauvreté que connaît le continent africain. Ce continent a le taux de pauvreté le plus élevé de toutes les régions du monde. À l'intérieur de ce continent, la proportion de personnes vivant avec un revenu de moins d'un dollar par jour se situe à 46 pour cent, ce qui dépasse de 17 points le taux de pauvreté en Asie du Sud, la deuxième région la plus pauvre de la planète (PNUD 2006). Au Congo-Brazzaville et en République Démocratique du Congo, cette proportion est respectivement de 70 pour cent[7] et de plus de 80 pour cent.[8]

La République du Congo fait partie des pays d'Afrique qui, dans la période charnière entre la fin du XXe et le début du XXIe siècle, ont connu à la fois une situation économique et financière difficile et des conflits armés récurrents. La crise économique et structurelle qui remonte au début des années 1980 et qui s'est aggravée notamment avec l'échec des programmes d'ajustement structurel, auquel se sont greffés les conflits armés des années 90, a considérablement détérioré les conditions de vie des individus. Au plan macroéconomique, la période qui s'ouvre à la fin de la première moitié de la décennie 80 est marquée par, d'une part, un fort ralentissement de la croissance dont le taux moyen est de 0,5 pour cent entre 1985 et 1997 et, d'autre part, une crise d'endettement (au 31 décembre 2000, la dette de l'État représentait 170 pour cent du PIB). L'accumulation des arriérés est devenue le principal mode de financement des déficits publics (UNICEF 2008).

À cette contreperformance économique se juxtapose la crise du secteur de l'emploi, qui se caractérise par la tension qui prévaut sur le marché du travail du fait du désajustement persistant entre les offres et les demandes de l'emploi. Ainsi, le chômage et la pauvreté se sont aggravés en dix ans, avec une chute de 58 pour cent du pouvoir d'achat. Les jeunes paient le plus lourd tribut, avec plus de la moitié de pauvres de toute la population congolaise (PIPC 2002).

Toutefois, pour des raisons diverses, la pauvreté des personnes handicapées motrices est celle qui demeure plus préoccupante à côté de la pauvreté des femmes et des enfants. Cette pauvreté se caractérise plus ou moins par leur non-accès aux services sociaux de base comme l'enseignement, la santé, le logement, le transport, l'information, la formation professionnelle, le recensement et surtout l'emploi. Selon le Rapport sur la situation des personnes handicapées en République du Congo-UNHACO-Brazzaville (1999), les personnes handicapées sans emploi représentent 88 pour cent de la population totale des personnes handicapées ; 97 pour cent vivent dans des logements inaccessibles ; 75 pour cent sont exposées aux maladies diverses associées au sida (Miankenda 2001).

Le cas du Congo-Kinshasa semble plus complexe. Les indicateurs de son état de pauvreté sont alarmants alors qu'il regorge de ressources naturelles avec notamment 49 pour cent de réserves mondiales de cobalt. En effet, la crise économique que connaît ce pays depuis les années 70, l'échec des programmes de stabilisation et d'ajustement structurel des années 80 initiés notamment par le Fonds Monétaire International (FMI), les deux pillages des années 90, ainsi que les guerres de 1996 et de 1998, avec les déplacements massifs de populations vers les grands centres urbains, ont profondément modifié la physionomie de la pauvreté urbaine dans les 12 provinces du pays.[9]

La pauvreté est élevée et elle a tendance à s'accentuer. Plus de la moitié des Congolais sont privés d'accès à l'eau potable (57%) et aux soins de santé de base (54 %), plus de trois enfants sur dix sont mal nourris, et la probabilité pour un Congolais de décéder avant de fêter son 40ᵉ anniversaire s'élève à 47 pour cent.[10] Kinshasa et Lubumbashi sont actuellement plus pauvres que Matadi et Mbuji-Mayi. Les observateurs qui s'intéressent de près à la RDC ont le même constat : « pays riche, mais jeunesse pauvre[11] », un véritable paradoxe. C'est autant dire que dans les temps présents, la jeunesse (congolaise) africaine, bien plus qu'à l'époque de leurs ainés, est bridée par des contraintes multiples que produit une conjoncture historique particulièrement défavorable ; et que les difficultés actuelles qui assaillent l'ensemble du continent touchent encore plus durement les jeunes qui ne voient pas l'horizon de leur vie s'éclaircir (Olukoshi et Ouédraogo 2005). Dans les pays en voie de développement, en plus du fardeau imposé par le poids démographique, il est plus difficile pour les adultes d'accéder aux revenus sûrs, ce qui affecte à la fois leur capacité à s'occuper des enfants et à payer les impôts pour les services gouvernementaux (Bourdillon 2009 : 44).

Il se développe dans les deux villes des marchés et des économies de misère. Pour essayer de remédier à cette situation lamentable qui menace dangereusement la vie de plusieurs jeunes urbains, des stratégies existentielles sont mises en œuvre par les jeunes handicapés physiques eux-mêmes dans les deux villes capitales congolaises. Mais à côté de ces facteurs conjoncturels existent, *stricto sensu*, des facteurs culturels qui justifient la dynamique commerciale des jeunes handicapés moteurs de Brazzaville et de Kinshasa.

Le poids des stéréotypes traditionnels soutenus collectivement en milieu urbain en crise

Selon les régions, l'imaginaire collectif des sociétés traditionnelles congolaises (RDC et Congo-Brazzaville) distingue différentes catégories d'enfants. Parmi ces catégories, nous avons : l'enfant dit normal, qui est intégré dans la société suivant le processus de socialisation ; les jumeaux, qui sont des êtres sacrés, « des êtres exceptionnels, le don des ancêtres » (Tshingi 1999 : 66) ; les enfants dits « sorciers » (Ernoult 1995 : 149), parce que présentant des signes extérieurs[12] qui intriguent la communauté villageoise ; et les enfants malades, ceux naissant avec un handicap.

Les deux premières catégories d'enfants font la joie de la société. Des cérémonies rituelles, des fêtes sont par exemple organisées à l'honneur des jumeaux. À l'époque coloniale, les « enfants sorciers » étaient directement exclus de la société, par leur mise à mort systématique. Selon toute vraisemblance, il était reproché à ces enfants d'être les principaux responsables des malheurs qui frappaient leurs familles et leurs villages. En revanche, les handicapés n'étaient pas exclus du cercle et du processus vitaux, mais étaient plutôt marginalisés à cause de leur infirmité. En effet, « la conscience collective s'exaspère en se manifestant en des drames qui décrivent des mythes ou de systèmes de croyance » (Duvignaud 1973 : 43). L'enfant handicapé ne peut faire la joie de la famille ; il en constitue plutôt une honte, une souillure difficile à laver. Le handicap de l'enfant symbolise, soit la colère des mânes contre la famille, soit la punition infligée par les dieux à cet enfant à cause de son indocilité, sa témérité et sa turbulence. Les personnes handicapées seraient donc envoyées sur terre par les dieux afin de persécuter et d'importuner les gens normaux.

Ces conceptions relevant des sociétés traditionnelles des siècles écoulés ont été malheureusement récupérées puis insérées tacitement dans le tissu urbain actuel. L'une des conséquences majeures de cet imaginaire social est sans doute la tentative récurrente de vouloir dissocier les personnes handicapées de tout processus qui conduit à la satisfaction et à la jouissance intégrales du corps. L'insertion effective dans les différents canaux qui mènent vers le bien-être est quotidiennement hypothéquée. Moins qu'à Brazzaville, la situation des handicapés semble être plus difficile à Kinshasa où, à cause de la précarité socio-économique, les croyances traditionnelles sont rendues à la fois omnipotentes et omniprésentes dans le champ social urbain par les discours théologiques, depuis la fin des années 80. La diabolisation sociale des handicapés et des enfants qui devrait être tempérée par l'Église est malheureusement rendue plus efficace par elle. En effet, plusieurs églises de tendance pentecôtiste assimilent l'infirmité au démon, à Satan, au sorcier, au tourmenteur. Cet imaginaire se structure habilement aux dépens du rôle crucial de rédemption que devrait jouer l'Église, en tant que cadre de mise en confiance des cœurs désespérés.

Toutefois, malgré ces schèmes qui s'apparentent à un procès des forts contre les faibles, nombre de citadins ressentent l'envie de vivre que les handicapés manifestent au quotidien. Ils ressentent aussi en ces personnes des capacités créatrices inouïes. Et, l'un des terrains sur lesquels les handicapés s'illustrent est la débrouille commerçante. Plusieurs jeunes d'âges variés ont donc choisi volontiers ce créneau.

À la vérité, les facteurs explicatifs de l'engagement de jeunes handicapés moteurs dans le circuit commercial entre les deux métropoles congolaises peuvent se justifier, globalement, selon le modèle théorique des « logiques de l'action » proposée par Michel Lallement (2000). Sans les détruire, Lallement compartimente la diversité des mobiles rationnels et compréhensibles qui justifient les « raisons d'agir » des individus à l'intérieur d'une société. Cette logique tient compte du discours d'acteurs, car il explique leur propre conduite.

Les jeunes commerçants et les activités marchandes entre Kinshasa et Brazzaville

L'économie de misère[13] qui s'est installée tacitement à Brazzaville et à Kinshasa s'explique moins par la crise des valeurs qui se manifeste, stricto sensu, par la décomposition des liens traditionnels au profit d'autres liens selon les intérêts des individus, mais, davantage par la pauvreté qui la secrète. À l'analyse, cette économie de misère structure les activités par sexe, par âge et par catégorie sociale. Mais il faut saisir dans cette apparente contradiction l'idée du refus de l'inertie. Et justement, plusieurs handicapés des deux métropoles refusent de s'asseoir et d'attendre que tout leur tombe du ciel. Pour essayer de trouver des alternatives à leur précarité, ils interrogent leur conscience. Pour répondre à ces interrogations, ils disent avec courage[14] : « il faut faire la *coop*[15] ». Venant du verbe coopérer, la *coop* exprime l'idée qu'un individu en quête d'argent recourt à la débrouille pour résoudre ses problèmes de survie quotidienne. Elle constitue un système qui traverse tout le champ social et concerne toutes les activités quotidiennes (Trefon 2004 : 23 ; Nzenza Bilakila 2004 : 33). La coop renvoie donc à un système de négociation perpétuelle, en recourant parfois à la ruse, à l'espièglerie et au charme. À Brazzaville comme à Kinshasa, on associe la coop à un autre synonyme, le *topo*. Et le *topo*, en tant que forme de négociation de la vie pour certains jeunes handicapés, se réalise entre Brazzaville et Kinshasa. Pour le cas particulier de ces jeunes handicapés moteurs, il se fait sous forme de commerce, par des allers et retours sur le majestueux fleuve Congo, selon des articulations bien définies.

Capital et modalités d'engagement dans le commerce entre les deux villes

Le tout commence par une ingéniosité qui permet d'acquérir un petit capital de départ. Selon les résultats de nos enquêtes, sur 100 pour cent de jeunes des deux villes interrogés, environ 67,11 pour cent affirment avoir réussi à capitaliser leur fonds de départ grâce aux gains du petit commerce, celui qui se fait devant la parcelle de la maison. Ce petit « commerce de maison », selon les témoignages de plusieurs jeunes, prend le maximum de temps possible pour réussir à épargner une somme qui puisse permettre de se lancer dans un autre type de commerce plus envieux, celui qui se fait entre Brazzaville et Kinshasa. Pour certains jeunes handicapés, après plusieurs années, leur situation financière, du point de vue de l'épargne, reste comparable à celle du départ. Cette précarité d'amorçage se justifie par le fait que pour certains d'entre eux, au même moment qu'ils épargnaient, ils devaient aussi se prendre en charge, c'est-à-dire se nourrir, se soigner, s'habiller et faire face à d'autres petits besoins avec le même petit fonds « de commerce de maison ». Assez régulièrement, ces jeunes se sont privés d'autres exigences vitales pour atteindre l'objectif suprême qu'ils s'étaient fixé dès le départ, comme le témoigne Mambo[16] de Kinshasa :

> J'ai dû consentir d'énormes sacrifices pour arriver à atteindre le montant de 300 dollars qui m'a permis d'engager fébrilement une activité commerçante de grande envergure. Aujourd'hui ma situation économique est mieux qu'auparavant.

Toutefois, en dehors des jeunes qui font intervenir directement leur propre ingéniosité pour commencer le trafic transnational entre Kinshasa et Brazzaville, d'autres jeunes affirment avoir vendu et géré des produits pharmaceutiques et/

ou alimentaires pour le compte d'autres personnes. C'est donc petit à petit qu'ils ont réussi à épargner jusqu'à s'autonomiser. Le temps d'épargne pour cette catégorie de jeunes dure plus longtemps que celui de leurs homologues qui ont commencé à partir de leurs propres capitaux. Joël de Kinshasa affirme avoir vendu des médicaments pour le compte de son oncle pendant plusieurs années. Plus d'une dizaine au total. C'est à l'issue de cette longue durée d'années seulement qu'il a pu thésauriser puis financer ses propres activités commerciales. Joël[17] nous livre les raisons qui ont fait qu'il travaille dorénavant pour lui-même :

> J'ai travaillé pour mon oncle, mais j'ai constaté que ce qu'il me donnait ne correspondait pas au service rendu, même si je suis pour lui un neveu. J'ai fait prospérer ses affaires sans qu'il ne songe à modifier ma rémunération ; alors que je grandissais et que mes besoins se faisaient de plus en plus sentir. Et plus je grandissais, plus je me rendais compte que je dois me prendre en charge, car je mangeais chez mon oncle et que mes rapports avec sa femme s'affaiblissaient progressivement. C'est comme si cette femme me prêtait des intensions qu'elle seule peut justifier. Dès que j'ai atteint vingt-trois ans, j'ai donc décidé de me débrouiller seul.

La décision de Joël de se débrouiller pour son compte personnel manifeste moins un sentiment de révolte à l'endroit de son oncle, qu'une prise de conscience volontaire de la nécessité de négocier individuellement sa vie hors de la sphère familiale. Cette démarche traduit la « logique de l'action » telle que défendue et soutenue par Boltanski et Thévenot (1991). Faisant une lecture critique de l'action sociale, ces deux auteurs soutiennent que les personnes sont dotées de réelles capacités cognitives et morales pour justifier la nature d'une situation quelconque et pour ajuster leur action à cette situation. C'est en fonction de valeurs et d'intérêts qui sont multiples, que les personnes définissent leurs actions.

Néanmoins, certains jeunes (environ 17% de notre échantillon) ont affirmé que leur capital financier de départ leur a été donné directement par leurs parents. Ces jeunes représentent la catégorie de personnes qui ont atteint un niveau scolaire assez élevé. Pour l'essentiel, ils sont du Congo-Brazzaville.

À Brazzaville comme à Kinshasa, les filles paraissent plus nombreuses que les garçons à s'atteler aux tâches domestiques. Dans un contexte de pénurie financière, de précarité alimentaire et de décomposition de relations familiales, plusieurs filles se voient contraintes de combiner les activités domestiques à la débrouille commerçante. L'entrée en activité des filles handicapées, dans la plupart des cas, est la résultante d'une contrainte de leurs époux.[18] Il existe donc tant de dynamiques commerçantes qui relèvent parfois d'un genre composite et les modalités, puis le capital d'entrée dans un commerce trans-spatial sont très variables. Mais, pour tous les trafiquants, quel que soit le sexe, ancien ou nouveau dans cette activité commerciale, les traversées entre les deux villes imposent les mêmes exigences d'organisation des opérations et de transport des marchandises.

Les maillons organisationnels des opérations marchandes

Le capital étant réuni, la phase qui suit est celle de l'achat d'un vélo tricycle. Plutôt que d'un achat, il s'agit en réalité d'une commande de vélos fabriqués localement par les soudeurs. Ces tricycles sont fabriqués de sorte qu'ils soient capables de supporter des charges bien lourdes, sans inquiéter leurs propriétaires tout au long des différentes opérations marchandes. Selon les ateliers de fabrication desdits vélos, leurs prix varient entre 80 et 120 000 F CFA. Les raisons de cette cherté sont simples, selon les justifications de Paul,[19] un jeune commerçant handicapé de Brazzaville :

> Ceux qui nous fabriquent ces vélos savent pertinemment que ces vélos ne nous servent pas pour de simples promenades dans la ville, mais plutôt pour exercer le commerce. Or, pensent-ils, le commerce nous procure beaucoup d'argent. Tu as beau discuter, mais il est difficile qu'on te diminue le prix. Ce qui fait que nous payons l'argent en deux mensualités, voire trois.

Le vrai travail commence avec l'achat des articles au grand marché de Kinshasa, car cette étape exige non seulement une maîtrise des produits préférés par les potentiels clients, mais aussi la manie dans la négociation des prix[20] auprès des grossistes. Il s'agit donc d'une maîtrise au plus haut degré du marché d'approvisionnement. Les jeunes commerçants qui ont déjà une expérience de plus de dix ans ont leurs fournisseurs. Ce sont eux qui initient les nouveaux venus dans l'univers commercial. Depuis le début des années 90, l'approvisionnement pour certains jeunes s'accompagne de prêts. Cette stratégie consiste à vendre gros afin de gagner aussi gros. C'est ce que les jeunes de Brazzaville appellent volontiers faire le « *nkala* ». Dans le vocabulaire linguistique local, *nkala* renvoie littéralement au crabe. Selon toute vraisemblance, il traduit ici l'idée de maximisation du gain/ du profit.

La marchandise souvent achetée à Kinshasa est composée de cartons de savons, de biscuits, de pax, de papiers hygiéniques, de brosses à dents, de pâtes dentifrices, des produits de beauté, des produits pharmaceutiques, d'alcool, de sachets, de sucre et bien d'autres produits divers. Ces produits relèvent, en grande partie, de la fabrication locale. Ils s'imposent à ceux venant d'Europe et/ou d'Asie. À cause de leurs prix qui sont très abordables sur les marchés de Brazzaville, les produits de fabrication locale sont préférés à ceux venant d'autres horizons dans les ménages à revenu précaire et/ou moyen. Prisonniers du cycle et du schéma de production (fabrication) de ces produits dans les industries de la République Démocratique du Congo, ces jeunes n'ont pas d'autres alternatives en dehors des produits disponibles sur le marché. Ce qui fait qu'ils sont monotones et invariables. Cela gêne un peu ces jeunes commerçants handicapés qui cherchent parfois à surprendre leurs clients, en leur proposant d'autres types de marchandises.

De ce point de vue, la tendance à la spécification marchande est nulle. Tout le monde achète et vend les mêmes produits. Tout le monde a son ou ses « aides ». Les aides sont des jeunes valides d'âge variant entre 18 et 23 ans. Comme le mot l'indique, ces aides de sexe masculin sont des secours permanents de handicapés dans ce trafic difficile. Leur rôle est indéniable, car se sont eux qui poussent les vélos chargés de marchandises et de ces handicapés, depuis les lieux d'achat de ces produits jusqu'aux lieux de vente, c'est-à-dire à Brazzaville. Ces jeunes, déscolarisés précocement à cause d'un système éducatif exigeant dans le paiement des droits scolaires,[21] négocient à leur façon leur vie, en travaillant aux côtés de ces handicapés.

Toutefois, il est hors de question pour ces jeunes de se positionner en travailleurs des handicapés, leurs relations avec ces derniers étant de type conjoncturel et circonstanciel. À n'importe quel moment, ces relations se construisent et se déconstruisent. Les enquêtes menées sur la nature de ces relations mutuelles prouvent qu'il existe parfois plusieurs dissensions en leur sein. Ce qui engendre plus de conflits entre handicapés et personnes valides reste et demeure avant tout l'irrespect des clauses et des modalités de paiement (compensation financière par rapport au travail réalisé par les aides), comme l'affirme Mabi[22] de Kinshasa :

> Travailler avec ces gens, c'est difficile. Quand vous vous entendez qu'il doit vous payer chaque fois que vous traversez, mais, il arrive parfois qu'il ne vous donne que la moitié d'argent de ce qu'il devrait normalement vous remettre, alors que sur le terrain tu réalises que vous avez bien vendu. Parfois même il ne vous donne que ce qui peut vous permettre de vous nourrir, prétextant qu'il va régler un problème urgent.

Seulement, ne trouvant pas mieux ailleurs, ces jeunes valides sont contraints bien malgré eux de travailler et de supporter les multiples caprices des handicapés. Ces jeunes assurent l'embarquement et le débarquement de la marchandise, entre les beachs de Ngobila (Kinshasa) et celui de Brazzaville.

Les épreuves des beachs et de la traversée sont difficiles pour ces jeunes handicapés moteurs. Bien qu'exemptés de toutes taxes marchandes, il n'en demeure pas moins que ces jeunes handicapés moteurs subissent les épreuves de la rançon. En effet, ces beachs fourmillent d'une multitude de services de douane, de police, d'émigration, de garde-côtes, de service d'hygiène, etc. Il est donc difficile d'échapper à la tentation des gens atteints d'anomie. L'anomie, selon la théorie de Durkheim, est un état de déconstruction, de désorganisation et, sans doute, de déstructuration d'un groupe, d'une société, consécutive à l'élimination temporelle ou totale des normes et des valeurs communes à ses membres. Ceci « engendre le sentiment que les comportements socialement inacceptables, comme la corruption, la fraude, la violence soient admis et nécessaires pour répondre aux besoins élémentaires et vitaux » (Nzeza Bilakila 2004 : 34) des individus au sein de la société.

La prospérité des affaires, pour ces jeunes handicapés moteurs, dépend de leur sécurité ainsi que celle de leurs marchandises. Et afin de garantir cette prospérité, ces jeunes sont obligés de relever d'énormes défis : tensions entre commerçants, conflits entre commerçants et personnel des beachs, « affrontement » entre commerçants handicapés et personnes normales. L'intervention aux côtés de ces jeunes handicapés des « Bana lunda » peut s'expliquer de cette façon. Les « Bana lunda » constituent une frange d'individus composés de jeunes qui font le négoce entre Brazzaville et Kinshasa. Ils ont un « pouvoir » dans les bateaux et les beachs.

Arrivés à Brazzaville, les produits sont vendus selon un réseau de distribution bien connu des commerçants eux-mêmes. À partir du beach de Brazzaville, ces produits rentrent en éventail dans la ville suivant les itinéraires : la grande gare-Moungali, la grande gare – Bacongo, la grande gare – Ouenzé, la grande gare-Mpila. Une bonne partie de cette marchandise est vendue aux petits commerçants depuis le beach, l'autre est distribuée chez les commerçants grossistes dans les boutiques ayant pignon sur rue.

Selon les témoignages de plusieurs jeunes commerçants handicapés, les activités marchandes entre Brazzaville et Kinshasa se font selon un agenda bien arrêté. Trois jours sont arrêtés pour la traversée : les lundis, les mercredis et les vendredis ou bien les mardis, les jeudis et les samedis. Dans les marchés de Brazzaville, les pagnes semblent être la marchandise que ces jeunes handicapés achètent et revendent à Kinshasa. Analysant avec minutie cette activité, on peut conclure que certains jeunes handicapés moteurs jouent le rôle de négociants entre plusieurs acteurs inconnus les uns pour les autres, dans la mesure où l'achat et la vente des marchandises ne nécessitent toujours pas un versement direct d'argent.

Cette stratégie magnifie l'ingéniosité de ces jeunes qui ont su s'insérer dans le monde néolibéral. Certains d'entre eux travaillent en réseaux, en mettant sur pied des tontines de cinq à huit membres. Ces tontines commerciales fonctionnent selon le principe d'échange, déjà analysé par divers anthropologues depuis Mauss avec le potlatch ou la kula avec Malinowski, le principe de l'échange réciproque. Toutefois, comme le souligne si bien R. Guidieri (1984), cet échange n'est pas de l'ordre du simple don et contre-don gratuit, mais plutôt de l'ordre du « prêt ». Ceux qui donnent leur argent à leur collègue ne fournissent qu'un effort de prêt. Ce dernier a l'obligation de le leur rendre, le moment venu. La taille humaine des tontines est sexuellement composite et numériquement variable, et peut compter jusqu'à huit personnes. Le versement individuel de la somme convenue collectivement par les membres se fait généralement tous les samedis. Cela suffit-il pour conclure que ces jeunes handicapés ont réussi leur vie ?

Niveau de vie et perspectives des jeunes commerçants de Brazzaville et de Kinshasa

Les jeunes commerçants handicapés moteurs des deux Congo semblent manifester un sentiment d'indépendance et d'autonomie vis-à-vis des autres couches sociales. Jour après jour, ces jeunes impulsent une nouvelle dynamique marchande sur l'espace transnational. Le courage et l'envie constants qui animent leur décision de transcender les obstacles[23] réels et supposés sont, entre autres éléments majeurs qui peuvent aider à apprécier le niveau de vie et d'évaluer les perspectives de ces jeunes commerçants handicapés moteurs.

Niveau de vie et recomposition sociale des jeunes commerçants handicapés

L'appréciation du niveau de vie des jeunes handicapés moteurs qui exercent des activités commerciales entre Brazzaville et Kinshasa peut se faire en considérant systématiquement leur passé et leur présent. Pour rendre vivace ce passé, il faut se nourrir continuellement des témoignages, voire des récits de vie des jeunes eux-mêmes. Toutefois, deux remarques s'imposent quant à la reconsidération du passé de ces handicapés. La première est celle qui intègre ces jeunes dans un environnement familial différent les uns des autres. Il est donc inapproprié de comparer la précarité vitale d'un individu à partir de celle de l'autre. Cette constatation mène droit à la deuxième remarque qui a « précisément trait aux ressources » dont Lopez 2009 : 124) a disposé chaque jeune dans son engagement pour le commerce entre les deux villes capitales. Le seul terrain où la situation des handicapés est univoque est celui de l'imaginaire collectif négatif que la société construit autour de leur état physique. Cet imaginaire, nous l'avons vu, a laissé glisser tranquillement l'espérance de plusieurs handicapés physiques, comme l'affirme Gilbert[24] de Kinshasa :

> Il y a plusieurs handicapés à Kinshasa qui traversent des situations difficiles. Pour n'avoir jamais souhaité ou voulu leur condition physique, ils croient vivre l'enfer sur terre, et beaucoup des gens les critiquent. (…). Ils préfèrent mourir plutôt que de supporter les insultes des gens.

Ce rejet, les handicapés le ressentent même au sein de leurs familles biologiques, surtout celles qui subissent les assauts récurrents de la crise économique. L'évocation que fait Mamie[25] à cet effet est révélatrice :

> Je suis fille d'une famille de sept enfants où j'occupe la deuxième position. Chez mes parents, à cause de mon infirmité, tout le monde croyait que je suis sorcière. Ils me regardaient comme un vulgaire étranger. Manger et se revêtir étaient difficiles. Mes frères refusaient même de dormir dans le même lit que moi. J'ai beaucoup souffert. Aujourd'hui ils ont changé de regard vis-à-vis de moi, simplement parce que je suis devenue autonome et indépendante.

Ce témoignage est corroboré par plusieurs récits de vie livrés à notre connaissance par les jeunes handicapés de Kinshasa.

Pourtant, en se positionnant dans la dynamique commerçante transnationale, ces jeunes handicapés ont progressivement restauré leur image et leur niveau de vie. Moins que dans la société, certains parmi eux sont devenus des piliers dans leurs familles. Selon notre échantillon et les résultats de nos enquêtes, trois personnes (garçons) ont commencé cette activité dans les années 70, 16 hommes pour 7 femmes s'y sont intéressés dans les années 80, 12 jeunes garçons pour 9 femmes s'y sont intéressés au cours de la décennie 90 et, 16 hommes plus 13 filles s'y sont intéressés pendant la décennie 2000. S'agissant des jeunes femmes, 5 se sont intéressées au commerce entre Brazzaville et Kinshasa dans les années 80, contre 11 pendant la décennie 90 et 9 au cours de la décennie 2000.[26] Il y a véritablement une tendance croissante vers cette activité devenue stratégique pour plusieurs jeunes handicapés moteurs.

La vie de ces jeunes handicapés moteurs est passée de la condition de précarité socio-économique à l'état de prospérité matérielle.[27] Grâce donc à ce commerce, ces jeunes ont réussi à réinventer leur identité, à soigner leur statut et à améliorer leurs rapports avec le reste de la société. Tentant de comparer leurs avoirs aux salaires mensuels de certains fonctionnaires de l'État, ces jeunes commerçants handicapés moteurs affirment sans embages que « *coop eleki* salaire », c'est-à-dire la coopération ou la négociation de la vie en dehors du cadre administratif et professionnel dépasse le salaire. La croissance quasi exponentielle des hommes et des femmes dans cette activité marchande, depuis la décennie 70 jusqu'aux années 2000, justifie non seulement l'intérêt particulier que les personnes handicapées motrices accordent à cette activité, mais aussi leur mépris d'envisager ou de convoiter, pour certains, un travail professionnel.

Cependant, en réussissant à soigner leur image au sein de la société, d'autres jeunes n'arrivent pas à inverser leurs conditions matérielles. Malgré plusieurs années d'expérience et d'exercice commerciales, que de jeunes – surtout les hommes – donnent l'impression de se situer encore au début de leurs affaires. Il se pose sans doute le problème crucial de leur encadrement, puisqu'ils ont démontré leurs talents à l'intérieur des villes (Brazzaville et Kinshasa) où la vie est de plus en plus perçue par leurs habitants respectifs comme une apocalypse.

Quelles perspectives pour ces jeunes handicapés moteurs ?

La plupart des « petits métiers » issus de l'imagination populaire ne permettent pas à ceux qui les exercent d'être autonomes. De même, il ne faut pas perdre de vue les conditions de vie souvent déplorables de ceux qui pratiquent les activités informelles (Sévédé-Bardem 1997 : 156).

Les jeunes handicapés que nous avons interrogés savent avec pertinence que leur activité relève du monde informel, qu'elle n'assure point une pleine garantie pour le reste de leur vie. Sur des jeunes interrogés, 13 pour cent à peine préparent ce qu'il est convenu d'appeler l'après commerce. Plus de 70 pour cent d'entre eux ne vivent que de cette activité. Quelque 21 pour cent seulement de jeunes essaient de diversifier leurs avoirs, en ajoutant à leur activité principale (le commerce transnational) une ou deux activités parallèles. Pour l'essentiel, il s'agit de boutiques de taille modeste ouvertes devant la porte de la parcelle, d'une table achetée au marché où un parent ou une parente y est placé(e) afin de vendre des produits divers, de salons de coiffure pour femme ouverts au coin d'une rue, etc. Ces jeunes préfèrent garder leur argent à la maison. Ils pensent qu'avec les banques de la place tout peut leur arriver, en particulier le pire. Prenant l'exemple des guerres fratricides que Brazzaville a connues de façon cyclique, entre 1993 et 1999, certains de ces jeunes ont affirmé avoir perdu beaucoup d'argent à cause des pillages.

En dehors des guerres qui sont directement évoquées comme raison de non placement de capitaux dans les banques de la place, il y a aussi la faillite et l'incapacité de certaines banques à rembourser l'argent aux-ayant-droits si elles venaient à fermer. Anne-Marie de Brazzaville dit avoir perdu la somme de 150 000 F CFA qu'elle avait placée, en 1999, chez Salut Umberto Brada. À l'analyse, il y a un sentiment de prudence qui traverse la pensée de ces jeunes commerçants handicapés. Ont-ils raison de penser ainsi ?

Il semble que ces jeunes, pourtant pleins d'enthousiasme, ne soient pas capables d'inventer d'autres paradigmes, d'imaginer des scénarios susceptibles de préparer l'après- commerce transnational. Il se pose donc un problème d'encadrement de ces jeunes ; lesquels s'interrogent au sujet de leur futur, notamment de leur vie d'adultes et vieux. Les pouvoirs publics des deux Congo devraient chercher comment garantir l'avenir de ces jeunes handicapés qui luttent jour et nuit pour leur bien-être quotidien. Maintenant qu'ils sont encore jeunes et qu'ils ont encore la capacité d'agir et de gagner plus d'argent, on devrait les encourager à financer leur (pension) retraite, en leur donnant la possibilité d'accéder dans les différentes structures nationales qui s'occupent des questions de retraite.

En plus de la question de retraite qu'il faut normalement assurer à ces jeunes commerçants handicapés, les pouvoirs publics devraient aller au-delà des premiers efforts fournis par les présidents Mobutu et Marien Ngouabi en direction des personnes handicapées. La suppression des taxes commerciales pour ces handicapés devraient s'accompagner de l'octroi des crédits et d'assurance maladie. Au-delà des témoignages donnés par les acteurs eux-mêmes, l'observation directe de leur activité montre que ces jeunes sont exposés à des dangers parfois imprévisibles. La négociation de la vie loin du cadre familial implique une prise en compte d'autres logiciels conjoncturels. Or, ces jeunes handicapés n'ont toujours pas les moyens de les prévenir.

Conclusion

Quelques appréhensions éparses suffisent pour conclure cette réflexion. La parenthèse de la crise socio-économique qui s'est ouverte dans les deux Congo au lendemain des indépendances a profondément désarticulé l'équilibre social. La lutte pour l'autosubsistance dans laquelle les jeunes handicapés moteurs des deux villes jumelles se sont lancés constitue sans doute une réponse réelle à la pauvreté multidimensionnelle. Un véritable challenge. Le commerce entre Brazzaville et Kinshasa semble donc offrir des opportunités à ceux qui entendent les saisir. Les jeunes handicapés, qu'on croit être de simples mendiants, ont su exploiter ce créneau et relever le niveau de leur vie.

L'enthousiasme avec lequel ils trafiquent entre les deux métropoles signifie qu'ils ont conscience des responsabilités qui sont les leurs. La recherche quotidienne des solutions pour satisfaire les besoins vitaux fait que plusieurs jeunes handicapés moteurs s'intéressent au commerce transnational. Leur nombre dans cette activité croît de façon significative. Ce qui devrait donc inviter la société à nuancer son regard vis-à-vis de cette catégorie de personnes.

Si la fréquence des jeunes commerçants handicapés moteurs a sensiblement augmenté ces dernières années, cela n'est nullement lié à l'environnement propice de l'activité commerçante entre les deux villes jumelles, mais plus à la conjoncture socio-économique difficile. Aussi, faut-il reconnaître que l'engagement de ces jeunes dans le monde de l'économie informelle est une réaction face au resserrement de l'étau du secteur professionnel. D'autres variables telles que l'envie de se prendre seul en charge et, surtout, le souci d'inverser la tendance handicap-charge lourde dont les handicapés sont collectivement victimes dans l'imaginaire collectif, peuvent aussi justifier l'attrait de nombreux jeunes dans l'activité commerciale transurbaine. Cette dernière hypothèse ne fait certainement pas consensus, dans la mesure où les personnes handicapées constituent en elles-mêmes une problématique globale. Néanmoins, les handicapés eux-mêmes ont une claire conscience des nombreux défis socio-économiques et culturels auxquels ils doivent régulièrement faire face. En se débrouillant à l'intérieur d'un espace gourmand qu'est la ville, les jeunes commerçants handicapés moteurs de deux villes ont certainement trouvé dans le commerce la magie libératrice des chaines de leur déconsidération et la declassification sociales. C'est de cette façon qu'il faut certainement comprendre et justifier l'entrée en scène de nombreux jeunes valides dans l'activité commerciale entre Brazzaville et Kinshasa.

Il faut reconnaitre cependant que les pouvoirs publics des deux Congo ont encore un devoir de mémoire de stabilisation et d'assurance de cette catégorie de personnes. Le succès effectif de leurs affaires et, sans doute, celui de leur insertion dans le système (monde) global passe par leur intervention. Car, ces jeunes contribuent à leur manière au bien-être de l'économie locale et au renforcement des relations socioéconomiques entre les deux Etats.

Notes

1. Nous devons à Charles Didier Gondola l'expression de « villes miroirs », notamment dans un de ses ouvrages (1997) qui porte le titre *Villes miroirs*.

2. http// www.itu.inti/ITU-D//sis/PWD/seminar. Site consulté le 24 septembre 2009.

3. http//www.handifestival.com/spip.php?article 90. Site consulté le 24 septembre 2009.

4. http//www.congo-siteportail.info. Site consulté le 24 septembre 2009.

5. http//www.ilo.org/public/french/employment/skills. Site consulté le 13 juin 2009.

6. Cette période est à considérer avec précaution, car nous n'avons trouvé aucun document officiel qui indique avec précision la date au cours de laquelle cet accord était signé. Les personnes interrogées à cet effet dans différentes administrations congolaises (Ministère du plan, Ministère du commerce, Ministère de l'administration du territoire et de la décentralisation, Direction générale de l'immigration) et en milieu universitaire (Faculté des Lettres et des Sciences Humaines) ont majoritairement hésité entre ces deux dates, c'est-à-dire 1971 et 1973.

7. http://www. Facebook.com/note.php?note-ide. Site consulté le 13 juin 2009.

8. http://fr.wikipedia.org/wiki/Economie-de la République-démocratique-du-Congo. Site consulté le 13 juin 2009.

9. http:// congoforum.be/fr/analysedetail.asp?id=172. Site consulté le 13 juin 2009.

10. http://lejalconcongolais.blogs.courrierinternational.com/archive/2008/12/17/pauvreté.html. Site consulté le 13 juin 2009.

11. http// : www.hns-info.net/article.ph3?id-article. Site consulté le 13 juin 2009.

12. Dans son étude *Les spiritains au Congo de 1865 à nos jours* (1995), Jean Ernoult mentionne qu'au sein de la société Kongo de l'époque qu'il étudie, est considéré comme enfant sorcier, tout enfant dont la peau est recouverte par endroit des taches rougeâtres, celui qui a des incisives qui accusent une proéminence quelque peu suggestive, etc.

13. Ce que nous appelons par économie de misère brasse diverses activités qui relèvent du secteur informel. Ces activités sont à la fois visibles et invisibles, et permettent de définir la ville comme cet espace complexe, mais ouvert qui offre à ses habitants diverses opportunités.

14. Ce courage, ces handicapés le manifestent sur le terrain, car ils rivalisent d'égal à égal avec leurs homologues qui sont physiquement normaux.

15. Plusieurs jeunes handicapés interrogés sur leur engagement dans le commerce entre les deux villes ont affirmé et soutenu cela.

16. Vibidila Mambo, E. O n° 57 du 9 avril 2009, Brazzaville.

17. Welepele Joël, 25 ans, E. O n° 21 du mars 2009, Brazzaville.

18. Certains de ces époux sont handicapés et choisissent d'initier leurs épouses dans le commerce entre les deux villes pour leur permettre de prendre parfois leur repos. D'autres encore sont valides, mais profitent de l'état physique de leurs épouses pour trafiquer entre Brazzaville et Kinshasa. C'est pour se mettre à l'abri des taxes commerciales que ces jeunes valides exercent le commerce via leurs épouses. Il faut rappeler que les handicapés ne paient ni de taxes, ni de billets entre Kinshasa et Brazzaville.

19. Loumingou Paul, 28 ans, E. O n°7 du 24 mars 2009, Brazzaville.

20. Ces prix varient généralement avec la hausse ou la baisse du dollar, car à Kinshasa, le franc Congo, qui est la monnaie locale, n'a véritablement pas une influence économique.

21. Ces droits sont plus difficiles à supporter à Kinshasa où les enseignants sont presque à la charge des parents. Ces droits sont versés trimestriellement ou mensuellement, selon les écoles. Les parents d'élèves n'ont souvent pas les moyens et la capacité de faire face à ces droits exorbitants et élastiques. Au Congo-Brazzaville par contre, les droits scolaires ont été levés depuis bientôt deux ans. Ce qui permet aux parents de souffrir moins dans la préparation et la scolarisation de leurs enfants.

22. Mabi Jules Pascal, 24 ans, E. O n° 83 du 2 juin 2009, Brazzaville.

23. Nous avons distingué les sexes ici sans toutefois distinguer les nationalités.

24. Lussekela Gilbert, 28 ans, E. O n° 18 du 26 mars 2009, Brazzaville.

25. Luzayadio Mpassi Mamie, 26 ans, E. O. n° 71 du 28 mai 2009, Brazzaville.

26. Certaines personnes qui étaient jeunes quand elles ont commencé ce trafic entre les deux villes, dans les années 70 et 80, sont devenues adultes. Toutefois, ces personnes nous ont livré leur expérience.

27. Certains jeunes nous ont cité les biens mobiliers et autres qu'ils ont acquis grâce au commerce.

Références

Adebayo, O. et Ouédraogo, J.-B., dir, 2005, *Sciences sociales et l'avenir de l'Afrique*, Dakar, Codesria.

Blanchet, A. *et al.*, 1985, *L'entretien dans les sciences sociales*, Paris, Dunod.

Bourdillon, M., 2009, « Enfants et travail: examen des conceptions et débats actuels », in *Contre le travail des enfants ? Point de vue du Sud. Alternatives Sud*, Vol.16, Paris, Syllepse, pp. 37-69

Copans, J., 1999, *L'enquête ethnologique de terrain*, Paris, Nathan.

Doury, J.-P., 1992, *L'art de mener un entretien de recrutement. Déceler une perle rare*, Paris, Les Éditions de l'Organisation.

Duvignaud, J., 1973, *Fêtes et civilisations*, Genève, Weber.

Ernoult, J., 1995, *Les spiritains au Congo de 1865 à nos jours*, Études et documents n°3, Paris, Congrégation du Saint-Esprit.

Gondola, Ch. D., 1997, *Villes miroirs. Migrations et identité à Kinshasa et Brazzaville 1930-1970*, Paris, L'Harmattan.

Guideri, R., 1984, *L'abondance des pauvres; six aperçus critiques sur l'anthropologie*, Paris, Seuil.

Lallement, M., 2000, « A la recherche des logiques d'action », in Philippe Capin et Jean-François Dortier, dir., *La sociologie. Histoire et idée*, Paris, Sciences humaines, pp. 256-257

Lopez, R. P., 2009, *Vivre et survivre à Mexico. Enfants et jeunes de la rue*, Paris, Karthala.

Miankenda, G., 2001, Conférence-débat, « La décennie Africaine des personnes handica-pées. Une action de solidarité contre la pauvreté », Brazzaville.

Morelle, M., 2007, *La rue des enfants. Les enfants des rues*, Paris, CNRS.

Nzeza Bikakila, A., 2004, « La « coop » à Kinshasa: survie et marchandage », in Th. Trefon, dir., *Ordre et désordre à Kinshasa. Réponses populaires à la faillite de l'État*, Paris, L'Harmattan, pp. 33-46.

PIPC, 2002, *Programme intérimaire post conflit du Congo (PIPC) 2000-2002*, Pointe-Noire, Multipress-Congo.

PNUD, 2006, *Les économies de l'Afrique centrale*, Paris, Maisonneuve et Larose.

Sévédé-Bardem, I., 2007, *Précarités juvéniles en milieu urbain africain. « Aujourd'hui, chacun se cherche »*, Paris, L'Harmattan.

Trefon, Th., 2004, « La réinvention de l'ordre à Kinshasa », in *Ordre et désordre à Kinshasa. Réponse populaire à la faillite de l'Etat*, Paris, L'Harmattan, pp. 13-32.

Thevenot, L. et Boltanski, L., 1991, *De la justification : les économies de la grandeur*, Paris, Gallimard.

Tshingi, K. Nd., 1999, « Cérémonies et fêtes à Kinshasa depuis la période coloniale », in Goerg Odile, dir., *Fêtes urbaines en Afrique. Espaces, identités et pouvoirs*, Paris, Karthala, pp. 65-83.

UNICEF, 2008, République du Congo, La pauvreté multidimensionnelle des enfants et des femmes, Geranda Notten, Brazzaville.

8

Youths' Poverty and Livelihood Strategies in Fegge, Onitsha Urban Local Government Area, Nigeria

Peter Ezeah

Introduction

The world has in recent times been experiencing rapid urbanization. Presently, over 80 per cent of children and youths live in urban cities of Africa, Asia, and Latin America (Unicef 2002:21). Sub-Saharan Africa is said to have the most youthful populations in the world. An estimated 200 million young people between the ages of 12 and 24 years live in Africa's urban cities today. This rapid rate of growth has pushed the absolute size of the youth population in Sub-Saharan Africa beyond that of many other regions. By 2030, youths will account for 28 per cent of the population, making Sub-Saharan African the 'youngest' region in the world (Garcia and Fares 2008:5).

The implication of this scenario is that the growth of the population of children and youths is bound to outstrip the coping capacity of poorly resourced governments and economies in developing nations, such as most nations in Africa, to absorb new residents and provide them with adequate jobs, shelter and services. In these circumstances, many if not most children and youths may end up in substandard housing in unserviced and marginal locations with exposure to health hazards and poor nutrition as well as other livelihood challenges.

In Nigeria, an estimated 20 per cent of children and youths are found in cities (Wikipedia, accessed 10th October 2009). Many of the urban youths live in squalid slum dwellings with poor basic infrastructure and social services. Given the situation they are confronted with, the youths are bound to initiate and construct various forms of adaptation as livelihood strategies to enable them to survive and stay in the city. Onitsha is a densely populated city and has a very high percentage of its population made up of youths that migrated from the many communities that make up the South East geographical zone of Nigeria. Livelihood opportunities are the major attraction of youths to the city.

Conceptual Issues

Around the world the terms 'youth', 'adolescent', 'teenager', and 'young person' are interchangeable term, often meaning the same thing but occasionally differentiated: 'youth' generally refers to the time of life that is neither childhood nor adulthood, but rather somewhere in between (Wikipedia, accessed 10th October 2009). The age varies at which a person is considered a 'youth' and thus eligible for special treatment under the law and throughout society. The United Nations defines youth as those persons between the ages of 15 and 24, while for the World Bank, youth generally refers to those between the ages of 15 and 25 (Wikipedia, accessed 10th October 2009). The African Union defines youth as persons between the ages of 15 and 35 (African Union Charter 1999). United Nations and Commonwealth Association of Nations Charters (2000) defined youth as persons between the ages 14 and 30. For the purpose of this work, youth is defined as those persons aged between 14 and 30. This is the accepted definition of youth in Nigeria which informs the pegging of the maximum age for the National Youth Service Corps programme at 30 years.

The recent attention paid to urban livelihoods follows from a wide recognition that significant proportions of urban poor in developing countries are vulnerable in terms of their sustainable livelihood systems. Because of the absence of formal employment opportunities in the city, youths take to various forms of informal economic activity as livelihood strategies in order to survive. Urban poverty in developing countries is predicated on the fact that the major urban centres in these countries face tremendous pressure of population with insufficient infrastructure and social services (Hossain 2005).

The urbanization of poverty and the impacts of structural adjustment programmes have lead to a situation in which for many of Africa's poor, urban spaces provide opportunities as well as fears and economic hardships in livelihood provision. Anan (2000:29) captures this succinctly:

> Cities are often described as cradles of civilization and sources of cultural and economic renaissance but, for the roughly one third of the developing world's urban population that lives in extreme poverty, they are anything but that. Most of these urban poor have no option but to find housing in squalid and unsafe squatter settlements or slums. And even though the population of cities like countries has on the average become older, slum dwellers are getting younger.

The most accepted definition of poverty is provided by scholars who attempt to combine both material and non-material dimensions of poverty (Chambers 1982, 1992; Sen 1981, 1997). According to Hossain (2005:45), poverty is not defined solely in terms of low income, but should include broader concepts of deprivation and insecurity. Deprivation occurs when people are unable to reach a certain level of functioning or capability. In this sense, Chambers (1983: 1989) includes 'physical weakness, isolation, vulnerability and powerlessness in addition to lack of income and asserts'. A pyramid starting from income poverty as the most measurable, to access to common pool resources, state-provided commodities, assets, dignity, and autonomy are identified (Hossain 2005:46).

In this chapter, poverty is conceived as a multiple concept, including economic and social deprivation particularly for urban poor youths in Nigeria. Thus, poor urban youths are persons who are not able to maintain secure and positive livelihoods due to their limited economic and social resources in the city.

A livelihood is generally defined as comprising the capabilities, assets, and both material and social resources and activities required for a means of living. A livelihood framework may be used as a basis for analyzing, understanding and managing the complexity of lives (Carney 1998, cited in Rakodi 2002:9). In the livelihood framework, poverty is not only characterized by lack of assets and inability to accumulate a portfolio of them, but also by the lack of choice with respect to alternative strategies. The livelihood framework suggests that people can choose, and choices make a difference, despite the economic or social constraints they face. By pooling resources, by working in both formal and informal economies, by self-construction of shelter, and by the use of social networks, youths avoid entrapment in a self-perpetuating culture of poverty (Roberts 1994 cited in Hossain 2005:45).

The livelihood framework is therefore a very useful guide for research and intervention on poverty. It proposes thinking in terms of strength or assets as an antidote to the view of the poor as 'passive' or 'deprived'. Central to the approach is the need to recognize that those who are poor may not have cash or other savings, but they do have other material or non-material assets such as their health, their labour, their knowledge, and the natural resources around them. Livelihood approaches require a realistic understanding of these assets in order to identify what opportunities they may offer, or where constrains may lie.

In a livelihood framework, the poorest and most vulnerable households and individuals are forced to adopt strategies, which enable them to survive but not to improve their welfare (Hossain 2005:46). In urban areas in developing countries, households as well as individuals seek to mobilize resources and opportunities and to combine these into livelihood strategies, which comprise a mix of labour market investment, pooling of labour and assets, and social networking (Rakodi 2002:47). Households and individuals adjust the mix according to their own circumstances and the changing context in which they live. Economic activities form the basis of a household and individual strategy, but to them, and overlapping with them, may be added migration movements, maintenance of ties with rural areas, such as education and housing, and participation in social networks. The 'livelihoods' concept is a realistic recognition of the multiple activities, in which households and individuals engage to secure survival and improve their well-being (Ellis 1998, cited in Hossain 2005:46). In other words, livelihood strategies are those implicit principles that guide youths when seeking livelihood opportunities for coping with adverse urban conditions.

In a study conducted in the city of Dhaka in Bangladesh, using the livelihood framework, Hossain (2005:50) found how poor communities cope with urban life through 'household strategies' such as putting more family members into the work force, through petty trading, avoiding many basic goods that represent luxuries to them, increasing household size by inducting more relations, withdrawing their children from education, constructing their own shelters, using kinship as social capital, and establishing patron-client relationships with local leaders. These findings provided important indicators for this present study in investigating how youths in Fegge, Onitsha, utilize both economic and non-economic resources to overcome poverty. Urban youths in Onitsha utilized a mixture of economic and social strategies to fight poverty in the city. Economically, the youths are engaged in various informal activities to improve their low-income status and in the process spend their meagre financial resources only on cheap essential commodities so as to encourage savings. They also utilized social networks as social capital as a strategy to boost their limited social resources.

In recent decades the issue of urban poverty in Nigeria has attracted attention from scholars as the major cities in the country face serious challenges of population growth and poverty. Studies by Gugler (1997) and some others in Nigeria used micro- and macro-level data to explain the trend and pattern of urban poverty, as well as the spatial and economic characteristics of the urban poor. However, few studies have focused on the coping mechanisms of poor urban youths in adverse urban settings using the livelihood framework in Nigeria. This is the gap in knowledge that this study sets out to fill. This study therefore investigated the strategies adopted by poor urban youths in response to the challenges of securing livelihoods based on the livelihood framework, in Fegge, Onitsha. To this end, the study focused on the different economic and non-economic resources and activities which the youths in Fegge have developed for adaptation to enable them cope with their livelihoods in the city. The following research questions guided the study.

(i)   What are the different livelihood activities available and accessible to youths in Fegge?

(ii)   In what ways do youths in Fegge utilize economic strategies in overcoming poverty?

(iii) What are the non-economic strategies adopted by youths in Fegge in dealing with poverty?

(iv) What are the perceptions of youths in Fegge about their livelihood strategies?

(v) What are the constraints facing youths in Fegge in their livelihood strategies?

The Study

This study is located in Fegge, Onitsha. Onitsha is one of the largest cities in Nigeria. It is made famous by the River Niger and the Onitsha market, which is one of the biggest markets in West Africa. Onitsha is the gateway to Eastern and South-Eastern Nigeria through the River Niger Bridge. The Onitsha market makes the city the second largest commercial centre in Nigeria, coming after Lagos. Commerce is thus the major factor behind the ever-growing population of Onitsha. A majority of the residents are traders, although manufacturing, crafts, fishing, and different informal economic activities also thrive. A few of the residents are engaged in white-collar employment.

Fegge is one of the settlement areas in Onitsha. It is an over-crowded area with a very high population density, with poor infrastructural facilities and social services. Negotiating livelihoods by residents of Fegge, particularly by children and youths, is often challenging on account of the poor social condition in the area. Fegge is purposively chosen for this study because it has the largest proportion of typical poor urban youths in Onitsha.

According to the Nigerian population census figures (2006), Onitsha had a population of 261,574. This figure is generally perceived to be very low given the fact that the 2006 census exercise in Onitsha was disrupted by violent protests by the Movement for the Actualization of the Sovereign State of Biafra (MASSOB) leading to the under-counting of Onitsha residents. Wikipedia (accessed 10th October 2009) estimated the population of Onitsha at 700,000. A breakdown of this figure for the various settlement areas that make up Onitsha including Fegge is not available. However, it is estimated that Fegge has about 150,000 and 45 per cent of this figure is made up children and youths (LEEDS document 2008). The sample size for this study is 220 youths made up of 20 respondents for in-depth interview and 200 for questionnaire data. The respondents were purposively selected from ten different informal economic activities on the basis of availability sampling technique. The informal economic activities are as follows:

(i) Newspaper vending

(ii) Food processing and sales

(iii) Fashion and designing

(iv) Hair dressing

(v) Music vending

(vi) Motorcycle transport *(okada)*

(vii) Petrol attendant

(viii) Mobile telephone operators

(ix) Barrow/truck pushing

(x)   Video/cinema house operators

Two respondents who were not amongst those administered the questionnaire within each of the ten informal economic activities were selected and interviewed. Data for the study were collected in two phases between October and December 2009. Firstly, 20 youths were interviewed based on their different informal economic activities. Secondly, a structured questionnaire was constructed utilizing the information obtained from the in-depth interview on the various forms of adaptation and livelihood strategies by youths in Onitsha. Thus, the structured questionnaire focused on the various forms of adaptation by poor urban youths in Fegge, such as their informal economic activities, expenditure and purchasing patterns, shelter and environmental services, use of social services, rural-urban ties, social networks, urban food production, and community participation

The data from the in-depth interviews were analyzed based on the narratives of the youths on their perspectives and constraints in their livelihood strategies; while descriptive statistics (simple percentages) were used to analyze the questionnaire data.

Data Analysis

Analysis of the socio-demographic characteristics of the respondents shows that a large proportion of the youths (39.5%) are aged 24 to 28, with 54.5 per cent males and 45.5 per cent females. The respondents are fairly educated: about 53 per cent have completed secondary education. Over 96.5 per cent are Christians; and 98 per cent of the Igbo ethnic group. The rates of income and wages for the youths are very low. Their average monthly income is only ₦8,000.00 (US$55), which is less than US$2 per day, signifying low-income status of the youths.

The main survival strategy of the urban youths in Fegge is engagement in various informal economic activities listed above. The youths adopt the following strategies within their informal economic activities.

The survey indicated that poor urban youths mostly spend their earnings to meet basic needs of cheap items. They cannot afford to buy expensive items liked meat and milk on regular basis. Some 65 per cent of the youths buy meat or poultry once or twice a month. The youths rarely buy new clothes: most of them buy second-hand clothes. They also depend on other cheap household goods with low prices. Sometimes some of them receive discarded items such as clothes from relatives or friends.

Housing is as major problem in Onitsha generally and particularly for poor urban youths. Some of the youths (25%) live in makeshift shelters that they have built themselves on vacant private and government land, making them squatters in the city. Most of the youths (78%) live in single-roomed housing. In some cases more than four youths live in one congested room. Only 6.5 per cent live in their family houses of more than one room. The majority of youths (57%) cook inside their rooms or in open spaces. They more often cook with firewood, charcoal, and sometimes with kerosene stove. Access to public electricity supply is inadequate and irregular. Sewage systems are poor. Some youths sometimes defecate in fallow lands, which gives pollutes the environment. Similarly, solid waste disposal facilities are lacking. Waste is generally disposed of very close to their settlements, which also poses serious challenges to the physical environment.

The youths have limited access to formal health facilities: only 33 per cent utilize health services from the formal sources. Accessibility and affordability of formal medical services, as well as less attention from physicians, are some of the reasons for the urban poor accepted youths not using government hospitals. Half of them buy their medicines from chemist shops without consulting trained physicians. Some (15%) make use of local herbs and medicines. Urban transportation is chaotic and expensive for poor youths. A large proportion of the youths (41.5%) walk up to six kilometres to their places of business, while 25.5 per cent, use the motorcycle transport system known as *okada*. The youths have little access to outdoor game facilities in the city and they spend their leisure time by playing few indoor games like 'ludo', drafts, and card games. Some of the youth pass their leisure time on most Sundays by watching television or movies, particularly at local television viewing centres (see Omotosho in this volume for a description of these in another south-eastern Nigerian town). There are no zoos, parks, or museums for recreation and leisure in the area.

The level of urban migration to Onitsha affects lives in the city. Only 5 per cent of the youths were born in the city. Others migrated from different rural communities. The major reasons for their migration include poor income in rural areas, and more job opportunities in the cities. However, migration to the city often leaves the youths disappointed when their expectations are not fulfilled. But they do not want to move from the city where they earn some income.

In spite of the fact that they have lived in the city for a while, they do not generally loose their bonds with their kith and kin in their villages of origin. They therefore maintain a dual system as a source of support and sustenance to poor urban youths in the city (see Gugler 1997). Of the urban youths in the survey, 65.5 per cent maintain links with their villages from time to time. One major reason for the youths visiting their villages is farming. The youths bring back such food items like rice, yams, cassava, palm oil, and vegetables cultivated by them or by their relatives to the city. This is an important source of food security for them.

One major source of 'social capital' for these youths is social networking. According to Hossain (2005:46), social networks play an important role for the poor to cope with urban life. The youths in the study maintain various kinship ties while in the city. These networks become social capital in the context of migration to the city by providing the youths with information relating to accommodation, work, and employment opportunities, and to enable them adapt to city life. Neighbourhoods where the youth live also provide social capital to them. Many of the youths (43%) have close relationships with their neighbours. Similarly, landlordship and employment play crucial role for social networks for the youths. Some landlords provide temporary accommodation and care for new migrants. Social networking as a social capital helps to perpetuate reciprocity in the microeconomic life of the youths. Over 70 per cent of the youths visit and invite each other on social occasions. Relatives, friends, and neighbours help poor urban youths to mitigate their economic and social crisis. More than 43 per cent of the youth receive financial assistance from their kin, friends, and neighbours, while 33 per cent of them receive non-financial support such as used clothes, food items, and sundry personal effects from these friends and relatives.

The urban youths utilize structures within their communities to mitigate their problems in the city. More than 53 per cent of the youths are members of different community-based and voluntary organizations. Ethnic affiliation is the basis for group identity, which helps youth to survive in the city. Belonging to a community association is a form of social insurance as these ethnic and community associations render various services to their members – especially in times of adverse life challenges, including death.

A considerable proportion of the youths (56%) take part in party politics: 20.8 per cent served as election monitors and 8 per cent provide security services to politicians. Onitsha is one the hotbeds for political activities in Nigeria. Poor urban youths in the area engage in various political activities as a form of livelihood strategy in the city. For example, for the 2010 gubernatorial election in the state, some of the youths could provide security services (thugs) to politicians for a fee. Thugs are hired by politicians to harass and intimidate political opponents during elections. In many cases thugs contributed to electoral violence and electoral malpractices. Youths serving as security agents or thugs are a common phenomenon in Nigerian political culture. Thuggery is often seen as a lucrative business for youths during elections and many youths get themselves involved because of the financial rewards involved. Youths enjoy doing this job because of the immediate financial remuneration and the hope for employment opportunity at the end of the election should their political master win. However, despite participating in different political activities and maintaining contact with political leaders, the youths complain of being ignored by politicians because their aspirations and expected goals for employment opportunities and provision of social services are often not met.

Perception of the Youths about their Livelihood Strategies

The perception of the youths in Fegge about their livelihood strategies is drawn from what the youths themselves have said, particularly in the in-depth interviews. The general notion in literature is that the roles children and youths play in the labour process in Africa are considered inhumane, exploitative, and degrading (Agbu 2009). However, the findings in this study show that while some youth see their involvement in informal economic activities as undignified, a good number of the youths interviewed (over 60%) perceive their livelihood strategies positively.

One remark made by a 23-year-old University graduate elucidates this point. When asked how he felt working as a motorcycle (*okada*) transport operator, he replied:

> Why should I not be happy? I am happy as an *okada* rider. I was doing nothing in my village for two years after my National Youth Service programme. I had no source of income and no support because my parents passed away shortly after my graduation. Since I came to Onitsha and started this motorcycle transportation, my life is changing. It has not been easy, but I am managing to survive.

An 18-year-old female hair dresser/designer shared similar optimism and hope. When asked if she would prefer to return to her village in view of the many difficulties of life in Onitsha, she said, 'I don't want to return to my village even though life in the city is tough. I am making a living here and I am happy with what I am doing.'

One possible explanation for the positive perception of some of the youths about their livelihood strategies is that the poor youths in Onitsha develop bonds of friendship and an ethnic network as social capital to cushion the effects of urban life amongst themselves. According to Reynolds (2007), urban youths are active agents, consumers, and recipients of social capital. Some 70 per cent of the respondents interviewed for this study shared high expectations of their close personal friendships and they were strongly interested in these relationships. Friendship values of reciprocity, trust, equality, honesty, support, loyalty, and mutual understanding recurred in most of the young people's narrations, thus driving home the positive influence of social capital in sustaining poor youths in the city. For example youths share thoughts, aspirations, advice, and hopes together. Some keep custody of property and money for one another with mutual trust.

On the other hand, some of the youths interviewed quite frankly expressed their negative perception about their livelihood strategies in the city. Two of the youths interviewed lamented, 'Life is not easy in Onitsha because there are many difficulties facing residents. Onitsha town is chaotic and disorganized. Lack of basic infrastructure such as electricity affects livelihood in the city.'

With regard to wages, a 19-year-old female petrol attendant stated, 'My monthly wage is very poor and irregular I barely exist. If I get something better, I will quit.'

For her part, an 18-year-old female mobile telephone operator said, 'My work makes me weak and tired. At the end of each day's work my legs are weak for running after customers. The work is hard. I don't want to stay longer doing this work.'

Socio-economic conditions in Onitsha were identified by some of the youths as the major sources of their misgivings about their livelihood strategies. A 20-year-old boy expressed this view: 'Onitsha is overpopulated and many youth are not properly placed in the city. This is why many youths are involved in crimes like armed robbery, human trafficking and other social vices.'

The gender dimension of the perception of the youths about their livelihood strategies was explored. Interestingly, some of the female youths interviewed were quite happy about their informal economic activities. A 25-year-old female newspaper vendor expressed joy about her job. In her words, 'This job has exposed me to many prominent and influential men in the city. Some people whom I am in relationship with are helping me to survive in the city through this job and I am happy about it.'

The study also reveals some challenges in youths' livelihood strategies. For instance, sexual harassment echoed prominently during the interviews with some of the young girls as the major challenge facing them in the city. According to one 22-year-old female mobile telephone operator interviewed:

> I have been sexually harassed on different occasions by some men who pretended to be genuine customers. One day a man lured me into his car at about 7.30 in the evening pretending to buy a recharge card from me. I was shocked when he put his hands inside my dress and… My initial reaction was to maintain a distance from male customers. However, one day one of my female friends and a colleague told me that male customers could help improve my livelihood if I agreed to enter into a relationship with them. I am still thinking about it.

> Other challenges were also identified as including extortion of money by touts and law enforcement agents; unsafe working conditions that damage health; carrying heavy loads; dangers of motor accidents; harassment and intimidation by law enforcement agents; insecurity of life and properly; refusal of some customers to pay for food they have eaten; and accommodation problems.

Conclusion

The inabilities of poor urban youths to access employment in the formal sector push them into different informal economic activities as sources of livelihood in Fegge. The youths consequently utilize economic strategies such avoiding the purchase of luxury goods and items, and living only on basic goods such as food for survival in the city. They also use non-economic resources or social networks as social capital including ethnic and friendship bonds, participation in urban politics and serving as security agents to politicians during elections, belonging to community/neighbourhood organizations, etc., as strategies to deal with their condition of poverty in the city. These strategies are in line with the livelihood framework, which considers the use of economic resources and other material resources for the enhancement of the well-being of urban poor youths in city.

In addition, the youths in Fegge also perceive their livelihood strategies positively. Some youths do not see themselves as engaged in degrading and exploitative informal economic activities. Indeed, some female respondents in the interview contended that their work has helped to expose them to many prominent men in the city who have helped them maintain positive livelihoods. In the same vein, some of the male youths asserted that informal work in the city has helped in raising their status out of unemployment, which they suffered prior to their migration to the city. In spite of these positive perceptions, however, youths are faced by some challenges such as sexual harassment, extortion of money by touts and law enforcement agents, insecurity of life and property, etc, in their livelihoods in Fegge.

References

Agbu, O., ed., 2009, *Children and Youth in the Labour Process in Africa*, Dakar: CODESRIA Book Series.

Anan, K., 2000, 'We are the Peoples', New York: United Nations.

Carney, D., ed., 1998, 'Sustainable rural livelihoods: What contributions can we make?' London: DFID.

Chambers, Robert, 1982, 'Vulnerability, coping and policy'. Cited in S. Hossain, 2005, 'Poverty, household strategies and coping urban life: Examining Livelihood Framework in Dhaka City', *Bangladesh e- journal of Sociology*, Vol.2 No.1.

Chambers, Robert, 1983, *Rural Development, Putting the Last thing First*, London: Longman.

Ellis, F., 1998, 'Household Strategies and Rural Livelihood Diversification', cited in S. Hossain, 2005, 'Poverty, household strategies and coping urban life: Examining Livelihood Framework in Dhaka City', *Bangladesh e-Journal of Sociology*, Vol.2, No.1.

Garcia, Marito H., and Fares, Jean, eds, 2008, '*Youth in Africa's Labour Market*, Washington: World Bank.

Gugler, J., 1997, 'Life in a Dual System Revisted. Urban–rural ties in Enugu Nigeria, 1961-1987', in Josy Gugler, ed., *Cities in Developing world*, London: Oxford University Press.

Hossain, S., 2005, 'Poverty, household strategies and coping urban life: Examining Livelihood Framework in Dhaka City, *Bangladesh e-Journal of Sociology*, Vol. 2, No.1, pp. 11-15

LEEDS Document. 2008, Onitsha Local Government Area.

Rakodi, C., 1995, 'Poverty Lines or Household Strategies?, *Habitat International*, Vol.19, No.4, pp. 402–426.

Rakodi, C., 2002, 'A Livelihood Approach-Conceptual Issues and definition' in Carole Rakodi and Tony Llyod-Jones, eds, *Urban Livelihoods: A people Centered Approach to Reduce Poverty*, London: Earthscan.

Reynolds, T., ed., 2007, *Social Capital*, London: Routledge. Available online.

Roberts, B., 1994, 'Informal economic and family strategies', *Journal of Urban and Regional Research*, 18:6-23.

Sen, Amartya K., 1981, *Poverty and Famine: an essay on entitlement and deprivation*, Oxford: Clarendon.

Sen, Amartya K., 1997, *Inequality Re-examined*, Cambridge (Massachusetts): Harvard University Press.

UNICEF, 2002, 'Poverty and Exclusion among urban children', Florence, Italy, United Nations Children's Innocent Digest 10, Research Centre.

9

Hunting and Gathering by Children and Youths in Owerri Urban, Nigeria: Negotiating Dietary Supplements

Okechi Dominic Azuwike

Introduction

In the suburbs of Owerri, children's struggle to survive comes to the fore when one observes the phenomenon of bands of chattering children and youths browsing the bushes on some nights with their local light sources and gathering snails for food or for sale. On occasional nights, in the rainy season, they may gather flying termites. In the daytime, other forms of hunting may also be practised. These children's perception of their hunting activities differs from the perceptions of those who have developed the mindset of saving the children from themselves by opposing these activities. Work forms that appear unpleasant for children in popular perception may be perceived as fulfilling by the children concerned (see Bourdillon, 2009:20).[1]

Hunting children relate with the home as well as the street. This suggests that these two platforms of children's existence are not necessarily mutually exclusive but rather coexist in the lives of children. The 'street child' may be interpreted more broadly than only to cover street residents.[2] Gimsrud and Stokke (1997: 21) include as street children, 'those living within the family whose earnings (on the streets) contribute to household survival'. The child hunters described in this chapter provide an example of children who combine activities on the streets with life in their homes.

A further question is whether or not economic hardship, which in many cases drives foraging behaviour, predisposes households to factor such informal engagements as children's hunting in their survival toolkit? The rewards of the children's enterprise are managed by adults, who are considered most capable of resource management. In hunting, children therefore largely remain a factor of adult's production processes. Surrendering their earnings is necessary for retaining critical adult protection.

Should hunting among children be called work or play? If it is work, is it exploitative work? What are the hazards involved in this form of work? The fact that child hunting is usually informed by enlightened self-interest on the part of the child and is at times approached with excitement tends to hide aspects that might be deemed abusive. The family can in some circumstances be a subterfuge that masks the exploitative nature of activities which children may successfully be cajoled or cowed into only in the authoritarian environment of the family. Thus, Lange (2000) interprets use of children's work as 'processes geared towards production and domination'. Is this generally or ever a true interpretation?

Do children involved in hunting perceive that they are being exploited? Rather than exploitation they tend to perceive an opportunity for self-expression and agency in general. In many quite different circumstances, attempts to protect children by stopping them from working have failed to attend to the positive difference that working made to their lives: stopping the work sometimes leaves them worse off than when they were allowed to work (Bourdillon 2009: 6-7). While night hunting may be deemed hazardous and while the hazards may be acknowledged by the participants, the willingness among them to meet the challenge of hazards is very real. Is this indicative of possible benefits that outweigh perceived risks? The children have invented strategies to cope with culturally imposed work requirements and to negotiate their existence in a largely adult-controlled world. In this study, we look at the phenomenon of child hunting as a social activity and in the context of urban social ecology of space contestation.

Contexts

This study deals with urban people who are rural in orientation, having been generally raised in rural areas surrounding urban Owerri and having migrated to the urban area. It also deals with children who may have been born to these migrants in the urban area as well as non-migrant indigenous populations that have been swamped by urbanization. The process of urban acculturation is scarcely completed among these groups, most of whom maintain a strong link with their rural roots.

In the 1980s, Gugler (2002) repeated studies he carried out in Nigeria in the early 1960s on urban people's connection to their rural roots. He found that urban people who expressed strong reservations about visiting their villages in the 1960s when they were children or youths, often established strong connections to their rural roots in their adulthood. The urban experience did not translate into the erosion of rural folkways in the African context, and many livelihood options of rural areas were replicated in the urban areas. Most urban dwellers involved with these livelihood options are found at the urban fringes that serve as their points of reception in the urban destination – an urban zone that might pass for a fresh migrants' zone, with its characteristic mixture of urban and rural lifestyles. This zone seems to be a cultural frontier that retains rural immigrants for a gradual assimilation into mainstream urbanism and eventual spatial relocation of successfully acculturated and usually empowered persons to more urbanized zones.

While many residents of this zone are wealthy persons who have located in this environment to avoid crowding disincentives associated with the urban core, many other residents are poor people who have responded to cheaper housing and lower municipal standards obtainable in the urban fringe. This creates a fertile ground for contestation of the urban space between the two distinct income groups.

A further feature of the Owerri context is that children are expected to make contributions rather than being barred from meaningful work or being restricted to only play and learning. The distinction in the lives of children between play and work as mutually exclusive phenomena is often associated with western thinking (Woodhead 1999:24). In the context in which this study is set, however, children are seen to combine play activities with work activities: play and work are fused. In this way, children yield to a biological inclination to vent their abundant psychomotor potentials while accommodating culturally imposed values of hard work and utilitarian engagement of their time. Beyond this, children often learn to perform tasks competently by playing at them first. This can be observed among Owerri urban poor.

The urban poor in Owerri have limited options in their quest for survival. There is scarcely enough industrial capacity in either the formal or informal sector to absorb them, as their number is swollen through migration from surrounding rural areas. They are therefore innovative particularly in informal economic arrangements. They have tended to deploy children in economic ventures in a bid to adjust to the high challenges for survival that the city presents. In different parts of the Owerri urban area, night-time hunting of snails and flying termites is quite common among children and youths. While flying termites are highly seasonal, being restricted to the rainy season months of May to August, snails are observed for a much longer period in the year. In the rainy months of April to October, snails forage at night and are exposed to gatherers who move in droves, wielding mostly crude light sources. In the dry season, they are hunted by day in cool environments such as under the shady ambience of banana and plantain growth. Flying termites, on certain cold nights, seek out light sources and invade human habitations in their craving for warmth. Through the provision of attractive light, they are lured and gathered in large receptacles. These activities take a good part of the night hours, and sometimes the entire night, featuring particularly children and youths who brave several hazards (discussed below) to hunt and gather these small creatures.

The focus here is on the activity of hunting and its place in the lives of the children that participate in it. The article also considers the dominance of children and youths in these hunting and gathering activities despite their hazard-prone nature; the challenges faced by the children in the activity and adjustments they make to meet these challenges; and the children's interpretation of the activity and of their involvement in it. Some hunting children participate as a form of agency, taking control of their lives. Uche, a 16-year-old boy said:

> Our parents do not approve of our joining [in night hunting] but when we see the boys and girls with their lights in the nearby bushes, we are really tempted to join them and we do join. Our parents do not mind when they see the snails we have collected. It is theirs you know.

Evidently, we are also dealing with a context in which children may initiate livelihood strategies.

Methods

Children and youths involved in night-time and daytime hunting and gathering were studied through in-depth interviews and participant observation of their activities. Selected parents or guardians of such children were also interviewed. The study included characterization of the research subjects, motivating factors, social networks, etc. Information acquired generally relates to age and gender of the subjects, amount of money made, extent of commoditization of the proceeds of hunting, occurrence of hazards, conflicts with urban agencies, time cost of the hunt, size of hunting parties, opportunity cost of the hunt, level of domestic application of gathered proceeds, etc.

A total of twelve children who participate in the activity were selected from twelve different hunting groups identified in different parts of the urban area. Grouping among hunters is more pronounced in snail hunting, which features a greater mileage along the roads or through the bushes and bush paths. Termite hunting does not have as great a nomadic component as it is largely point-specific, being highly associated with dwelling units that tend to attract mainly children in their immediate environments. Another reason is that while snail hunting proceeds over a fairly long period, allowing usually fluid groupings time to consolidate, termite hunting is only for a short time and is impossible to plan in advance given the uncertainty of timing in termite activity. Thus hunting parties transcending dwelling units hardly evolve in termite hunting. Study subjects were selected through the purposive sampling technique using the snowball method. Five parents or guardians of the children were also selected through the same process.

The process of identification of respondents was plagued by a denial syndrome. Some of the potential respondents who were identified denied their involvement in hunting. The problem was solved by paying individualized attention to respondents outside public view. Some preferred to trivialize the practice by falsely submitting that it was only younger members of their households that were involved. Participant observation helped gain their confidence and also elicited responses. Responses were mainly in the Igbo language, at times poorly flavoured with English, and have been translated into English.

Study Subjects and their Hunting Activities

Children and youths involved in the hunting and gathering of snails and termites are usually aged between 9 and 26. There are some older persons who also participate, but the indicated age cohort dominates the activity. The study population is made up of six boys and six girls aged between 13 and 18 years and only insightful responses from them have been highlighted here. The three male and two female parents or guardians included in the study are aged between 48 and 63 years. They are all artisans and are involved in bricklaying, food vending, carpentry, and trading.

The hunting activity is a social activity in the sense that factors such as need for company compel group behaviour. In snail hunting, favourable weather parameters such as diurnal heavy rains followed by rain-free nights indicate good nights for snails' foraging activity and promote preparations, which may include networking among hunting persons and preparation of light source and receptacles for the hunt. If the weather is good, there could be up to three night hunting sessions in a week. The usual destinations that promise good snail occurrence are refuse dumpsites and other areas of vegetal decomposition.

In the dry season, hibernating snails may be found encysted under cover in cool moist places while some others may be shaken off dry plantain leaves. Night hunting parties spend as much as three hours between 9 pm and 12 am in search of snails – moving from one area of anticipated snail activity to another. This movement may take them up to 5 to 10 kilometres away from home, through bushes that may be interspersed by human habitations. In the course of this movement, they encounter various forms of opposition from home owners apprehensive of their trespass and security guards wary about the security risk they pose and the potential cover their presence can offer miscreants. Security guards therefore confront these hunting groups and refuse to yield space to them. Encounters of the two groups are always unpleasant, with the children complaining of various forms of victimization including beatings.

Children's hunting cannot be scheduled to fall at weekends or with some regularity so as to reduce its disruptive tendencies, because snail foraging activity is not controlled by the hunters. Snail hunting may therefore disrupt schooling in terms of sleep deprivation costs. Sometimes children are reluctant to disrupt their lives in this way and are pressurized to take part by parents or guardians. However, hunting children are largely willingly motivated by the utilitarian value of hunting and recreational and social opportunities they derive from it. Consequently, in some cases, the children participate in snail hunting against parental advice.

Children who participate in hunting snails include both domestic servants and children living in their own homes. Households that participate in these activities tend to maximize returns by mobilizing as many members of the household as possible.

In termite hunting, hunters are usually taken unawares by the termites, which have uncertain swarming regimes. It is therefore difficult for some to prepare in advance. When termites swarm close to midnight as is common, many households may not have fuel to maintain lighting and attract the termites. Termites are also known to gravitate towards strong light sources in a neighbourhood. This habit is usually to the disadvantage of the poor who may not have electric power – the usual source of strong lighting. While most households tend to gather termites incident on their dwelling units, some households do take advantage of stronger light sources existing elsewhere in the neighbourhood. This may involve movements that may extend up to eight kilometres from their dwelling units in search of strong security lights or street lights. Gathering flying termites may take up to nine hours between 11pm and 8am, although gatherers may decide to call off the activity at any time. While adults may choose to participate only at the peak of termite swarming, it is usual for children to endure until after the swarming when they pick up descended wingless termites that are scurrying for cover. Children may hunt up to 8am, lifting objects off the ground to expose these termites. For children therefore termite hunting can be quite disruptive of their activities, including schooling. Scheduling of the activity is out of the question as termite hunting can only take place while swarming lasts. Children compete among themselves over gathering of large quantities of termites. Household mobilization for termite gathering includes most members of the household.

Social Networks of Hunting Parties and the Power of Grouping

The grouping of snail-hunting parties among children is of fair regularity. Obinna, a 14-year-old boy said, 'I hunt with two of my siblings. We are usually joined by three or four others. So five or six of us gather before we move'.

The children value company and its role in dispelling fear. The social grouping of hunting parties mirrors the group mentality of other street-level groups. They tend to be reactions to a collective fear and/or shared sense of social disapproval. Though each hunting child is as helpless as any other in the face of any real danger, their group mentality provides them with a feeling of mutual assurance of safety. In analyzing psychosocial impact of child work, Woodhead (2004: 323) observed:

Most types of work do not impact on a lone child but on children as part of a work group, a family group, a peer group etc. These wider groups can be important in providing a shared sense of identity and support, buffering the impact of difficult circumstances.

Shared impacts are more manageable by children and therefore leave less psychological injury on them. Thus, UN HABITAT (2006) noted that 'quality relationships are important to youth who can provide peer support and guidance to others....' The phenomenon of grouping among hunters is not free of usual regimentation associated with human groups. In night hunting, leadership requirements come into decisions on movements, timing, conflict management, and moderation of play; and without forms of social control, the activity cannot go on. Snail-hunting groups have to be large enough to form critical mass that will transcend the children's fear threshold and provide adequate and mutual support for rewarding deep forays into the bushes. They also have to be small enough to guarantee per capita pickings large enough to justify forgone night rest. Thus, all sorts of intra-group and inter-group intrigues involved in recruitment and dropping of hunting mates are encountered in maintaining optimum group strength.

Children's Hunting and Urban Space Contestation

Besides intrigues among themselves, hunting children must sometimes contest for urban space. In every contest, the more resourceful and endowed have an advantage over others. Children and youths suffer disadvantages since urban space use is also a social construct based mainly on adult world-views. Children's recreational and work activities may be deemed inferior to adult activities and be forced to give way in the contest for urban space, even to adult leisure activities.

Chawla (2002:228) outlined indicators of environmental quality from children's perspectives to include peer-gathering places, green areas, variety of activity settings, freedom of movement, freedom from physical dangers, and freedom from social threat. A breach of these indicators occasioned by adult applications of the urban space is common in many areas and it affects children's use of the urban area for activities like hunting. Based on experience in South Africa, Samara (2005) contended that perception of street children as a threat to social order indicates 'ongoing struggle over public space'. In suburban Owerri, there is elite resentment over the night-hunting behaviour of low-class children and youths. The tendency is for the elite to be intolerant of these 'excesses' of peasant children/youth, and to employ urban management agencies, like the hired security guards.

A 15-year-old girl, Ada, reported:

> I used to participate fully [in hunting snails] but since the neighbourhood hired a night vigilante outfit, we have had a couple of unpleasant skirmishes with them on the hunting trail, and as a result, my parents stopped me from further participation in it.

Also, a parent, 60-year-old James, a male bricklayer said:

> I would rather that my children do not join the hunting, but they seem to enjoy it.
> We did all these things while growing up in the village. The children are in the urban
> area which presents a whole lot of challenges. The idea of having children out in the
> bushes at night is becoming scary in the face of kidnappings for ritual purposes.
> The world has changed.

Children are not, however, always losers in contests for urban space. In some circumstances, children are quite able to negotiate their use of it. Citing the experience in conflict situations in which children may be allowed to forage and scavenge in areas controlled by security forces where adults are barred from doing so, Boyden (2003) noted that children do not always have more limited options for survival than adults. Could adults convince local vigilante or security groups that they are actually hunters if confronted while wandering at night? They would not have the same measure of success achievable by children. Children more easily establish innocence of their motives. This contributes to children and youths' dominance of these activities. There is a strong youth presence in night life consumption as elsewhere in the world (Chatterton and Holland 2003:68). Youths tend to look out for justifications for their usual tendency to retain an outdoor presence far into the night, longer than older people, and hunting may provide this opportunity. Another dimension of urban space contestation is therefore that of adults' insistence on clearing the outdoor nightscape of human presence against a youth inclination to populating and enjoying such nightscape which is usually free of 'irritating' adult content.

Distinctions in the Street Experience

I have pointed out that perceptions of street children comprise part of the contest for urban space. What is the public evaluation of the child hunter and particularly the night hunter? Does the usual stigma of the street child apply to the child hunter, who is usually domesticated? The sentiments expressed in the interview responses mirror the perception of street children and their activities and the usual public hesitation to accommodate them. A 14-year-old boy, Emma, discussing the wisdom of group effort in hunting, comments in a mode common with street children:

> The night time is a fearful time as it is dark all around. Anything can happen. If you
> are alone hunting in the night, you are looking for trouble. You could be targeted by
> miscreants or accused of sundry criminality.

Also Maretha, a 48-year-old food vendor maintained:

> Gathering termites around the house? Yes, my children get into that, but hunting
> for snails in far away bushes? No I don't think I have the heart for that. The children

> may however pick snails from around the house. Poorly minded children used to the outdoors are more competent for the long-range hunts.

Hunting children tend to suffer the perceptions of others due to the street orientation of their activities. Many therefore deny the hunting status because survival on the street is easily linked to negative behaviour. Do these children share the usual characteristics of street children? Adoption of socializing and survival strategies among street children such as existing in clusters (Rizzini and Butler 2003) is also seen among child hunters. Their similarity to street children does not arise from family dysfunctions commonly associated with street children, but rather from their apparent reckless abandon associated with street life.

However, there is no sharp dividing line between street life and domestic life of children in Africa. Most children are situated at some point of a gradation along the domestic–street spectrum. Many domestic children periodically share the life world of street children, that is, the street experience. Hawkers and night hunters are in this category. Since many children outside those categorized as street children are involved in street life to various degrees, classification of those involved in street life should be based on the extent of domestication of the youths.[2]

Resort to the streets by otherwise domesticated children like those usually involved in hunting, betrays a discontent with whatever domestic provisions are available. Children who look forward to outdoor succour, entertainment, and survival in night hunting are usually the ones repelled by scarcely conducive dwelling units. The children involved in these hunting activities are mostly from poor artisan parents operating in the informal sector, who can hardly afford decent housing. To these children, meaningful outdoor engagements come as a relief. Emma, quoted earlier, sums up this observation:

> Even on non-hunting nights, I do not usually retire indoors until very late. There are six of us that sleep in that little room and it is suffocating even in the rainy season.

Children of the low-income group are generally, compelled or induced by different circumstances to maintain a presence on the streets even as they maintain a domestic livelihood. This fact is also made evident in the lives of child hunters who may leave home at night to negotiate livelihood on the streets. The street experience is evidently, for most children, a continuum of situations rather than a discernible framework of inclusiveness and exclusivity as regards who is a street child and who is not. This leads to a discussion of the household characteristics of hunting children.

Hunting Behaviour and Household Characteristics

Most child hunters, and all in this study, share the characteristic of coming from poor households, where per capita consumption is low. Such economic factors push them to engage in this activity. Nnenna, a 60-year-old female petty trader relates:

> Termites and snails are no longer poor people's food. The rich access them better. I made about N4000 selling flying termites last year. How many poor people can afford to spend as much as N500 on these things like some of my rich clients do? The rich has pushed the poor out of the market for these things. Hunting is the best bet of any poor family that still has a taste for them.

Poverty pushes households to go into this foraging behaviour as a means of supplementing their diets and raising cash income. Though these are regarded as delicacies, some households that produce them do not consume them as they prefer to sell for cash. On the other hand, the buyers are usually from better-off households from the same neighbourhoods, who would not make the sacrifice to hunt but have disposable income to buy proceeds from the producers. Hunting behaviour – participation or otherwise – is a function of household characteristics.

Togunde and Richardson (2006), working on the relationship between child labour and household variables in urban Nigeria, found that size of household, number of children in the household, and number of children contributing to household income are positively correlated with children's hours of work. Children are relied on or co-opted into the survival game where household characteristics indicate requirement of a concerted effort. Large poor households are hardly able to make adequate welfare provisions for members while they enjoy a large pool of labour.

In this study, of the twelve identified households of hunting respondents, nine have more than four children aged below 25 years. All these nine households constitute initial units of hunting parties around which hunting teams crystallize. Small households tend to be able to provide for the household's needs and are less inclined to seek extra income from hunting. The observation supports the household production theory that resource constraints drive parents to maximize household wealth (Togunde and Richardson 2006). This can involve deployment of children in productive activities.

Generally, vulnerability predisposes a family to reliance on children's labour to supplement family income. At the same time, where housing is poor, household members tend to maintain an outward orientation and an affinity for the outdoors that may culminate in foraging behaviour. Apart from housing, a household characteristic that predisposes children to night hunting is poverty, the dominant factor that drives child labour (Bass 2004:182). Related to this is the decline in urban diets which affects protein and calorie intake among the poor in the face of declining wages (Potts 1997). The poor have reacted to this situation by sourcing food from outside the market, including such activities as hunting termites and snails.

Although children take part in night hunting spontaneously and for fun, the productivity of this activity and its importance in the household economy give it characteristics of work. Indeed, children find their working day extended at times by four to six hours, sometimes extending to 2 am or even daybreak.

The uncertainty in the timing of termite swarming means that constant vigilance is required. Nkechi, an 18-year-old girl recalled:

> On one occasion last two or three rainy seasons, we [she and her household] woke up in the morning only to realize that the termites had a field day through the night. The large heaps of shed termite wings testified to it. Unfortunately our neighbours had helped themselves without alerting us. It was a sad day for us and we blamed our neighbours for their selfishness. Since that time, we have learnt to watch out when the termite season shows up. At times, you may just have to interrupt your sleep to find out.

Mixed Work and Play

While hunting has some characteristics of work, this does not compel children to compromise their playful side. Child hawkers in Nigeria, for instance, are seen to insert fun into the various activities involved in their trade. There is the usual exercise of balancing wares on the head with cultivated inattentiveness while the hands are totally free or engaged in some trivia like computer games. Those that hawk chilled beverages make music from running bottle openers against their plastic crates. A lot of others, wares on their heads, watch videos playing in shops that sell records. The tendency to spice up non-play economic activities also appears in night hunting. Felix, a 16-year-old boy said, 'I enjoy it (snail gathering). Every one of us does. It is as much work as play. We like the competition involved. It is a lot of fun to gather snails because there is joy in their discovery, at times in unlikely places.'

The largely non-coercive and self-motivated nature of participation in these activities is evidently due mainly to the play and social derivatives from them. On the other hand, spicing up work with play could be a way of managing inescapable, unsatisfactory work occasions. The tendency to marry work with play may also be stimulated by environmental conditions operating outside the intrinsic nature of work itself.

Woldehanna, Jones, and Tefera (2008) drew attention to how work can violate children's rights to leisure, socializing in the community, and rest. Night hunting may compromise rest, but it supports aspects of children's leisure and socializing requirements.

Night Hunting as a Hazard

Although in hunting, children mix work and play, this does not remove potential hazards from the activity. While James, quoted earlier, raised fears about the danger of kidnapping night child hunters for ritual purposes, Ngozi, a 15-year-old girl, had other fears. She said:

> The danger is much. Neighbourhood dogs that bark at us might bite somebody. There could also be snake bites, and some dangerous wild game. We simply hope that our light sources will repel them. Oh well, we are usually many and that helps.

Uche (quoted earlier) said:

> There is a real fear that some may mistake us for thieves and possibly shoot at us. We hear of such mishaps, though there has not been any such incident I know of. Robbers do not wield local candle like we do of course. This factor makes hunting with torch light confusing and dangerous. I guess it is because we [child night hunters] chatter a lot that the public differentiates us from night marauders.

It can be seen that it is not all fun for the children even as children tend to extract some form of excitement from situations of uncertain security.

Sleep deprivation is one of the consequences of night hunting that may impact on health and other activities. Julie, a 15-year-old girl noted, 'Termite hunting...can take an entire night. You are useless for school or anything else the next morning.' The focus in literature has been on effects of child work on education. Other areas of livelihood are also affected.

I have pointed out that children of poorer households are more likely to take part in this productive activity. The propensity to judge such activities as hazardous is also related to households' level of welfare. In highly constrained households, risk awareness assumes a form of cognitive dissonance as the pressure for survival overrides safety concerns. In richer households, on the other hand, risk aversion is high and small risks may be overblown, and protection from hazards is emphasized.

Benefits of Children's Hunting in the Home

There are advantages to compensate for the hazards. Apart from the enjoyment, hunting can provide economic and social advantages to urban youths. It may not be possible to identify persons who have been significantly enriched by earnings from night hunting, but we cannot deny the differences it may make in the family menu and income profile of poor households.

The usual major breadwinners, parents, benefit from any freely obtained supplement which they might otherwise have paid for. Beyond benefiting parents, some children target personal items that also usually fall under parental responsibilities, which may come as a relief to parents. Iyke, a boy of 17 years said, 'I keep my snails till they are plenty. Then I sell them and make money. Last year I bought myself a pair of sandals from the money I made.'

The place of hunting in the diet of households is also significant. Children's efforts towards their survival through activities in the subsistence sphere of the peasant economy are highly acknowledged in literature (e.g., Nieuwenhuys 1996). Termites in the diet add an element of luxury to the family menu. Josiah, a 58-year-old male carpenter, commented, 'Who does not consider the *aku ebe* (flying termites) delicious? All my life, I have eaten it. I don't know why it is so appealing. Perhaps it is due to its high seasonality.'

Beyond the utilitarian function of night hunting in participating households, there are other psychosocial aspects to it. Nnorom, a 63-year-old male trader, commented:

> You cannot compare the resourcefulness of those that engage in these enterprises [hunting activities] with that of those who do not. These activities build discipline, social harmony and realistic adjustments to expectations. The mere fact that you cannot predict what you are going to get from the bush is a humbling experience. Your colleague may gather far more than you and in that realization, you grow to appreciate the spirit of fair competition.

In line with value orientation, Woodhead (2004) identified survival, distraction from main vocation, and a way of learning responsibility or of attaining greater autonomy, as functions of work in children's life. These are all relevant to the experience of child hunters.

The Paradox of Children's Agency in Hunting Activities

Children's activities to enhance their survival are not entirely free from adult control and supervision. Concerns about the 'impropriety' of children's night hunting occasioning institutional and other constraints against the practice restrains children's choice on their diet and income pursuit. The unpopularity of these restraints among children is seen in the willingness of some to get around them, for instance in hunting in defiance to parental disapproval.

In many cases, the child works but the parents or guardians take charge of the proceeds. Jane, a 16-year-old girl, had this to say:

> You think I know how much money is made from the hunts. Well, I do not. All I know is that everything we get from the bush, mine and my siblings' go into the common pool. Mother dispenses as it pleases her. We eat much of what is collected and scarcely have enough to sell.

Although children exercise some agency in this field, parents and guardians control the produce. This orientation tends to interpret children as competent wage earners and incompetent resource managers. Thus, children only have choice, constrained by age and gender-appropriate behaviour, and by those related to access to key resources (see Whitehead, Hashim and Iversen 2007). In Igboland generally, it is said that the child owns hunted game only while in the bush, because on his or her arrival from the bush, ownership becomes that of the homeowners. Children's production activities are, however, facilitated by granting them pseudo-ownership. Parents speak of the proceeds of the hunt as 'the child's', conferring on the children status and pride of ownership. This does not bar their parents or guardians from exercising full ownership rights over the same materials. According such recognition to a child is merely a social construct that promotes their agency. Children may, however, use such recognition to negotiate appropriation of their materials for personal use. Having been socialized in this way, children do not necessarily want to be in control of their earnings. Those studied appear contented with being acknowledged. Ijeoma is a 13-year-old girl and she had this to say about what she realizes from her hunts:

> I don't sell. All I know is that my mother keeps some of it for us and sells most of it in the market. She buys things for us from the money she makes. I feel proud to contribute to family income and I enjoy the blessings I get from my parents.

Children may derive fulfilment from activities the adult world considers negligible or unpleasant. This calls for a need to look at these children's activities from their perspective.

Conclusion

Children and youths opt to exercise agency to negotiate their sustenance in the Owerri urban area by hunting and gathering small game for food and or for sale. Children's agency in this activity is, however, restricted to the extent that adults usually exercise control over the enterprise and proceeds from it. The study analysed the practice as a livelihood option and as a phenomenon of interest exhibiting varied forms of contestation in urban social ecology. These hunted natural resources provide avenues for engagement in both work and entertainment, allowing children to enjoy being productive.

Hunting children, despite their domestic derivation, are able to enjoy life of the streets, characterized by the rugged confidence to meet the challenge of hazards. This leads us to a rethink of popular definitions of the street child to accommodate irregular persons that may occasionally stray into street life from their domestic base.

Household characteristics of poverty tend to give children an outdoor outlook that favours foraging behaviour, both for the rewards it offers and for the escape from crowded homes. Hunting children acknowledge the existence of varied forms of hazards, but they do not see themselves as exploited persons, irrespective of this difficulty and the involvement of adults as beneficiaries. Most of them participate willingly in hunting driven by, among other factors, the play and social aspect of it. From the high level of motivation observed among hunters, hunting can be said to be a form of improvised recreation activity, justified as work by its material productivity component. Also children's agency as exemplified by hunting operates within adult-erected child disempowerment structures.

Percy-Smith (2002) documented many young people's views of their neighbourhoods and the emphasis is on conditions that tend to reduce their application and enjoyment of urban space, including restrictions on young peoples' use of neighbourhood space. In our study area, absence of designated neighbourhood parks and recreation/playgrounds might have occasioned the combination of work and play in bush foraging activities. In this regard, there is a reinforcement of the idea that night hunting may also be seen as a form of improvisation by children to attain desired recreational goals in environments that have not made adequate arrangements to accommodate their youthful exuberance. Hence, wherever children find themselves, they tend to invent opportunities for play. Urban development is pushing children's play activities out of the environments where they are of potential nuisance value to the adult world and at times out of safe spaces. Play is therefore being taken to non-play areas. However, the attitude of children in making play a part of livelihood pursuits like hunting shows that negotiating the social and environmental space is a part of environmental awareness/cognition which is an important part of child/youth development.

Notes

1. Nieuwenhuys (2000) reported that factory girls who travelled for seasonal work in prawn factories in Gujurat and Maharashyra perceived the work as desirable while others saw it as exploitative and abusive.
2. On-the-street status of street children appears in several classifications: 'floaters' and 'runaways' identified by English (1973), 'missing children', 'absconders', 'homeless children', and 'drifters' identified by Richter and Van der Wall (2003). Categories such as 'seasonal street child' or 'diurnal/nocturnal street child' that can let one into the extent of detachment of the street child from the domestic life are not emphasized.

References

Bass, Loretta E., 2004, *Children Labour in Sub-Saharan Africa*, Boulder Co: Lynne Rienner Publishers.

Bourdillon, Michael, 2009, *A Place for Work in Children's Lives?*, PLANCanada. Available at http://plancanada.ca (accessed on 24 January 2010).

Boyden, Jo, 2003, 'Children under Fire: Challenging Assumptions about Children's Resilience', *Children, Youth and Environment*, Vol. 13, No. 1.

Chatterton, P. and Hollands, R., 2003, *Urban Nightscapes: Youth Cultures, Pleasure Spaces and Corporate Power*, London and New York: Routledge.

Chawla, L., 2002, 'Toward Better Cities for Children and Youth', in L. Chawla, ed., *Growing up in an Urbanizing World*, Earthscan, UNESCO Publishing, MOST, p.228.

English, C., 1973, 'Leaving Home: A Typology of Runaways', *Society*, Vol. 10, pp. 22-24.

Gimsrud, B. and Stokke, L. J., 1997, *Child Labour in Africa:Poverty or Institutional Failures? The cases of Egypt and Zimbabwe*, Fafo-report 233, Fafo Institute for Applied Social Science.

Gugler, J., 2002, 'The son of the Hawk Does Not Remain Abroad: The Urban-rural connection in Africa', *African Studies Review*, Vol. 45, No. 1, pp 21-41. Also available at www.jstor.org/stable/1515006

Lange, Marie-France, 2000, 'The Demand for Labour within the Household: Child Labour in Togo', in B. Schlemer, ed., *The Exploited Child*, London, ZED Books. pp. 268-277.

Nieuwenhuys, Olga, 1996, 'The paradox of Child Labour and Anthropology', *Annual Review of Anthropology*, Vol. 25, pp.237-251.

Nieuwenhuys, Olga, 2000, 'The household economy in the commercial exploitation of children's work: The case of Kerala', in Bernard Schlemmer, ed., *The Exploited Child*, London and New York: Zed Books, pp. 278-91.

Percy-Smith, B., 2002, 'Contested Worlds: Constraints and Opportunities in City and Suburban Environments in an English Midlands City', in L. Chawla, ed., *Growing up in an urbanizing World*, Earthscan, UNESCO publishing, MOST.

Potts, D., 1997, 'Urban Lives: Adopting new strategies and adapting rural links', in C. Rakodi, ed., *The Urban Challenge in Africa: Growth and Management of its Large Cities*, Tokyo: U.N. University Press, pp. 447-494.

Richter, Linda M. and van der Walt, Michelle, 2003, 'The Psychological Assessment of South African Street Children', *Children Youth and Environment*, Vol. 13, No. 1.

Rizzini, Irene and Butler, Udi, 2003, 'Life Trajectories of Children and Adolescent Living on the streets of Rio de Janeiro', *Children, Youth and Environment*, Vol. 13, No. 1.

Samara, T.R., 2005, 'Youth, Crime and Urban Renewal in the Western Cape', *Journal of Southern African Studies*, Vol. 31 No. 1. pp. 209-227.

Togunde, D., and Richardson, S., 2006, 'Household Size and composition as Correlates of Child Labour in Urban Nigeria, *Africa Development*, Vol. 31, No.1, Dakar: CODESRIA, pp. 50-65.

UN-Habitat, World Youth Forum, 2006, 'Youth in Urban Development: Bringing Ideas into Action', Discussion Paper, World Urban Forum 3, UN-Habitat.

Whitehead, Ann, Hashim, I. M., and Iversen, Vegard, 2007, *Child Migration, Child Agency and Inter-generational Relations in Africa and South Asia*, Working Paper T24, Development Research Centre on Migration, Globalization and Poverty.

Woldehanna, T., Jones, N., and Tefera, B., 2008, 'The invisibility of Children's Paid and Unpaid Work: Implications for Ethiopia's National Poverty Reduction Policy', *Childhood*, Vol. 15, No. 2, pp. 177-201.

Woodhead, Martin, 1999, *Is there a place for Work in Child Development?* Stockholm: Radda Barnen.

Woodhead, Martin, 2004, 'Psychosocial Impacts of Child work: A Framework for Research, Monitoring and Intervention', *Psychosocial Journal of Children's Rights*, Vol. 12. No.4, pp. 321-377.

10

Youth Livelihoods and Karaoke Work in Kampala's Nightlife Spaces

Joseph Wasswa-Matovu

Introduction

Youth, most frequently defined as those between the ages of 15 and 24, comprise a major part of the urban population in Uganda. It is estimated that about 17 per cent of Uganda's population falls in the 15 to 24 age group (Uganda Demographic and Health Survey – UDHS – 2006). In urban and rural areas, this age cohort represents respectively 25 and 16 per cent of the population. The preponderance of this age cohort in urban areas points to processes of rapid urbanization that impose an imperative on governments and communities to create and promote viable and sustainable livelihoods for urban youth. In Kampala, Uganda's administrative and commercial capital, the UDHS (2006) provides data that shows youth as suffering the highest rate of economic inactivity and that this rate is heavily gendered. Thus, on average females are three times more likely to be redundant compared to their male counterparts. At the same time, urban youth, especially in Kampala, are more likely to be redundant compared to their rural counterparts (see Table 1).

Nevertheless, for a substantial number of unemployed youth in Kampala's poor and low-income neighbourhoods, 'Karaoke' has come to provide a semblance of productive work. Karaoke work refers to the activities of youths co-opted into entertainment groups to provide a host of nightlife entertainment acts in numerous venues around the city. While distinct from karaoke as conventionally practised in up-market entertainment venues (with its arsenal of teleprompters and lyrical materials); here the karaoke work of the youths shows up as a range of stage acts, which include singing (both actual and lip singing or mimicking), dancing, comedy and striptease by female group members.[1] In its expression, karaoke adopts some of the latest local, regional, and international musical genres and entertainment acts.

Table 1: Percent Distribution of Unemployed Persons Age 15-49 in 12 Months Preceding the Survey

Background Characteristic	Male	Female
Age		
15-19	13.3	32.1
20-24	5.6	15.4
25-29	1.1	7.6
30-34	0.8	5.9
35-39	0.7	4.1
40-44	0.3	4.0
45-49	1.8	4.0
Residence		
Urban	12.0	32.3
Rural	3.3	9.7
Regions		
Central 1	4.4	25.3
Central2	2.1	19.1
Kampala	12.3	37.7
East central	11.1	15.8
Eastern	0.2	2.6
North	3.4	4.7
Western	6.0	6.0

Source: UDHS (2007:44-45)

However, notwithstanding the opportunities karaoke work affords the youths to negotiate some livelihood, anecdotal evidence points to a number of risks youths face in the occupation. Thus, many are cheated and not paid for services rendered; working hours are known to be long, with managers lining up group members to perform at various venues in a night; in-group competition strains the youths who have to put on exceptional performances to earn the crowd's approval and the accompanying tips. Youths in karaoke groups are also susceptible to sexual harassment or abuse and to face risks of acquiring sexually transmitted infections (STIs) when working in spaces that bring them into contact with older and possibly less well-meaning individuals. Finally, it has been suggested that karaoke group members (especially the females) mask their prostitution activities as karaoke performers and are stigmatized as prostitutes by family, friends, and the community, who see their work as decadent.

Yet, for youths facing prospects of prolonged unemployment because they lack skills and/or education, or because jobs are unavailable, Kampala's nightlife spaces appear to offer opportunities for negotiating some form of livelihood out of karaoke work. This chapter explores the agency karaoke work affords youths to negotiate their livelihoods in Kampala's nightlife entertainment spaces. The following two sections provide the study's methodology and the theoretical framework within which karaoke work and the livelihoods of urban youth can be conceived. The subsequent two sections present an analysis of the views of the youths on how karaoke work affords them opportunities to negotiate livelihoods by focusing on the production, regulation and consumption processes that underpin the karaoke phenomenon in Kampala. The chapter closes with a section synthesizing results and a conclusion.

Methodology

A case study approach was used to solicit the views of youths in two karaoke groups, namely VIP and Ocean Stars, on a range of issues pertinent to karaoke work using a discussion theme guide. Information on group members' attributes, work history and lived experiences in karaoke work was collected. In total, twenty-eight individuals in both groups were interviewed, five males and eight females from the Ocean Stars Group and eight males and seven females from the VIP group. These individuals comprised all youth performers in the groups. The average age of youths in the groups was 22 years, with females slightly younger (between 18 and 20) than their male counterparts (between 18 and 25).

The two groups differed slightly in the way they operated. The Ocean Stars group appeared more marginal, possessing less attractive attire (costumes) and banners. The group had operated in the karaoke business for less than three years in the city's more marginal nightlife spaces and was apt to employ more transient and younger youth. Finally, all youths in the group cited karaoke to be the main and possibly only productive work they undertook in the city.

On the other hand, the VIP group was a more longstanding group, having been in the karaoke business for over eight years and, as such, had seen a greater turnover of youth performers compared to the Ocean Stars group. Compared to their counterparts in the Ocean Stars group, VIP group members also appeared slightly older, especially the males, and were more self-provisioning with some possessing personal costumes and laptops on which music was played during rehearsals. Some youth in the group also claimed to be students and/or to hold other part-time jobs.

Theoretical Considerations

Following from Chatterton and Hollands (2002, 2003:5), Kampala's nightlife spaces can be conceptualized as an integrated 'circuit of culture' comprising the three processes of production, regulation and consumption. In this context, one needs to simultaneously explore who and what is involved in producing them (designing, marketing, selling, property markets, corporate strategies); who and what is involved in regulating them (laws and legislations, surveillance, entrance requirements, codes of conduct); and, who and what is involved in consuming them (lived experience, perceptions, stereotypes). Nightlife entertainment spaces are also understood to constitute a mixture of mainstream, residual and alternative spaces as shown in Table 2. This analytical framework provides a neat tool for mapping out spaces where karaoke might be undertaken in Kampala and to explore how the production, regulation and consumption processes of karaoke articulate in these spaces.[2]

Table 2: Types of Nightlife Spaces and their Modes of Analysis

	Mainstream	Residual	Alternative
Production	Corporate brand Profit-oriented Global/national	Community Need-oriented National/regional	Individual Experimental Local (global networks)
Regulation	Entrepreneurial Formal (CCTV, bouncers) and informal (style, price)	Stigmatized Formal (police)	Criminalized Informal (self-regulated)
Consumption	Profit-oriented Divided consumer– producer relations (brand/lifestyle)	Community-oriented Traditional consumer- producer relations (product)	Creative-oriented Interactive consumer- producer relations
Spatial location	Gentrified/up market Dominant centre	Down-market Under-developed centre	Alternative/resistant Margins

Source: Chatterton and Holland, 2002:6.

While in recent years Kampala's nightlife landscape has seen the proliferation of the mainstream that constitutes sanitized and overpriced entertainment venues frequented by the city's elite[3] ; conceiving karaoke work and youth livelihoods within the 'mainstream' is inappropriate since karaoke as understood here is rarely undertaken in these spaces. However, the karaoke activities of the youth described in this chapter take place in nightlife spaces that can be considered residual and/ or alternative because they are situated in low-income neighbourhoods on the fringes of the city centre and/or venues in these spaces serve a less affluent clientele.

In varying degrees, for all involved in producing, regulating and consuming the activity (youth performers, venue owners/managers, venue patrons/clients, the larger community etc.), karaoke meets felt and material needs for income, leisure and entertainment, belonging (to a youth community or culture), skills acquisition, future prospects for work and education. In its expression, karaoke appears experimental, and employs creative entertainment content that transcends the national by embracing regional and global musical genres (reggae, rap and hip hop). In some cases the activity is stigmatized, especially where it degenerates into disorder or misbehaviour. Consequently, nightlife space managers have come to rely on informal (the application of various rights of admission rules) and formal (use of security guards and bouncers) methods to regulate behaviour in these spaces. It is also plausible that karaoke work represents expressions of resistance for youth excluded from the 'mainstream' to project new identities of consumption, which mirror those from which they are excluded.

Production and Consumption of Karaoke in Kampala's Nightlife Spaces

The Experience of a Karaoke Night Out

Over the last ten or so years, karaoke has taken root in many privately owned entertainment venues in Kampala where venue patrons and clients have come to appreciate its interactive forms as a mode of nightlife entertainment. Within the venues, karaoke has come to blur the division between its producers and consumers through the exchange of music, shared ideas and values. Different categories of patrons have come to meet their felt needs for certain genres of music, dance cultures, clothing styles, or sexual identity and/or to be more casual. At the same time, because karaoke tends to be performed in some of Kampala's more marginal neighbourhoods, its consumption has come to invariably reflect patrons' conscious identities and lifestyles.

The production of karaoke usually occurs in single-site music, club and bar venues. These are located in neighbourhoods that teem with hordes of the city's unemployed youth and others with varying forms of employment in the informal sector. The venues exhibit anti-aesthetic exteriors, although some have attractive interior decors and beguiling names like T-cozy, Chez Johnson, Mambo Jambo, Honey Pub and Club 24, among many others. Many are enclosed bar shades with a capacity to hold up to 300 individuals. The venues may also be partitioned to accommodate dancing space, several bar stands (counters), and a general sitting area where tables and chairs are arranged in a number of configurations to cater to the ambience and comfort needs of different clients. Besides karaoke, clients also patronize these venues to watch English Premier League football games that are broadcast via satellite on a number of television screens in the venues.

Featuring prominently in these venues is a raised stage upon which karaoke is performed. In some of the venues this stage is fitted with all manner of lighting (flash and neon lights, dark- coloured fluorescent lights, etc.) to enhance stage performances. The venues are also equipped with the latest music sound systems, which blare out music at high decibels making simple conversation difficult: even the most marginal nightlife spaces are supported by state-of-the-art musical equipment. The managers also ensure that the venues are dimly lit through the use of dark-coloured florescent lights to ensure the privacy of clients. The venues also afford free entry to clients although it is common for them to charge fees ranging between Ugandan shillings 2000 and 5000 (US$ 1-US$ 2.60) on days karaoke is performed at the venues.

Venues usually use bouncers to keep the peace and ensure clients comply with entry requirements. A key requirement is that clients purchase a drink (a beer or soda) before they are granted entrance. This measure ensures that idlers are kept out and congestion is kept at a minimum. Some venues also buttress these security measures through the use of armed security guards hired from registered security firms. These are particularly valued by clients with vehicles who for a fee task these guards with overseeing their vehicles as the vandalization of vehicles and the stealing of car parts are common around these venues.

Karaoke performances begin around 9 pm with a comical curtain raiser act performed by a member of a karaoke group or a performer that is independently hired by the venue management. The opening performer normally rants over a diverse range of topical issues, which in the main revolve around sex and other controversial (political, cultural and social) issues of the day. A common subject is women and relationships. In particular, women are portrayed as opportunistic lovers (gold-diggers) and also the major carriers and transmitters of the HIV/AIDS virus. Women who constitute a substantial number of clients in these venues, in turn can be seen engaging the performer in animated gestures denoting objections to his assertions. Political and social debates of the day also feature prominently in these presentations. All in all, no hard feelings ensue from this good-natured interactive discourse between the performer and venue clients.

Having made his presentation, which lasts for about 20 minutes, the opening performer introduces the karaoke group and invites the in-house Disc Jockey (DJ) to commence with the musical programme he has previously worked out with the karaoke group. The first performers then appear on stage dressed in all manner of flashy costumes. By this time, the crowd is frenzied and some can be seen joining the youths on stage and engaging them in dance or throwing money at favoured performers. A variety of musical genres is performed, which include the local and regional (including localized forms of Reggae and Hip hop, called Ragga and Lugaflow respectively), and Western (Hip-hop, Rhythm and Blues – R & B). Performances which last for about three hours have intermissions that see the performer in the curtain-raiser return to work up the crowd and allow the youths to rest or to rotate performances. At the show's close, the youths retire backstage, remove their costumes and later can be seen leaving the premises in pooled transport or individually, or to melt into the crowd and join in the merry-making. Post-performance, the in-house Dj takes over and the venue turns into a free for all dance fest till the early hours of the morning.

In a nutshell, nightlife spaces where the youth undertake their karaoke work form the basis of more localized nightlife production-consumption clusters, which are characterized by an independent ethos that provides a counterweight to the uniformity of consumption one is likely to observe in venues that serve an elite clientele. For example, the mainstream (elite nightlife spaces) are frequented by young corporates, university students and other fairly well-to-do people, who may desire to create a community of like-minded people in spaces imbued with certain styles and behaviours that are expected and accepted and enforced through door policies and technologies such as CCTV.

On the other hand, marginal nightlife spaces epitomize a more democratic form of popular culture, with the affordability of technologies (lighting systems, musical equipment, etc.) allowing the lived experience of a karaoke night out to be enhanced in these otherwise drab spaces. To echo *Hesmondhalgh* (1998), the affordability of technologies appear to make Kampala's residual and alternative nightlife spaces more alluring by countering the 'big-name' artist in the mainstream, whose valorisation to a large measure depends on a 'star system'.

The Value of Karaoke to the Youth

The karaoke work of the youth in Kampala is an upshot of what Biaya (2005; 216) termed the 'crisis of unemployment', which has affected African youth over the last two decades. Karaoke appears to allow youth to explore new means of affirming their identities, assert popular demands and develop the makeshift economy. To this end, 'nightlife spaces' should draw our attention to the role the youth play in using them to rework disparate signs, forms and materials and convey powerful counter messages, subaltern identities, and disruptive mimicry to demonstrate positive, assertive and authentic voices (Weiss 2005; Miller 1994; Friedman 1990; Hansen 1999; Herault and Adesanmi 1997).

For karaoke performers, nightlife spaces are both places of work and public spaces, which for the youth embody the social crisis of neo-liberal economic reforms that have destroyed traditional, familial and ethnic solidarities. For the youth, these spaces also exemplify the broken promise of belonging to the class of urban petty bourgeoisie suggested by current modes of education in Uganda. The spaces also typify the disappearance of the providential state and the increasingly extreme precariousness of living conditions (Biaya, 2005). Conceived as such, the spaces appear as sites of marginality and opportunity for young karaoke performers, although their work serves, as Weiss (2005; 108) would put it:

> to promote (the spaces) as attractive, contemporary establishment(s) and also to demonstrate that (they) are of the public, (and) are hooked into a reality beyond even the here and now …

It is in this light that the karaoke activities of the youth in Kampala's nightlife spaces need to be understood, with young – people both males and females – creating the makeshift economy that manifests as a means of survival, games, postures and attitudes of consumption and leisure.

All the youths in the karaoke groups claimed to have dropped out of school before completing their secondary education. This in the Ugandan context meant that all of them had no tangible technical skill to engage the formal labour market or create their own employment. In their majorities, the youths also claimed to have engaged with karaoke for two to three years. Thus, given their average age of 22 years and considering that all left school in or about grade 12 at about 16 years, this meant most had been out of school for about six years and to have suffered at least three years of sustained unemployment. One female member of the Ocean Stars group narrates:

> I dropped out of school after I got pregnant. I was shunned by my family and sought all manner of employment to earn money and feed my child, all in vain. For a long time I had to depend on friends until one suggested I join a karaoke group where she performed. The work was initially stressful and I had to move between groups as work conditions in some groups were poor and payments delayed or not made at all. Am happy now in this group, where I have performed for two years and learnt a lot as a performer.

Thus, karaoke may for these youth constitute the 'makeshift economy' that provides a means of survival through the games, postures and attitudes of consumption and leisure it encapsulates. Youths in both groups, and in particular the females, saw their engagement with karaoke as the only productive activity open to them to legitimately earn a living in the city. Equally important was the opportunity the work afforded the youths to acquire skills and talents in the dramatic arts (that is, dancing and singing).

Youths in the Ocean Stars group claimed to perform at least six shows a week at different venues around the city. They also claimed that at any one time, their group had standing contracts with entertainment venues, which ranged in their duration from two to three months. On the other hand, youths in the better resourced VIP group claimed to undertake four performances at different venues around the city in a week. Nevertheless, both groups also claimed to perform at more than one venue in a night. The VIP group also engaged the corporate sector when hired to perform at promotions for key companies in the brewery, tobacco and cosmetics sectors and at functions where agencies combating the HIV/AIDS epidemic distribute free condoms and disseminate information related to HIV/AIDS. These promotions were highly valued by the youths, who in many cases received free clothing (T-shirts and caps draped in company labels and insignia) and other products (beers, alcoholic spirits, cigarettes, etc).

However, despite slight differences in the groups' outlooks, wages earned by youths in both groups appeared competitive. In the Ocean Stars group, one youth earned on average Ugandan shilling 10,000 (US$5) and 7,000 (US$3.60) for weekend and weekday performances respectively; wages that mirrored those for each youth in the better-resourced V.I.P group at Ugandan shillings 10,000 (US$5) and 8,000 (US$4.10) for weekend and weekday performances respectively. Thus, on average, each youth earned Ugandan shillings 49,000 (US$25.25) a week, or Ugandan shillings 196,000 (US$101) monthly.

For youths facing few prospects of finding full-time employment, such income is not trivial. Youths in the VIP group all stated that they lived away from their parental homes in rented premises and student hostels. Money earned from karaoke work was critical to meeting their rental obligations, food, clothing and other basic needs. Nevertheless, while some youths in the group felt that given the alternatives a monthly take of close to 200,000 Ugandan shillings was sufficient, some felt it was not and that income gaps were bridged by the additional work that the group was able to procure during busy seasons (e.g., during the Christmas and Easter periods) and privately (such as at birthday parties).

For youths in the less resourced Ocean Stars group, managers claimed to cover some group members' costs, which in the VIP group were borne by individual group members. These included the costs of transport to and from entertainment venues, the costs of meals and, for the females, the costs of pooled housing as a security measure to avoid the dangers they face moving alone at night. However, while female group members did not directly claim to be abused or exploited by group managers, the fact that Ocean Stars Group managers claimed to have pooled housing always stocked with food, fuel and water – 'to ensure the girls are comfortable and feel well cared for' – pointed to some control managers wielded over these youths. Nevertheless, these subsidies, together with payment the youths received for their karaoke work, appeared lucrative despite, as shown subsequently, the stigma female performers faced in this line of work.

According to the VIP group manager, while it was desirable for karaoke groups to claim a share of revenues collected at venue gates from clients, such arrangements rarely worked and were fraught with difficulties. Most groups therefore resorted to charging venue managers a flat fee. However, even under this arrangement they were still faced with some problems. The VIP manager, for example, claimed that,

> (there is) …too much exploitation by venue managers. The managers fluctuate (adjust) payments to the group. Sometimes managers stop us (from performing) without your awareness and this costs us and is a sign of disrespect

However, both group managers claimed to charge a flat fee of Ugandan shillings 150,000 (US$77.32) for each performance. On the basis of information gathered from the two groups, Table 3 draws out the income positions for the groups on a weekly basis in Ugandan shillings.[4] It is clear that karaoke work is lucrative for group owners, who can be expected to take in Ugandan shillings 256,750 (US$132.35) every week or about Ugandan shillings 1,027,000 (US$529.38) a month, which is 76% of the net pay of a university lecturer at a publicly-funded university in Uganda.

Table 3: Karaoke Groups' Weekly Income Statements

VIP		Ocean Stars	
Income	600000[1]	**Income**	1,050,000[2]
Expenses		**Expenses**	
• Wage	(336,000)[3]	• Wage	(539,0000)[4]
• Transport	(0)	• Transport	(140,000)[5]
• Housing (Rent)	(0)	• Housing (Rent)	(37,500)[6]
• Food/Fuel/Water	(0)	• Food/Fuel/Water	(84,000)[7]
Net Income	**264,000**		**249,500**

1. 4days* 150,000/=
2. 7 days*150,000/=
3. 4days*12 persons*7,000/=
4. 7days*11 persons*7,000/=
5. 7days*20,000/=
6. 150,000/= /4 weeks
7. 7days*8 persons*1500/=

In addition, there does not appear to be great divergences in incomes earned between these groups even as they exhibit subtle differences in outlook as previously suggested. Nevertheless, these subtle differences explain why the VIP group has been able to transcend residual and alternative spaces and to attract business from the corporate sector (the mainstream). At the same time, by mastering a range of musical genres (including Western Hip-hop and R & B, local and regional genres such as Raga and Lugaflow), the group has been able to tailor its performances to meet the particular musical tastes of clients in given venues and garner a loyal fan base. As one member of the group asserts, 'We are motivated by our fans who like our system.' The income figures given above thus mask what could be higher or additional earnings the VIP group receives from its corporate engagements; and for the youth individually, the substantial tips from adoring fans.

When asked what attributes one needed to join a karaoke group, the majority of the youths made prominent mention of: being able to dance and sing; to learn and improve on one's dancing and singing skills; reliability; commitment; discipline; respect; being considerate; and having love for one's work. Thus, beyond providing income for the youths, karaoke appeared to play a role in building their characters as focused and responsible individuals. For example, youths in the VIP group pointed out that their karaoke work made them self-confident, responsible, developed their leadership skills, and made them physically fit.

In its expression karaoke work is physically demanding and the youths, either individually or as a group, can be expected to commit 10 to 15 minutes in strenuous dance and song presentations, which the audience expects to be performed flawlessly. But attaining such standards of performance requires that the youths take their work seriously. Thus, VIP group members on average committed up to eight hours a week on rehearsals undertaken on Tuesdays and Thursdays at their centre of operations, T-Cozy Bar and Restaurant. Similarly, youths in the Ocean Stars group rehearsed for at least two hours every weekday at their centre of operation, Club 24, with the in-house DJ providing accompanying music. In all cases, the youths were expected to commit the necessary time to the rehearsals despite their other commitments. Absenteeism led to sanctions that included a group member being allocated no or less work and/or being paid less wages.

However, in both groups a sense of camaraderie appeared to exist, upon which the social capital that sustained the groups was based. Thus, beyond the sanctions group managers might impose for contravening set rules, the youths were more likely to conform to rules for the common good. Thus, one youth in the VIP group claimed, 'We act as a family, where everything is all about sharing.'

While group managers tended to allocate work to the youths based on how seriously they took their work (possibly based on the quality of their performances), even those assigned little or no work during an engagement were never completely left out. Thus, one Ocean Stars group member asserted:

> ... allocation of work depends on the seriousness in your performance. This improves performance through competition [among group members]. However, even though you do not present [are assigned no work] you may get money to eat [get paid]. No individuals are favoured.

Beyond the role karaoke plays in building the group's social capital, a key objective the youths pursue in the occupation is a desire to improve and develop what they call 'talents' as dancers and musicians. Karaoke work therefore provides a springboard for the youths to break into what in recent years has become a very lucrative music recording and open concert industry in Uganda. For example, female group members in the Ocean Stars group said:

> We like the karaoke activity and we hope to improve our talents like dancing and singing to become celebrities such as Juliana Kanyomozi[5] one day. Karaoke allows us to present ourselves as entertainers since our future lies in the entertainment industry.

These sentiments of the youths appear to echo the work of Weiss (2005: 107) in that in this case, karaoke work may project images (such as musical and dance styles, dress and personalities) that for the youths offer:

> … a wider familiarity with not only the 'images' but also the material forms of success, as well as … connection to persons who enjoy such success, in contrast with the declining real opportunities to enjoy these values and fully participate in the world they embody.

It appears then that karaoke eases the pain youths feel as marginalized people, with their karaoke work generating the future as an open prospect and knowable. Thus, for youths in tenuous employment as karaoke work, the profound gap between one's severely limited, or intractable present conditions and the limitless prospects of the future appear to be reconciled and eased by the lived experience of a karaoke performance.

However, this conception of the karaoke phenomenon as therapeutic masks other real benefits youths derive from it. First, the independent mode of karaoke production ensures that participation is more about 'active production' than 'passive consumption', which creates a fluid boundary between producers and consumers through the exchange of music, ideas, business deals and networks of reciprocity and patronage. For aspiring artists and those who wish to promote them, nightlife spaces create an 'authentic' outlet for the karaoke work of the youth and a meeting place for like-minded people. In fact, nightlife spaces in Kampala where karaoke is performed have become important scouting sites for those wishing to promote talented youths.

The development of skills and talents among the youths did not appear to be restricted to dancing and singing. In both groups, the existence of organizational structures meant individual group members could undertake additional tasks. For example, one male member in the VIP group was identified by other group members as the marketing manager with the responsibility of scouting for business and negotiating terms in the absence of the group manager.

Regulating Karaoke in Kampala's Nightlife Spaces

In the literature, residual and marginal nightlife spaces are said to offer the possibility of a less regulated, more fluid space defined by an absence or defiance of appropriate codes (Chatterton and Holland 2002). However, rather than being places of absolute freedom or disorder, marginal spaces and practices have their own modes of social ordering, rules and relations of power (Hetherington 1997). Thus, beyond normative rules such as health, licensing, noise control and others governments impose, rules are self-generated and communally agreed to demonstrate and envision less hierarchical ways of social and spatial ordering (Chatterton and Holland 2002). Among the most visible are entrance requirements, which are based around self-selection and sub-cultural knowledge. As well, underpinning such self-regulation is the geographical location of many residual and marginal spaces on the edge of central areas as a luminal twilight zone offering flexibility and anonymity.

However, a whole range of restrictive regulations have emerged to crack down on the unregulated nature of karaoke nightlife spaces in Kampala. In these spaces, nightlife has come to be viewed as deviant or abject and, in recent years, the spaces have been compelled to adhere to the National Environment Act, which has provisions setting noise limits in public spaces. The media has also fuelled moral panic, often stemming from the hedonistic nature of karaoke performances and the supposedly wayward nature of individuals who patronize these spaces. For instance, some of Kampala's residual and alternative nightlife spaces offer opportunities and avenues for infidelity, with married individuals using them to meet other partners. In addition, some of these spaces are known to be rendezvous sites for homosexuals who meet there with the tacit knowledge of establishment owners and venue clients and patrons.

Earlier, it was suggested that youths were bound to face a number of threats to personal security and health from their karaoke work. In both groups, however, the youths did not consider nightlife spaces to pose serious threats to their persons. Most were comfortable with existing security arrangements, especially the use of bouncers to control disruptive and drunk venue patrons. As youths in the VIP group asserted, 'We discipline ourselves and the bouncers keep the security at the place.'

Youths also saw their personal safety as the responsibility of the karaoke group managers who, as in the case with female group members in the Ocean Stars group, had made commitments to next of kin to ensure the personal safety of the girls. The girls asserted, 'Security-wise we are safe since managers commit themselves to ensure our safety by talking to our relatives.'

However, outside the venues, the youths still appeared to remain vulnerable to all kinds of threats to their personal safety. The youths in the VIP group claimed, 'Outside the venue everyone is on his or her own.'

Even here the youth appeared to draw solace from the fact that their groups provided them with identity cards (IDs) to mitigate the harassment they were likely to face from the police and other local security operatives, who might find them moving about at night from engagements. Thus, VIP members claimed to '… have ID cards to represent ourselves in case of trouble at night'.

On the other hand, the Ocean Stars group circumvented these problems through pooled transportation for its members and by informing local authorities of their presence in their jurisdictions. The Ocean Stars group manager thus asserted:

> Sometimes police disturb us especially when we happen to be found walking in the night. That's why we use the same transport, inform local leaders the times when we are to present in their areas of control and the main issue they raise is making unnecessary noise, which we avoid.

The youths also face a host of threats to their health in nightlife spaces where karaoke is undertaken. Many are susceptible to temptation when clients approach them with all manner of propositions. In the VIP group, female members claimed to have clients who ask them out after shows and/or who offer money as an incentive to this end. On the other hand, male performers are approached by older women and in some cases men, who provide them with their phone contacts with a view to setting up sexual rendezvous. The youth thus claimed, '… clients normally con [target] girls to sleep around and for the boys they are given numbers from old women and men'.

Nevertheless, the youths are generally aware of the dangers of STIs and they appear to have devised a number of strategies to deflect any negative advances from clients. 'Detoothing' (youth slang for free riding) constitutes one such adoptive strategy, which in its crudest form sees a youth playing along with the client making the unwanted advances and extracting as much from him or her (in drinks and/or money), only for the youth not to keep his or her side of the bargain. But some youths do succumb and get themselves involved in all manner of relationships with clients, which has stigmatized their karaoke work. As one female member of the VIP group pointed out:

> …. [youths] are … conned … this has made the karaoke activity stigmatized … (because) … clients involve group members in relationships. This has tarnished the karaoke activity especially when the same clients call us prostitutes after having an affair (with a group member).

Synthenzing the Results : Is Karaoke Valued Work or Decadence?

In this chapter I have explored a number of key questions, including who were the youth negotiating livelihoods out of karaoke work; what they negotiate for; and the agency nightlife spaces and karaoke work affords them to eke out a living in the urban milieu. As it turns out, Chatterton's and Holland's (2002) conceptions of residual and alternative spaces capture well Kampala's nightlife spaces and the karaoke activities of the youth undertaken therein, and offer insights on the agency the youth might exercise in earning a living in the spaces.

Karaoke has been shown to have value for the youths, not only in terms of incomes derived from it, but also as a springboard to future careers as professional entertainers. Its value in inculcating within the youths key beneficial attributes such as self-confidence, reliability, respect for others, discipline, hard work and leadership have also been noted. For the youth with very few opportunities to acquire these skills and attributes through formal and regular employment; karaoke and the spaces within which it is undertaken provide the perfect venue for their acquisition. Given that karaoke and the games and postures it encapsulates are by their nature interactive, the youths are pitted against a community of karaoke consumers bent on meeting their needs for different genres of musical entertainment. Borrowing a leaf from Foreman (2002:8), karaoke then becomes central for youth attempting to construct spaces of their own or a 'culture of compensation' or, according to Cashmore (1997:171), substituting for educational advancement and literacy.

Besides engendering interactive processes between the youth and karaoke consumers, which entail beneficial outcomes for the former, residual and alternative spaces are also shown to allow the youth to experiment and actualize themselves. To mirror Chatterton and Holland (2003; 210), the spaces 'in this sense are a source of creative innovation, revelling in a desire for novelty, conflict and dialogue'. For example, some of the musical and dance genres performed by the youth transcend the national and regional to encompass the global. Thus, for youth performing hip hop or rap, these genres cease to be viewed as expressions of African American culture and come to represent vehicles for global youth affiliation and a tool for reworking local identities. For older karaoke consumers, these novel, radical and possibly dangerous musical genres and their accompanying dress and speech codes would appear in the context of a karaoke performance to be appropriated, domesticated and rendered harmless.

The acquisition of an income was critical in motivating the youth to undertake karaoke work. Evidence has been presented to show that youths and group managers garnered appreciable amounts of income from the occupation. Groups appeared to be managed professionally, which allowed managers to earn incomes comparable to those of public servants in formal employment. The spaces also offered the youth a competitive environment and thus some agency to supplement their incomes with tips.

The venues and their managements also eased the karaoke production process for the youth by allowing them to access the venues and musical equipment for their rehearsals. Daytime rehearsals within these spaces also allowed what otherwise would have been idle youths to spend time in activities that they considered beneficial and thus to keep out of trouble. As places of work, the spaces also appeared to provide a safe environment for youths and their clients. The use of bouncers and armed security guards at venues was critical in ensuring the personal safety of the youth and in protecting clients' property. At the same time, karaoke appeared to possess in-built structures to ensure the safety of the youth and to legitimize their work in the eyes of the authorities.

But karaoke and the spaces where it is undertaken need not be overly romanticized. The spaces also pose real dangers to youths who face a double-edged sword when exercising agency to earn a living in these spaces. While they offer opportunities to youths to meet like-minded people, who in some cases may advance their prospects in their chosen lines of work, they are also places of debauchery, where less well-meaning people might congregate to prey on the youth. While youths have been shown to devise a number of mitigating strategies, many are drawn in and face serious risks of contracting STIs and engaging in unproductive relationships with clients. In particular, the latter has the effect of projecting these youths as prostitutes and to stigmatize their work.

Conclusion

It is clear that Kampala's residual and alternative nightlife spaces offer opportunities for the youth to eke out a living from their karaoke work. By their very nature as obscure entities, these spaces come to be frequented by those most likely to be excluded from the mainstream and who, as such, may wish to connect with it in ways that the games and postures of karaoke epitomize. For the youth, this scenario presents opportunities to meet this felt need and in the process negotiate livelihoods in the spaces by undertaking karaoke performances. Yet, even as these spaces pose challenges for the youth, their vivaciousness leads them to adopt mitigating strategies to overcome the challenges. More importantly, the spaces allow the youth to develop identities and ease their sense of marginality in ways that link them to a virtual world of opportunity and prospects of better future livelihoods.

Notes

1. See http://news.bbc.co.uk/2/hi/africa/3874359.stm. [last accessed: 16 February 2010] 'Uganda's dirty dances reveal all' BBC News online 8 July 2004.
2. However, Chatterton and Hollands (2002) use the framework of mainstream, residual, and alternative spaces to address processes of urban transformation in developed country settings by emphasizing the role corporate control plays in usurping and commercializing public space, segmenting and gentrifying markets, and marginalizing historic, alternative and creative local development.

3. Karaoke entertainment in its conventional sense, which may not apply in the African context, is the preserve of rich folk in Kampala and is enjoyed by them at only one venue in the up-market Garden City Mall. Yet, despite the proliferation of a nightlife entertainment scene that caters to the tastes of a small elite group (in the form of bars, restaurants and night clubs), its genesis is marginally related to wider economic, political, and socio-cultural changes as in developed countries. In the literature, these changes have variously been explained under such themes as Fordism, post-Fordism and neo-Fordism (see Kumar 1995; Amin 1994; Harvey 1989a; Lash and Urry, 1987); flexible specialization and accumulation (see Piore and Sable 1984; Harvey 1989b); the growing literature on (anti) globalization and corporations (see Monboiot 2000; Klein 2000); the move towards a service-based, cultural, and 'symbolic' economy (see Harvey 1989a; Jessop 1997; Burrows and Loader 1994) changes in the local/welfare state and the rise of the entrepreneurial city (see Hollands 2002; Warde 1994), and critiques of post-modern consumption and how it engenders processes of market segmentation, gentrification and branding (Chatterton and Hollands 2003).
4. That is, that Ocean Stars group maintains pooled accommodation for its female performers and provides transport to and from venues for all its performers while the VIP group does none of this.
5. Juliana Kanyomozi is a Ugandan-born local artist whose music has gained acceptance across the East Africa region, even though most of her songs are sung in a local vernacular that is mainly understood in Uganda.

References

Amin, A., 1994, *Post-Fordism: A Reader*, London: Blackwell.

Biaya, T.K., 2005, 'Youth & Street Culture in Urban Africa: Addis Ababa, Dakar & Kinshasa', in A. Honwana and F. De Boeck, eds, *Makers and Breakers: children and youth in postcolonial Africa*, Dakar and Oxford: CODESRIA and James Currey.

Burrows, R. and Loader, B., eds, 1994, *Towards a Post-Fordist Welfare State?* London: Routledge.

Cashmore, E., 1997, *The Black Culture Industry*, London: Routledge.

Chatterton, P., and R. Hollands, 2002, 'Theorising urban playscapes: producing, regulating and consuming youthful nightlife city spaces', *Urban studies*, Vol.39, No.1, pp.95-116.

Chatterton, P. and Hollands, R., 2003, *Urban nightscapes: youth cultures, pleasure spaces and corporate power*, London: Routledge.

Foreman, M., 2002, *The Hood Comes First. Race, Space, and Place in Rap and Hip Hop*, Middletown: Wesleyan University Press.

Friedman, J., 1990, 'Being in the world: Globalization and Localization Theory', *Culture and Society*, Vol.7, pp.311-28.

Hansen, K.T, 1999, 'Second-hand Clothing Encounters in Zambia: Global Discourses, Western Commodities, and Local Histories', *Africa*, Vol.69, pp.334-65.

Harvey, D, 1989a, 'From managerialism to entrepreneurialism: the transformation of urban governance in late capitalism', *Geogtafiska Annualer*, Vol.71B, No.1, pp.3-17.

Harvey, D, 1989b, *The condition of Post-Modernity*, Oxford: Blackwell.

Herault, G. & Adesanmi, P. eds, 1997. *Youth, Street Culture and Urban Violence*, Ibadan: IFRA.

Hetherington, K., 1997, *The Badlands of Modernity. Heterotopia and Social Ordering*, London: Routledge.

Hesmondhalgh, D., 1998, 'The British dance music industry: a case of independent cultural production', *British Journal of sociology*, Vol.49, No.2, pp.134-51.

Hollands, R, 2002, 'Division in the dark: youth cultures, transitions and segmented consumption spaces in the night-time economy. *Journal of Youth Studies*, Vol.5, No.2, pp.153-73.

Jessop, B., 1997, 'The entrepreneurial city: reimaging localities, redesigning economic governance or restructuring capital', in N. Jewson and S. McGregor, eds, *Transforming Cities*, London: Routledge.

Klein, N., 2000, *No Logo*, London: Flamingo.

Kumar, K., 1995, *From post-Industrial to Post-Modern Society*, Oxford: Blackwell.

Lash, S. and Urry, J., 1987, *The end of Organized Capitalism*, Cambridge: Polity.

Lash, S. and Urry, J., 1994, *Economies of signs and spaces*, London: Sage.

Miller, D., 1994, *Modernity: An Ethnographic Approach*, Oxford: Berg Press.

Monboiot, G., 1998, 'Reclaim the fields and the country lanes! The Land is Ours campaign', in G. McKay, ed., *DiY Culture. Party and Protest in Nineties Britain*, London: Verso.

Piore, M. J. and Sabel, C. F. 1984, *The Second Industrial Divide*, New York: Basic Books.

UBOS and Macro-International Inc., 2007, *Uganda Demographic and Health Survey 2006*, Kampala: Republic of Uganda.

Warde, A., 1994, 'Consumers, consumption and post-Fordism', in R. Burrow and B. Loader, eds, *Towards a Post-Fordist Welfare State?* Routledge: London.

Weiss, B., 2005, 'Consciousness, Affliction and Alterity in Urban East Africa' in A. Honwana and F. De Boeck, eds, *Makers and Breakers: children and youth in postcolonial Africa*, Dakar and Oxford: CODESRIA and James Currey.

11

Patronage of Local Cinema Halls among Urban Youths in Ado Ekiti, Southwest Nigeria

Babatunde Joshua Omotosho

Introduction and Statement of Problem

Globally, urban areas are noted for the provision of social and public spaces in terms of education, energy supply, leisure, recreation facilities in order to make life conducive for the urban dwellers. Nigerians are deprived of these facilities in urban centres due to poverty and failure to maintain the existing ones, among other reasons. However, in the words of Simone (2005:1), Africans ensure that they make the city conducive in spite of the challenges they face; they ensure that they make the city 'a platform to consolidate particular approaches to engaging a larger world'. Nigerian youths are no exception and appear to have played a crucial role in this process over time.

One of the means adopted among urban youths in Nigeria in the process of making urban centres conducive for living and meeting the expected status quo is the establishment of local cinema halls (viewing centres) usually constructed with planks and wood benches for the spectators, to accommodate fifty spectators or more. A large television set is usually placed in the hall and connected to cable networks. The proprietors of these cinemas halls (mostly youths) collect a token for tickets from spectators (youths) to watch international football matches and sometimes foreign movies. This is a welcome development considering the ability of youths to re-invent and transform the public space to their survival and satisfaction (Diouf 1996:228; Honwana and Boeck 2005:17; Biaya 2005:214). This further becomes interesting taking into cognisance the importance of recreation, games and sports in the socialization process among youths which unfortunately are not available for them (Cohen 1993; Calhoun 1987; Utuh 1999;

Callois 2001; World Youth Report 2003, 2005). An understanding of the youths involved; the kind of social relations existing among these groups and implications of their actions on the wider youths and the general society therefore becomes important.

Youths constitute 40 to 50 per cent of the population of the urban centres in Africa and they have undergone (and are still undergoing) series of changes and interventions (Amit-Talai and Wulff 1995:116; Chingunta 2002; Biaya 2005; Honwana and Boeck 2005:16). Youths have been involved in violence, trafficking (as victims and perpetrators), gangsterism, and revolutions of all kinds (Igbinovia 1998:134; Taylor 2002:19; Aghatise 2002:20), including Nigerian youths. One of the areas where activities of youths become interesting is in the area of leisure. Youths globally are increasingly seeking new ways to spend their free time, out of both necessity and interest (World Youth Report 2003:228). Studies have further revealed that youths, especially boys, often spend their leisure time outside the home with their peers (World Youth Report 2003:243). They are innovative and have contributed in many instances to the development of their communities. However, these positive roles do not usually receive attention as public attitudes, the media, and policies usually consider youth activities as problems to be solved rather than a potential to be observed and developed (World Youth Reports 2003, 2005; Honwana and Boeck 2005:7). For instance, studies often raise fears as regards social space of youths in terms of socio-political and economic issues (Sarr 2000; Economic Commission for Africa 2002; Okojie 2003). This perceived image has affected the type of responses to the youths and the type of studies conducted as regards them.

Understanding who a youth is would further lend a hand in appreciating their abilities in creating and recreating urban spaces. This framework provided by Chatterton and Hollandis (2005:7), while explaining youth nightlife in urban environment, further facilitates an understanding of the spaces in urban centre and how youth fit in and operate within it. They highlighted the urban nightlife as a mixture of *mainstream, residual,* and *alternative* spaces. Mainstream spaces are recognised and driven by commercial gain and profit motives. To these authors, key organizations are the dominant figure. Residual community are traditional spaces which have been in existence for a long time. This community exists, but is declining and no longer receives as much attention as before. The last space, the alternative, refers to spaces independently run and spaces which are self-organized and unofficial. This typology becomes relevant in this discourse considering the place of local cinemas in the urban space. The entertainment industry in Nigeria is well-developed and can be subsumed under the mainstream. Traditional cinema patronage as it obtained in typical pre-colonial and colonial Nigeria is gradually giving way as most cinema houses are becoming event or religious centres. Youths are very active in this area as they have created an alternative space in terms of local cinemas due to the failure of the existing body to provide the needed facilities; the cost involved in the provision of private cinemas; the excitement and the joy in creating spaces for their satisfaction.

A study of these youths become important considering the assertion of Biaya (2005) that brutal violence may not be the only means of expression among youths. To him, games, posture, consumption, and leisure also serve as instruments used by youths to affirm their historical presence as a social group and actors in their respective urban societies. He further argues that once leisure is spatialized, it becomes a founder of street culture. The question we need to ask at this juncture is: how far is this statement true regarding the youths that patronize these cinema halls? Are these youths affirming their presence? Are they likely to transform to other 'group' or association in future? What is the existing culture among these groups? Does their action have impact on the wider youths and society as a whole?

Attention appears to often focus on youth marginalization, negative roles and its implications without a proper examination of survival strategies embarked upon by the youths in urban society and ways of harnessing such activities for the benefit of youths and the larger society. These and other issues inform this study. These issues further become interesting based on the assertion that actors have goals, have intentions and are able to make decisions based on their ability to interact, which allows them to examine possible courses of action, considers their relative advantages and disadvantages and then make choices (Manis and Meltzer 1978:68). It becomes pertinent therefore, to investigate and understand issues that inform the actions of the youths regarding the patronage of local cinemas in Ado Ekiti metropolis.

Based on the above, the study aims at taking a look at the youths patronizing local cinema halls in the Ado Ekiti urban centre in Nigeria. Ado Ekiti became the study area based on the concentration of youths in this area and due to the presence of two tertiary institutions (University of Ado Ekiti and Federal Polytechnic) within the city. The University of Education and the College of Education are also within fifteen minutes drive from Ado Ekiti. Thus, youths who patronize the cinema halls to watch soccer in Ado Ekiti constituted the study population irrespective of their state of origin, religious affiliations or ethnic backgrounds.

The population of Ado Ekiti was 112,657 in 1991 (National Population Census 1991). Presently, the city comprises thirteen political wards as described by the Independent Electoral Commission (INEC). The study was carried out in Ado Ekiti, the capital of Ekiti State for a number of reasons; one of which is the fact that it is an urban area. Secondly, middle class youths were the focus of the study as upper class neighbourhoods could afford cable television network, hence the absence of such facilities within their neighbourhoods.

In a bid to further situate this study within a theoretical underpin, Weber's Social Action and Use and Gratification approaches became relevant. To Weber, action becomes social in as much as the actor attaches meaning to his action, 'when individual takes account of the behaviour of others and is thereby oriented in its course' (Weber 1921,1968:4; Ritzer 1996:321; Haralambous and Holborn 2001:961). The second approach (Use and Gratification Model of Mass Media) is concerned with what people do with media (Chandler 1994). It presents the use of media in terms of the gratification of social or psychological needs of individuals (McQuail 1987:284). These theories highlight social actions as rational, and goal-oriented, taking the social environment into consideration. Further, the theories explain the patronage of mass media as an instrument used by humans to satisfy their social and cultural needs. The youths therefore may visit these halls because of their need to achieve their desired goals, which may go beyond watching football. These sets of actions thus become social, since they are chosen after considering a series of alternatives. Aside from this, in the process of watching football matches, a series of social and cultural negotiations are expected to arise. It therefore becomes important in this study to understand these social negotiations within the space created by youths; what informed their choice of action in the first instance; the existing culture within the group; and implications on the society.

Research Methods

The study drew a sample of 120 respondents patronizing these centres. In selecting the sample, Ado Ekiti was clustered into three areas, namely: High-income communities, Middle-income communities, and Low-income communities. Middle- and Low-income communities were selected because the cinema halls are located in these communities. It appears that the majority of the High-income communities are able to afford cable television in their homes and have no need of such centres.

From the selected communities, three cinema halls were selected for interview. From each selected cinema hall, 40 respondents were selected for the survey, making a total of 120 respondents. Further, from this sample, three respondents from each cinema hall were selected for in-depth interviews. Three proprietors of the cinema houses served as key informants to give information regarding the issues in focus and this was complemented with a participant observation on repeated visits to the selected halls.

A survey questionnaire was developed and administered to the selected respondents. The questionnaires were administered after a pilot study to ascertain the validity and reliability of the instruments. The questionnaire addressed specific issues relating to respondents' socio-demographic characteristics such as age and sex. The questionnaires were administered to the respondents after consultation with them at the each of the cinema houses where they watch soccer matches.

Data Presentation and Analysis

Socio-economic and Demographic Characteristics of Respondents

The respondents' socio-economic and demographic characteristics are presented in Table 1. The study sample was dominated by young men aged 21 to 25, followed by boys aged 16 to 20. The dominance of males relates to the fact that soccer is largely a male sport, and girls appear not particularly interested in watching the game.

The fact that most of the respondents had received significant education (the two youngest being the only exceptions) relates to the fact that this is a middle class community. Regarding other age groups who were not youths and included in the study, they were included in the research because they claimed to be students and also, their appearances, attitudes and responses were like those of youths. The dominance of those in tertiary education is a reflection of the tertiary institutions in the neighbourhood. Besides this, the state is often referred to as a 'fountain of knowledge' due to its perceived educational history and status.

Reasons for Patronising the Centres

This section considers factors prompting the respondents to patronize the viewing centres. The respondents were interviewed on how they knew about the centre; and the majority said they got to know about it through their friends. Other respondents claimed they got to know about the centre through a deliberate search for any viewing centre around. A respondent had this to say during the in-depth interview about how he knew about the viewing centre:

> When I gained admission to the university, the first thing I tried to look for is any viewing centre around, as a fan of Manchester (Man U); I saw that a majority of the people in the place who were 'man u fans' so I just located the place and started patronising the centre to watch soccer(Male, 24 years).

Findings regarding the length of time they had been patronizing the centre showed that a minority of the respondents had been visiting the centre for more than three years. On why they visited the centre, half of the respondents claimed they visited the centre primarily to watch soccer matches; and a significant number of the respondents claimed that they patronized the centre just to catch fun and be entertained. This was buttressed by the response of one of the respondents during the in depth interview conducted on why he visits the centre. He remarked thus:

> Though the reason for coming here is to watch football since I cannot afford DSTV cable[1], but in recent times it's not just the soccer matches am interested in, I love to come here to watch people interact, make fun of themselves and more especially I am fascinated when different soccer fans argue over their clubs. To me it's the most entertaining aspect of while in the centre. (Male, IDI, Ado Ekiti, 2009)

Table 1: Socio-economic and Demographic Characteristics

Age	Frequency	Percentage
10 years and below	2	1.7
11-15 years	11	9.2
16-20 years	27	22.5
21-25 years	50	41.6
26-35 years	27	22.5
36-40 years	2	1.7
41 years and above	1	0.8
Total	**120**	**100.0**
Sex		
Male	101	84.2
Female	19	15.8
Total	**120**	**100.0**
Educational qualification		
No formal education	1	.8
Primary school	1	.8
Still in secondary school	3	2.5
Finished secondary school	22	18.3
College of education	3	2.5
Polytechnic student	9	7.5
University student	59	49.2
Apprentice	2	1.7
Graduate	20	16.7
Total	**120**	**100.0**
Marital status		
Single	111	92.5
Married	9	7.5
Total	**120**	**100.0**

Table 2: Reasons for Patronising the Centres

How they knew about the centre	Frequency	Percentage
Through a friend	67	55.9
While passing by	37	30.8
Others	16	13.3
Total	**120**	**100.0**
Length of time they have been patronizing the centre		
Less than 1 year	32	26.7
2-3 years	45	37.5
4-6 years	21	17.5
6 years and above	22	18.3
Total	**120**	**100.0**
Reasons for patronizing the centre Fun/entertainment	28	23.3
To watch football matches	60	50.0
I like the atmosphere	10	8.3
Can't really describe it	22	18.4
Total	**120**	**100.0**
What they enjoy most in the centre		
Meeting people	20	16.7
I love the arguments there	26	21.7
Love catching fun	14	11.7
The conducive atmosphere	22	18.3
Watching football	30	25.0
No specific reason	8	6.6
Total	**120**	**110.0**

Further, findings showed 8.3 per cent of the respondents visited the centre just to enjoy the atmosphere in the centre. The argument raised by some of these respondents was that viewing centres were such a nice place to relax since they were dominated by fellow youths. An in-depth interview captured this better:

> When I come to this place, it is not just watching football that gives me pleasure, there are different characters here. I love the way people sit down looking so serious as if they want to write examinations, and the way their mood changes when their favourite club scores a goal. Not that alone, at the end of the match you hear a lot of debates and gossips about players and their private lives, club side and so on. Some even tell us lies and gossips about the players. In fact, you listen to information and stories you have never heard about in your life in these centres. It's always a nice experience to me any time I find myself there. (Male, IDI, Ado Ekiti, 2009).

A small remainder of the respondents claimed they could not really explain why they patronized the centre. Some of them asserted during the in-depth interview that patronizing the place was a form of relaxation to them; however, they argued that they could not really explain their continued patronage of the centre. They were however sure that they derived pleasure coming to the centre. This assertion was further corroborated during the in-depth interview session with one of the respondents. Her comment is quoted below:

> I can't really say that there is anything special here but I still see myself coming here. When I first came in here it was my friend that asked me to follow him to this place. But now when I don't have much to do, I come here because it's close to my house. Apart from this reason, it is always interesting to see my friends argue and shout on one another because of the game and it always amuse me (Female, IDI, Ado Ekiti, 2009).

Assessment of the Existing Sub-culture among the Respondents

This section aims to understand the existing sub-culture in the group. The respondents were asked whether there existed any form of social activity within the group. In response to this question, about 45 per cent of the respondents said yes. Further, they were interviewed about the form of social activity in existence. In response, 20 per cent said chatting among friends was a major social activity, while 19 per cent said it involved playing games. A response in an in-depth interview threw more light on the existing activity:

> When we are waiting for a match to start, we gist (discuss) about our 'boys-to-boys' talk …hope you understand what I meant… we talk about school, our lecturers, the way our leaders govern and we talk about our female friends. (Male, IDI, Ado Ekiti.)

Table 3: Sub-Culture among the Respondents

Any social activity in the center	Frequency	Percentage
Yes	54	45.0
No	66	55.0
Total	**120**	**100.0**
If yes what kind of activity		
Talking/chatting	24	20.0
Playing games	23	19.2
Can't describe it	7	5.8
Total	**54**	**45.0**
Other activities apart from football in the centre		
Argument/debate	26	21.7
Avenue to meet new friends	30	21.7
Avenue to hear latest information	4	3.3
Watch local and foreign films	9	7.5
Play games	5	4.2
The youthful atmosphere	9	7.5
Listen and dance to music	37	30.9
Total	**120**	**100.0**
Have there been cases of violence, clash?		
Yes	34	28.3
No	86	71.7
Total	**120**	**100.0**

The researcher also observed the respondents unobtrusively before, during and after some of the matches. In the process, the respondents were observed talking about youthful activities, making fun of themselves, talking about politics and keeping themselves happy while waiting for a match to start or after the end of a match. Further on the perceived culture in the centre, the researcher observed a sitting arrangement reflecting the way club fans wanted to share both sorrows and joy together as occasion demanded. On some occasions, viewers within the centre hurled abusive language at each other which were meant to tease the other person, like 'go and sit down', 'what do you know about soccer': such comments usually occurred at intervals, when arguments ensued among spectators. Other viewers in the hall usually laughed at such abusive words, and any argument usually ended after the end of the match. The proprietors of these centres commented that the respondents hardly foughtt or engaged in any violent activity. One said spectators usually engaged in hot arguments and debates over players or coaches. This finding suggests that violence is not a feature of youths in these cinema halls: a large majority of respondents denied experiencing violence in the centre. When respondents were asked about other activities within the centre apart from watching football, they reported common and harmless leisure activities. A respondent had this to say regarding the issue of violence in the centre:

> We hardly experience violence. Of course we engage in hot arguments over matches but it hardly result to violence, we are here to watch match and enjoy ourselves almost all of us here are friends and yet belonging to different clubs. We are students, and we are matured and we are here to enjoy good soccer. I think the essence of coming here is to get ourselves entertained.

Another respondent had this to say:

> Well, I have heard that some of them have almost fought before, but I have seen them engaged in a very hot argument and to me this in itself is bad because any one can be provoked in the course of such hot debates.

Impact of the Group Sub-culture on the Wider Society

This section examines the impact of the group sub-culture on the society. The respondents were asked whether they believed the centre had any positive contributions to the society, and to explain what kind of contributions it had on their lives. In one of the in-depth interview sessions conducted, a respondent explained how the centre had contributed to his life and society:

> This centre has a lot of positive influence on my life. There has been several occasions in which I get a free ride to school when I see any fan of 'man u' [Manchester United]. The room apartment I occupy presently was rented through one of the guys coming to watch match here. I was even told of a situation in which somebody got a very good job through a centre like this elsewhere.

Table 4: Impact of the Group Sub-culture on the Wider Society

Whether they believe the centre has any thing to contribute to their lives	Frequency	Percentage
Yes	97	80.8
No	23	19.2
Total	**120**	**100.0**
If yes explain		
Meeting new people	73	60.8
It keeps me occupied	6	5.0
It could be a source of income	8	7.5
Cant really explain it	10	8.3
Respondents who said No and reasons for it		
It's a waste of time	7	5.8
Its only for fun and nothing more	16	13.3
Total	**120**	**100.0**
Whether they think they can learn anything from the centre		
Yes	83	69.2
No	37	30.8
Total	**120**	**100.0**
If yes explain		
Learn new things	48	40.0
Friendship/togetherness	30	25.0
Cant explain better	5	4.2
Respondents who said No	37	30.8
Total	**120**	**100.0**

On the other hand, a fifth of the respondents felt the centre had nothing positive to contribute to their society, and gave some reasons for their opinions, commenting that watching soccer is just fun or a waste of time.

The respondents were further asked whether they believed they could learn anything as a result of coming to the centre. A majority said that they could learn about the world around them, in terms of politics, current debate in the country; others said they had learnt about the art of making friends, while a few claimed they could now express themselves better unlike before. An in-depth interview buttressed this further as a respondent gave this remark about what he learned from the centre:

> If you want to listen to the latest news in the world, just come to this centre. Some of the information you don't hear in the media are discussed here, only God knows how and where they get such information. But it is a place where you are developed and initiated into manhood …

For the respondents whose opinion differed from the one above, their reasons for this were captured in a statement made by one of the respondents during the in-depth interview:

> I don't think I gain anything special here than watching football. Although they discuss about politics, girls and music… there was a time I listened to them and I discovered that they are all bunch of liars. Some of them say what they don't know just to keep themselves entertained.

The Place of Cinema Patronage in the Lives of the Youths

This section aims at understanding the place of cinema in the lives of the youth. A series of questions were asked on the activities within the centre and how it affected the youths who patronized the place. A large majority of the respondents claimed they had friends in the centre. This may imply that a network of interaction had been built and probably sustained within the centre. To support this, a respondent gave this comment during the IDI session:

> I have so many friends in the place now. If I don't go there to watch match in a particular time especially when my club has a match, they will either buzz me or probably come to check me at home. I also reciprocated this when any of my friends did not show up to watch soccer. In most instances now, some of them come to call me at home so that we can go together or vice versa… (Male).

As regards whether the respondents had learnt any new things within the centre, a large majority of the respondents claimed that they had learnt a lot of things in the centre. A slightly smaller majority explained that their behaviour had changed as a result of attending the centre. On what they had learnt, some of them during the in-depth interview claimed they had learnt the art of analyzing issues critically;

Table 5: The Place of Cinema Patronage in the Lives of the Youths

Whether respondents have friends at the centre	Frequency	Distribution
Yes	94	78.3
No	26	21.7
Total	**120**	**100.0**
There are rules guiding the centre		
Yes	89	74.2
No	31	25.8
Total	**120**	**100.0**
I obey all rules and regulations within the centre		
Yes	91	75.8
No	29	24.2
Total	**120**	**100.0**
I learn a lot of things in the centre		
Yes	107	89.2
No	13	10.8
Total	**120**	**100.0**
My behaviour has changed in course of visiting the centre		
Yes	74	61.7
No	46	38.3
Total	**120**	**100.0**

Table 5 (Continued): The Place of Cinema Patronage in the Lives of the Youths

Whether respondents have friends at the centre	Frequency	Distribution
I would still visit the centre if I had a DSTV cable		
Yes	86	71.7
No	34	28.3
Total	**120**	**100.0**
If yes explain		
Meeting people	54	45.0
Catching fun	23	19.2
Watching football	6	5.0
Cant explain	3	2.5
Respondents who said No and their reasons		
It's a waste of time being here	11	9.2
I value my privacy	23	19.2
Total	**120**	**100.0**

others opined that they are well informed regarding current affairs both within and outside the country. The in-depth interview report below further captures what the respondents had learned and how it had affected their behaviour:

> I think I have learned a lot of new things in the course of coming to this centre. When you hear how people analyse issues you cannot but appreciate the beauty of logical arguments. For me, I used to be shy before now but now I am gradually developing the confidence to contribute meaningfully to discussion; even I can do that now in classrooms when my lecturers ask me questions. I could not do all these before. I think I am trying now. (Male)

These assertions were further buttressed considering their responses on whether they would still patronize the centre assuming they could afford a DSTV cable. Over two thirds claimed they would still patronize the centre.

Summary, Conclusion and Recommendations

This study examined the patronage of local cinema halls among youths in Ado Ekiti, south-west Nigeria, and demonstrates the abilities of youths to reinvent and create spaces for leisure. The patronage of cinema halls was one of the means of achieving this in Nigeria. The study further revealed that the need to enjoy their discretionary periods was the main reason for patronage of these centres. Further, a majority of the youths interviewed became members of these viewing centres through their peers. A major activity in the place was enjoyment, meeting new friends and learning new things while they watched soccer matches in these centres. According to the respondents, social vices like violence within these centres were rare. Rather, the respondents claimed that the places were venues to relax and meet new people and they further claimed that the centres had contributed positively to their lives.

This study has demonstrated that patronizing the centres was primarily for the purpose of meeting their leisure needs which the government had not been able to meet. The places appeared to be avenues to interact, enjoy their youth stage and get initiated into youth behaviours. Patronage of cinema halls by youths and the sub-culture within the centres did not seem to pose any problem to the youths and the society. Youths in these centres were not engaging in anti-social behaviour at the time of the study. Besides entertainment, the centres served other social and cultural functions which enabled the youths to socialize and operate successfully in the phase of life they found themselves.

There is need to further explore and document other activities of youths in their bid to survive within their milieu. All these become important considering the assertion of World Youth Report (2003:214) regarding youths and leisure activities across cultures. Discretionary time plays an integral role in young people's individual development and the development of their communities; the availability of a range of constructive, voluntary activities and opportunities to engage is critical to young people's development and their contributions to the community; and the choice of institution is as critical as the choice of activity. This will further help to understand youths and their potentials within their worlds rather than seeing them as problems to their communities and agents of social vices. It would also help government to plan better to accommodate the needs of the youth for constructive leisure activities.

Note

1. This is the trade name of a cable Television network which provides access to virtually all available television stations across the globe through subscription.

References

Aghatise, E., 2002, 'Trafficking for Prostitution in Italy: Concept Paper', A Paper Prepared for the Expert Group Meeting on Trafficking in Women and Girls, New York, 18-22 November.

Amit-Talau, V., and Wullf, H., eds, 1995, *Youth Culture: A Cross-Cultural Perspective*, London: Routledge.

Biaya, T.K., 2005, 'Youth and Street Culture in Urban Africa Addis Ababa, Dakar and Kinshasa', in A. Honwana and F. Boeck, eds, *Makers & Breakers Children & Youth in Post Colonial Africa*, Dakar.: CODESRIA.

Calhoun, D.W., 1987, *Socialization: The Rules of the Game*, Champaign Il, Human Kinetics.

Callois, R., 2001, *Man, Play and Games*, New York: Free Press.

Chandler, D., 1994, 'Why Do People Watch T.V.?' www.aber.ac.uk/media/documents/short/usegrat.html 18 October 2009.

Chatterton, P., and Hollands, R., 2005, *Urban Nightscapes Youth Cultures, Pleasure Spaces and Corporate Power*, London and New York: Routledge & Taylor and Francis.

Chingunta, F., 2002, 'The Socio-economic Situation of Youth in Africa: Problems Prospects and Options', Paper presented at Youth Employment Summit, Alexandria Egypt, September.

Cohen, D., 1993, *The Development of Play*, London: Routledge.

Diouf, M., 1996, 'Urban Youths and Senegalese Politics Dakar 1988-1994' *Public Culture*, Vol 8, pp. 225-50.

Economic Commission for Africa, 2002, 'Youth and Employment in the ECA region', Paper Prepared for the Youth Employment Summit, Alexandria, Egypt, September.

Haralambous, M., and Holborn, M., 2001, *Sociology Themes and Perspectives*, London: Collins.

Honwana, A., and Boeck, F. D., eds, 2005, *Makers & Breakers: Children & Youth in Post Colonial Africa*, Dakar: CODESRIA.

Igbinovia, P., 1988, 'Perspective on Juvenile Delinquency in Africa', *International Journal of Adolescence and Youths*, Vol.1, pp. 131-156.

McQuail, D., 1987, *Mass Communication Theory: An Introduction* (2nd edn.), London: Sage.

Manis, J., and Meltzer, E. D., 1978, *Symbolic Interaction: A Reader in Social Psychology* (3rd edn.), Boston: Allyn and Bacon.

Okojie, C.E.E., 2003, 'Employment Creation for Youths in Africa: The Gender Dimension', Expert Group Meeting on Jobs for Youths. National Strategies for Employment Promotion, Geneva, pp. 15-16.

Ritzer, R., 1996, *Sociological Theory*, McGraw Hill International Editions.

Rose, A., 1982, 'A Systematic Summary of Symbolic Interaction Theory', in A. Rose, ed., *Human Behaviour and Social Process*, Boston: Houghton Mifflin, pp. 46-89.

Sarr, M.D., 2000, 'Youth Employment in Africa: The Senegalese Experience', Background Paper No. 3, UN/ILO World Bank Brainstorming Meeting on Youth Employment, New York: UN Secretariat, 25 August.

Simone, A., 2005, 'Introduction: Urban Processes and Change', in A. Simone and Abouhani, eds, *Urban Africa Changing Contours of Survival in the City*, Dakar etc.: CODESRIA.

Taylor, E., 2002, 'Trafficking in Women and Girls', Paper prepared for the Expert Group Meeting on Trafficking in Women and Girls, New York, 18-22 November.

Utuh, M.C., 1999. 'Traditional games in Nigeria: Ibibio Tribe', in L.O. Amusa, A.L. Toriola and I.U. Onyewadume, eds, *Physical Education and Sport in Africa*, Ibadan: LAP Publications, pp. 59-76.

Weber, M., 1921,1968, *Economy and Society*, 3 volumes, Totowa NJ: Bedminster Press.

World Youth Report, 2003, *Rethinking Leisure Time: Expanding Opportunities for Young People Communities*. www.un.org/esa/socdev/unyin/documents/ch08.pdf. 15 February 2010.

World Youth Report, 2005, *Leisure, Youth and the United Nations*. www.un.org/youth. Accessed 15 February 2010.

12

Dynamique urbaine et nouvelles formes de négociation de l'existence sociale : les jeunes et les « grins de thé » dans la ville de Ouagadougou

Ollo Pépin Hien

Introduction

Dans un contexte économique marqué par une forte dégradation du marché de l'emploi et un affaiblissement des liens sociaux, les jeunes de la ville de Ouagadougou inventent des stratégies de débrouille à travers des réseaux de sociabilité que sont les « grins de thé ». Dans cette ville en crise, l'expérience d'un processus de disqualification sociale vécue par les jeunes, les confine, en majorité, hors de l'univers du travail dans la sphère de l'inactivité et de la dépendance quotidienne. Ces « grins de thé » se présentent alors comme des formes sociohistoriques des réseaux d'interdépendance croissante entre les jeunes. Dans une ville dont le fondement repose sur des relations inégalitaires et parfois conflictuelles, ces clubs de thé sont l'expression de tensions, de déséquilibres, même de ruptures qui affectent et menacent par moment l'ordre social dans sa globalité. C'est aussi un mode de régulation des contradictions sociales cachées dans le tissu social et culturel de cette ville qui préfigure de nouvelles configurations communautaires et familiales.

En s'appropriant les rues de la ville à leur manière, les jeunes définissent un nouveau mode de gestion et de gouvernance des nouveaux espaces configurés à travers les « grins de thé ». En prenant en compte les positions marginales de la catégorie « jeunes » comme territoire d'investigation, la rue demeure le lieu idéal de questionnement des formes du lien social et de la recomposition des types de sociabilité. L'effritement des cadres anciens de socialisation retrace des parcours en zigzag dans le processus d'insertion sociale des jeunes.

En adoptant un recours rigoureux à l'analyse biographique, il convient cependant d'objectiver les nouvelles formes de négociation de l'existence quotidienne des jeunes de la ville de Ouagadougou à travers les « grins de thé ».

Les objectifs de notre recherche s'articulent autour des axes suivants :

- comprendre et expliquer comment le processus de déstructuration et de restructuration de l'espace urbain affecte le lien social dont le corollaire est la marginalisation croissante de la catégorie « jeunes » dans le secteur de la modernité ;

- analyser les nouvelles formes de recomposition du lien social à travers les réseaux de sociabilité des jeunes de la ville de Ouagadougou ;

- décrire les stratégies juvéniles de négociation de leur existence sociale dans une ville de plus en plus marquée par la dégradation continue du marché de l'emploi.

Démarche méthodologique

Notre méthodologie d'approche s'articule autour de deux axes principaux qui sont la recherche de terrain et le recueil de données.

La recherche de terrain

Le champ d'analyse de notre thème est circonscrit sur la ville de Ouagadougou en ce sens qu'elle est la plus grande agglomération urbaine du Burkina Faso et elle est composée en majorité de jeunes et d'enfants. Nous avons axé notre travail de terrain sur deux quartiers que sont : Zogona (secteur n°13) et Wemtenga (secteur n°29). Ces deux quartiers regorgent une forte majorité de jeunes en raison de leur proximité géographique avec l'université de Ouagadougou et un nombre assez élevé de « grins de thé » par rapport aux autres quartiers de la ville.

L'échantillon a été choisi de façon aléatoire. Au total une vingtaine de jeunes ont été enquêtés dans les « grins de thé ». La population d'enquête comprend essentiellement les jeunes des « grins de thé » qui foisonnent dans les quartiers populaires de cette ville. Nous avons tenu compte, dans le choix de notre échantillon, de la morphologie sociale de ces clubs de thé et des caractéristiques sociales des jeunes qui les forment.

Le recueil des données : l'entretien semi-structuré

Nous avons conçu à cet effet un guide d'entretien comme instrument d'observation de notre objet d'étude. Nous avons fait des entretiens libres, au moyen d'un dictaphone, qui nous ont permis de recueillir le maximum d'informations sur l'expérience du vécu des jeunes dans les « grins de thé ». En plus de l'entretien, nous avons procédé à une observation participante et à une participation observante des faits sur le terrain qui nous ont instruit à plus d'un titre. Moi-même, suis membre de plusieurs « grins de thé » de jour comme de nuit. Pour une exigence épistémologique, nous avons ménagé une position de recul et de distance critique qui nous a permis de rompre avec la réalité sensible, avec les catégories du sens commun. Nous avons construit de l'intérieur la logique propre des situations telle qu'elle est perçue et vécue par les acteurs eux-mêmes. Partant de là, nous avons pu découvrir les données implicites par rapport auxquelles seules leurs conduites prennent sens et significations.

Crise urbaine, crise du lien social

Les jeunes de la ville de Ouagadougou, pour la plupart fragilisés par la conjoncture économique, redéfinissent de nouvelles trajectoires par lesquelles ils pourraient s'insérer dans le secteur de la modernité. Suite à la crise du secteur moderne due en partie à la politique d'ajustement structurel mise en place par l'État, l'économie urbaine est entrée en récession prolongée ayant des répercussions directes sur les conditions de vie des ménages. Le secteur formel de l'emploi en quasi-stagnation se trouve dans une certaine mesure dans l'incapacité d'absorber la masse croissante des nouveaux actifs. On assiste alors à la montée du chômage et des emplois informels dans l'espace urbain. Dès lors, l'environnement urbain s'est caractérisé par la montée fulgurante de la pauvreté de masse et la dégradation continue du marché du travail. Le chômage, la précarité et la pauvreté constituent les problèmes transversaux dont sont victimes les jeunes générations. Néanmoins, une faible proportion des jeunes investissent le marché du travail. En effet, « le chômage n'est qu'une des manifestations de la fragilisation du statut des jeunes adultes à laquelle vient s'ajouter une précarisation croissante des emplois occupés, pour ceux qui ont trouvé un travail » (Antoine *et al.* 2001 : 30). L'insertion professionnelle difficile des jeunes atteste indubitablement qu'ils sont les premiers atteints par les restructurations du monde du travail. Les opportunités d'emploi dans la fonction publique se sont considérablement réduites au regard de la formidable poussée scolaire de la jeune génération. Dans ce contexte économique morose, récessif, les jeunes se trouvent contraints de négocier leur insertion professionnelle dans des conditions plus difficiles que celles connues par les générations antérieures au moment de leur entrée dans la vie active :

Jusqu'à la fin des années quatre-vingts, les jeunes qui sortaient diplômés de l'enseignement public étaient immédiatement intégrés dans la fonction publique. S'il le désirait, tout récent détenteur d'un titre universitaire trouvait ainsi rapidement un emploi dans l'administration burkinabè. Mais les dégraissages drastiques du secteur étatique imposés par la Banque mondiale et le Fonds Monétaire International, à travers des programmes d'ajustement structurel, ont donné naissance au chômage des jeunes diplômés. Ainsi, de nombreux jeunes sont désormais hésitants devant la poursuite d'études qui ne leur garantissent plus une insertion dans l'économie urbaine. (Isabelle Sévédé-Bardem 1997 : 137).

L'allongement de la scolarité tend à prolonger l'âge de la jeunesse et l'insertion non seulement difficile mais aussi tardive sur le marché du travail. La prolongation de la jeunesse a comme corollaire l'entrée tardive dans la vie adulte marquée par une autonomie financière et résidentielle difficiles à obtenir. C'est une période moratoire de tâtonnements au cours de laquelle les jeunes se construisent des identités. Les niveaux de vie faibles et décroissants obligent les jeunes à différer leur entrée en première union. Le mariage retardé est lié au recul de l'âge d'accès à l'emploi et à l'autonomie financière. Le retard dans le processus d'autonomisation maintient les jeunes dans une situation de dépendance vis-à-vis de leur famille. Certains commencent leur vie d'adulte plus tard dans des emplois sous-qualifiés, précaires et mal rémunérés en dépit des niveaux scolaires nettement au dessus de leurs aînés.

La mutation des conditions de vie des jeunes et les difficultés de leur insertion professionnelle les soumettent à une épreuve de déclassement social. On assiste à un tarissement des sources traditionnelles d'aide et d'entraide. Alors, la ville est devenue un lieu de lutte sociale qui engendre des processus structurels d'exclusion et de discrimination sociale. Cette situation s'explique en partie par l'effritement des bases traditionnelles de la solidarité, l'absence des cadres sociaux d'intégration traditionnelle dont le corollaire est la décomposition du tissu urbain. Le décloisonnement des structures sociales et la désagrégation progressive des appartenances sociales anciennes conduisent au relâchement quasi-total du lien communautaire qui caractérise la crise urbaine. La formation de la ville a opéré une segmentation de l'espace social général, révélatrice des nouvelles configurations qui entretiennent des rapports sociaux inégalitaires. La décomposition du lien social, née de la désagrégation du tissu urbain, entraine une chute de la densité morale, l'effondrement de l'ordre moral et l'évolution des pathologies sociales.

Cette ville consacre une rupture du « lien égalitaire » qui forme le principe dominant de la vie sociale. Le pauvre, en d'autres termes, « celui dont les moyens ne suffisent pas à atteindre ses fins » (Simmel 1998 : 91), est marginalisé, littéralement écarté des circuits de distribution des biens communs. La monétarisation croissante des relations sociales redéfinissent de nouvelles modalités de relation à autrui. Désormais, l'argent est la pièce maîtresse, l'enjeu du jeu social. La lutte quotidienne pour l'appropriation des biens rares éloigne les jeunes des moyens les plus communs d'accumulation. Ils se trouvent dans une incapacité à prendre part efficacement à l'échange matériel et de services, à l'univers de la production et de la consommation des biens rares produits par la société. Ces formes structurelles de l'exclusion des jeunes hors de la sphère de l'échange marchand consacrent la rupture du lien économique qui entraîne d'autres processus de l'échec social où ils ne parviennent pas à accéder à la hiérarchie sociale dominante et valorisante.

Face à la décomposition des liens communautaires provoquée par la dynamique urbaine, les jeunes citadins initient un réajustement de leur comportement à un environnement économique durablement défavorable. Alors, les jeunes investissent les rues à travers les « grins de thé », s'approprient un territoire en le marquant d'une nouvelle identité produite à partir de réseaux de sociabilité.

Les conditions sociales d'émergence des « grins de thé » dans la ville de Ouagadougou

L'émergence des « grins de thé » dans la ville de Ouagadougou constitue l'une des stratégies plurielles de recherche de survie que les jeunes inventent dans la rue.

> La ville est en effet le lieu par excellence des processus de transformation et de restructuration : de nouvelles solidarités de quartier et de voisinage naissent, des groupes d'intérêts communs se développent, (…), la crise éthique et la crise des valeurs sociales apparaissent. La mutation des liens familiaux, l'éclatement des modèles et la reformulation des rôles sociaux lancent à la jeunesse un défi inédit, les invitant à un remodelage des aspirations et des modalités d'insertion sociale et professionnelle (Bahi 2007 : 33).

L'appropriation de la rue par des groupes informels de jeunes confère à l'espace urbain de nouvelles dynamiques sociales et de nouveaux modes de solidarité-survie à travers les « grins de thé ». Les rapports interpersonnels construits dans la rue forgent de nouvelles sociabilités qui engendrent des recompositions sociales et provoquent parfois une rupture avec l'ordre établi. Ces univers de sociabilités que sont les « grins de thé », créatrices de nouvelles pratiques juvéniles réelles ou imaginaires participent à la construction des nouvelles identités urbaines et fonctionnent comme des structurants sociaux de l'espace urbain. Le nouvel usage et la nouvelle signification de la rue redéfinissent les pratiques informelles foncières urbaines en dehors de ces fonctions planifiées et délimitées dans le temps et dans l'espace officiels. Alors, la rue apparaît comme le « lieu de construction par les jeunes d'un monde à part autour d'une culture du contre-stigmate » (Callu 2005 : 20).

Les jeunes des quartiers populaires de la ville de Ouagadougou s'installent dans les rues à ingurgiter du thé à longueur de la journée. Ces « grins de thé » qui foisonnent dans les rues des quartiers déshérités se localisent au pied d'un mur, d'une concession, sous un arbre, sous un hangar, à l'intérieur des concessions. L'émergence de ces mouvements juvéniles que constituent les « grins de thé » est le fait de la migration scolaire et professionnelle des jeunes, de l'ouest du pays vers Ouagadougou la capitale, à travers le phénomène de la reproduction des pratiques informelles des jeunes de l'ouest du pays et le brassage du tissu urbain :

> C'est les fonctionnaires bobolais qui ont amené le thé à Ouagadougou. C'est quand les bobolais ont commencé à venir en masse à Ouagadougou que le thé a pris de

l'ampleur. C'est venu aussi du Mali. Les Maliens qui sont venus se sont installés à Djaradougou et à Accart-ville. C'est eux qui sont venus avec le thé et après ça pris de l'ampleur à Bobo. À Ouaga, l'ex-camp fonctionnaire qui a été rasé là, il y avait des bobolais et on prenait le thé là-bas. C'est vers les années 90 qu'on a commencé à voir les « grins de thé » à Ouagadougou avec surtout les étudiants venus de l'Ouest du Burkina. C'est avec le temps que la nouvelle génération des jeunes de Ouagadougou ont emboîté le pas des bobolais. C'est dans les quartiers d'étudiants comme Zogona et Wemtenga qu'on trouvait les « grins » avec les étudiants et puis la cité universitaire (Konseiga, secteur N°13).

Par les emprunts culturels des comportements juvéniles venus de l'Ouest du Burkina, les jeunes de la ville de Ouagadougou ont intégré progressivement, depuis les années 90 jusqu'à nos jours, les « grins de thé » dans leurs habitudes citadines. Ces groupes de jeunes sont pour la plupart des produits du système scolaire. Ce sont des jeunes déscolarisés, des sans-emplois, des chômeurs, des étudiants, des travailleurs du public et du privé : « dans le « grin », il y a des étudiants, des ouvriers, des élèves, des fonctionnaires. Mais pas de bandits, pas de voleurs, ni d'escrocs. Nous, on les déteste. Si tu viens ici bizarrement, on te chasse » (Rasmané, secteur n°13).

Le groupe se forme à travers les proximités sociales : relations de parenté, de voisinage, d'amitié, de camaraderie, d'ancienne camaraderie d'écoles ou du campus. En dehors des travailleurs du privé et du public, la plupart de ces jeunes vivent d'une « économie de la débrouille » à travers les petits métiers, le petit commerce, les « deals », les activités temporaires manuelles ou d'artisanat. On remarque une forte absence des filles dans les « grins de thé ». Ces « grins de thé » autrement appelés « QG » (quartier général) s'identifient par des noms de baptême qui révèlent les préférences et les références réelles ou imaginaires de ces jeunes. Ce sont : « bagdad », « afganistan », « Alquaïda », « le Forum », « carrefour du bonheur », « Agora », etc. Ces fonts baptismaux sont l'expression d'une idéologie du groupe portant la marque d'une symbolisation identitaire qui forge des croyances, des sentiments, des représentations communes du monde social.

À l'intérieur des « grins », on découvre une hiérarchisation des relations entre les membres et une répartition des tâches fondées sur le principe de séniorité. En général, ce sont les plus jeunes qui sont chargés de la préparation du thé. Ils sont aussi les coursiers de leurs aînés : « La plupart du temps, dans un « QG », c'est les kôrôs (grand-frère) qu'on respecte. J'ai 32 ans par exemple, on s'assoit au « grin », on ne peut pas servir le thé à un petit de 26 ans avant moi » (Soro, secteur n°13).

Il s'agit d'une reproduction des anciennes structurations communautaires en fonction des classes d'âge. Le « grin » fonctionne sur des normes, des codes de conduite édictés par les aînés qui veillent quotidiennement à leur respect par les plus jeunes. Il se présente comme un univers de socialisation qui inculque aux plus jeunes, les bonnes conduites morales. L'économie du « grin » est fondée sur la contribution volontaire de chaque membre. En général, un membre du groupe est chargé de la gestion du stock des biens du « grin » : théière, charbon, sucre, thé, etc : « Celui qui a l'argent, qui est fort (avoir le pouvoir d'argent) le jour là, il paye. Ça ne manque pas. Y en a qui viennent au « grin », ils peuvent payer cinq (05) ou dix (10) paquets de thé. C'est pas obligé, celui qui a l'argent paye » (Soro, secteur n°13).

Il existe d'autres formes de « grins » qui se caractérisent par des pratiques marginales et d'autodestruction : ce sont les « ghettos ». Ces pratiques de la marge qui inaugurent d'autres modes de vie sont en même temps une tentative de remise en cause de la rigidité de l'ordre collectif. Ces jeunes de la marge s'adonnent à des pratiques légales ou illégales : vol, viol, violence, drogue et alcoolisme qui ont des effets stimulants, dépresseurs ou perturbateurs sur le système nerveux central. Ils développent alors des comportements agressifs, violents en rupture avec la conscience collective courante. Dans les « ghettos », les rapports de force règnent sans véritable arbitrage. C'est le plus fort qui fait la loi. L'entraide est alternée avec la soumission et le sentiment d'appartenance est suffisamment fort. Ce « monde à la Hobbes » est une instance de production des normes, une démultiplication des possibilités de contournement des règles et des lois de la société. Il convient cependant de préciser que tous les jeunes pauvres ne se retrouvent pas nécessairement dans les « ghettos ». Il existe des enfants de classes moyennes ou aisées qui se laissent fasciner par l'expérience de la rue d'où surgissent les nouveaux styles de vie urbaine. Ce qui veut dire que la seule misère économique ou sociale ne saurait exclusivement expliquer l'existence des « ghettos ».

Les « grins de thé » et les « ghettos » ont en commun le partage des mêmes pratiques langagières : le nouchi, un argot produit en Côte-d'Ivoire et diffusé dans les villes du Burkina, oppose sans cesse à la culture officielle une contre-culture vigoureuse. Ce niveau de communication fabriqué par des jeunes de la marge dénote un sous-ensemble important du lexique hors de l'utilisation courante du français. On y rencontre fréquemment les mots suivants : dôgô (petit frère en dioula), kôrô (grand-frère en dioula) ; bramôgô (mon alter égo), môgôpuissant (homme fort), guèzemanchoc (un fin dealer), gamataire (un menteur), goder (boire l'alcool), un quaine (un deal), la djagaïe (la cigarette), etc. La tradition lexicographique ne peut à présent conserver les nouveaux mots des jeunes. Ce français conventionnel qui facilite la communication interpersonnelle des membres des « grins » et des « ghettos » reflète un contexte social, culturel et multiethnique favorisant. Sur la base de leurs expériences quotidiennes, les jeunes parviennent à opérer un changement de mots du fonds commun sémantique du français général. L'ingénierie de ces jeunes, tant dans le lexique que dans la phonétique, se repère par un argot qui fait usage de la syntaxe française avec quelques mots ayant une double racine traditionnelle et française. Cet argot est un véritable écart à la norme, un déplacement et un renversement des mots qui deviennent des codes secrets partagés par les jeunes de la marge.

Les « grins de thé » comme stratégie de survie quotidienne des jeunes

Les « grins de thé » se présentent comme une famille d'amis au sein de laquelle les membres trouvent entraide, réconfort morale, attention, écoute dans une cité de plus en plus marquée par l'atomisation sociale, la montée de l'individualisme. Ce sont des univers de partage, de soutien réciproque, affectif et matériel. La réciprocité est le principe dominant qui fonde les échanges entre les membres du groupe. Ce sont des réseaux d'interdépendance comme nouvelles stratégies d'innovation ou de survie face à la dissolution du lien social, à la décomposition du tissu urbain. Pour parer aux difficultés alimentaires que rencontrent les plus démunis, les repas communautaires sont organisés dans les « grins ». Nourriture, argent, cigarettes sont échangés quotidiennement entre membres d'un « grin ». Ceux qui ont déjà un emploi rémunéré viennent en aide aux sans-emplois lorsque ceux-ci sont confrontés à des difficultés de tous ordres :

> Y a des gens qui sont bien aujourd'hui à cause des « QG ». Dans le « QG » ici, il y avait des étudiants qui étaient là, ils n'avaient rien. On leur payait à boire, à fumer. Ils buvaient le thé, ils ne contribuaient pas. Même quand on a l'argent, on ne payait pa, souvent on vous donne à manger. Aujourd'hui, ils travaillent et ils sont bien. Et, ils reviennent nous payer la bière à boire. Donc, les « grins » c'est une bonne chose pour les jeunes. C'est ceux qui n'ont rien compris qui pensent que ceux qui sont dans les « grins » sont des voyous (Soro, secteur n°13).

En cas de décès d'un membre du « QG » ou dans une famille proche d'un membre du « grin », le groupe apporte son soutien affectif ou moral en aidant à creuser la tombe au cimetière et en présentant ses condoléances à la famille endeuillée en donnant une enveloppe contenant une modique somme cotisée par les membres du « grin ». Le même scénario est observé lorsqu'un membre du « grin » est malade ou quand sa femme ou sa copine accouche d'un enfant. Pour le mariage d'un membre du « grin », tout le groupe se mobilise et s'implique activement dans l'accomplissement des différentes tâches liées à la cérémonie du mariage. La contribution du « grin » est perceptible par des dons en matériel, en argent nécessaire à l'organisation et à la réussite du mariage. On trouve aussi des « grins de thé » qui se forment autour d'une entreprise commerciale détenue par un membre : atelier de couture, boutique, réparateur de chaussure et cireur, blanchisserie, kiosque (point de vente de café), etc. Dans ce cas, le groupe qui se forme autour de l'entreprise se mue en même temps en clientèle fidèle qui permet à l'activité économique en question de prospérer.

Nombreux sont les jeunes qui ont obtenu un emploi rémunéré grâce à leur « grin » d'appartenance devenu un capital social, une ressource qui leur permet de se tirer d'affaires : « Le grin a été une ressource que chacun a du exploiter d'une manière ou d'une autre pour réussir dans la vie » (Kambou, secteur 29).

Le « grin » est en même temps une école de formation et de préparation aux concours d'entrée dans la fonction publique. De même, ceux qui ont déjà obtenu un emploi œuvrent à ouvrir des opportunités d'embauche à leurs amis du « grin » :

> Le « grin » est comme une famille. Ceux qui premièrement avaient le job prenaient les cv des gars du « grin » pour voir au niveau de leur connaissance s'ils peuvent avoir des portes de sortie pour leurs gars. Grâce au lien du « grin », j'ai pu intervenir pour qu'un membre du « grin » ait du boulot dans un projet. Et à partir de ça, aujourd'hui, il s'est marié, il a une famille et il a construit. Le « grin » était comme une famille (Konseiga, secteur n°13).

Le « grin » étant un carrefour des jeunes, il devient le point de repère pour ceux qui vivent des activités informelles telles que : les « démarcheurs » de maisons, les électriciens, les maçons et toute autre activité de manutention. À défaut de posséder un atelier ou un bureau, le « grin » devient le lieu de la centralisation des demandes de travaux divers de manutention par les habitants du quartier.

Fonctionnant comme un espace public informel, les « QG » sont des lieux de diffusion des informations générales sur l'actualité nationale et internationale qui sont commentées, discutées par les membres du « grin ». C'est à travers ces regroupements de jeunes que nombre d'entre eux acquièrent petit à petit une culture générale sur les choses du monde. Les journaux sont lus et commentés par les membres d'un « grin ».

Il est tout aussi important de préciser que la précarité n'est pas le seul facteur de formation des « grins ». On y rencontre des « grins » formés de jeunes diplômés employés du public et du privé qui ont en commun l'ancienne camaraderie du campus. Pour lutter contre la dispersion sociale liée aux occupations professionnelles, ces anciens amis du campus ou des lycées se retrouvent dans un « grin » qui devient un forum de discussions, de débats contradictoires.

Par ailleurs, il est aisé aussi de constater que les clubs de thé qui jonchent les rues de la capitale sont des espaces de loisirs. Par manque de moyens financiers pour accéder à la vie mondaine qui caractérise le style de vie urbain (bars, maquis, boîte de nuit, etc), les jeunes se retrouvent dans les « QG » pour jouer aux jeux de société et écouter de la musique. Exclus de l'univers des loisirs publics, les samedis soirs, il n'est pas rare de voir des jeunes organisés une sorte de « bal poussière » dans les « QG ». Nuitamment dans un coin de la rue, parfois avec une ampoule allumée d'une lumière blafarde, on les rencontre entrain d'esquisser des pas de danse à l'aide des sonorités musicales du moment. Certains parmi eux ont fait leur apprentissage de la danse dans les « QG ». Compte tenu de l'inaccessibilité des bars dancing et des boîtes de nuit due au coût exorbitant à l'entrée, des « QG » organisent, dans la nuit de la Saint Sylvestre, des soirées dansantes dans les concessions à partir des cotisations de chaque membre. Une cérémonie de présentation des vœux à l'occasion du nouvel an se tient régulièrement dans certains « grins de thé » qui donne l'aspect d'un repas communautaire.

Pendant les grandes vacances, des tournois de football « intergrins » sont organisés. C'est aussi des moments de retrouvailles des anciens amis disséminés dans les « QG » d'un quartier donné ou dans d'autres quartiers de la ville. Alors, les « QG » se transforment en équipe de football.

Entre autres stratégies de survie des jeunes, il faut noter celui du modèle de gestion du corps des loubards qui révèlent leurs conditions quotidiennes d'existence :

> Il y a aussi des « grins » de loubards. Eux, ils misent sur leur force. Quand il y a un bal ou une manifestation dans le quartier, on vient les louer pour assurer la sécurité. Dans la journée, ils boivent le thé au « grin ». Le soir, ils font des exercices de musculation et la nuit, ils sont dans les maquis, les boîtes de nuit pour assurer la sécurité (Kambou, secteur n°29).

Alors, le corps devient un capital majeur qu'ils mettent en jeu pour assurer leurs conditions de survie. Ces loubards s'adonnent au développement, au maintien et à l'entretien des attributs du corps. Ils œuvrent pleinement à sa protection à travers l'observation de rites physiques tels que les exercices de musculation, le recours à des objets, des habits qui collent au corps, des attributs de force et d'agressivité âpres à semer la peur et à obtenir la soumission envers quiconque. Ils sont perçus comme des gens anormaux, difformes et étranges aux yeux du public. Ces loubards développent en eux le goût du risque. Ils assurent leur survie quotidienne en prêtant leur service aux gérants des bars, des maquis, des boîtes de nuit moyennant un salaire. Ils sont chargés de la sécurité des personnes et des biens à l'entré et à l'intérieur de ces lieux de loisirs. Ils doivent leur autorité à la crainte qu'ils inspirent par leurs corps difformes qu'ils exhibent publiquement.

L'échec ou l'abandon des itinéraires scolaires a suscité chez les jeunes des « QG » de nouveaux imaginaires de la réussite sociale. Il existe d'autres formes de « grins » que l'on rencontre dans la rue dont les membres s'identifient à des figures mythiques des arts musicaux : ce sont les rastas. Ils ont comme philosophie de base le « rastafarisme » et se spécialisent dans un des instruments musicaux tels que la guitare, le djembé (une sorte de petit tam-tam localement fabriqué). Les « grins » de rastas sont aussi des lieux de fabrication et de vente de djembé qui leur permet de survivre. En plus des prestations musicales que font ces rastas lors des cérémonies festives, ils entretiennent des relations étroites d'amitié avec des touristes en visite au Burkina Faso. Ils deviennent les guides des touristes en arpentant chaque jour les rues de Ouagadougou avec ces derniers. Le capital social qu'ils acquièrent leur permet d'emprunter les chemins de la migration vers l'Europe. Aussi, la mise en couple ou en union maritale de certains rastas avec des européennes est l'une des occasions réussies pour ces derniers de se retrouver en Europe pour commencer une autre vie peut-être meilleure par rapport à celle d'ici :

> J'étais dans un « grin » de rastas à Ouidi. Ils faisaient de la musique, ils avaient une troupe, ils jouaient dans les festivals. La musique était leur activité principale. Ils faisaient de la musique mixte : « djembé », balafon, guitare. C'est du « tradimoderne » qu'ils faisaient. Le « grin » était leur lieu de répétition. Le « grin » était leur famille. C'est là-bas ils mangeaient tous. Ils passaient tout leur temps au « grin ». Le plus diplômé avait un certificat d'études primaires. Y en a qui ne savaient ni lire, ni écrire. Ils parlaient souvent du » ratafarisme » et de l'actualité politique à leur manière. Après le « grin », ils sont à l'aéroport, devant les hôtels, les jardins pour rencontrer et nouer des contacts avec des touristes. En plus de la musique, ils sont des guides touristiques. Ils vendent des objets d'art aux abords des hôtels. Ils donnent aussi des cours de « djembé » aux touristes contre rémunération. Y en a qui ont profité de la musique et ils sont aujourd'hui en Europe et c'est ce qu'ils font là-bas comme activité (Adams alias Rasta, secteur 29).

Le mouvement hip hop foisonne aussi dans les « grins de thé ». La « rue donne, au premier abord, une image de liberté, d'universalité, d'invention » (de Latour 2001 : 153). Elle recèle les derniers frémissements culturels du monde. La ville, réappropriée par les jeunes devient un espace d'expression de culture urbaine tel que le mouvement hip hop : « Il s'agit là d'une expression publique affirmée haut et fort d'une génération qui refuse l'étouffement et le bâillonnement »; « il s'impose comme le cri venu des milieux urbains voués au silence » (Benga 2001:175).

Ce mode d'expression contestataire fait émerger progressivement une nouvelle identité juvénile. Cette expression musicale des jeunes est une forme de revendication sociale et politique par la volonté d'inscription au sein de la conscience collective les blessures dont ils sont porteurs qui sont des séquelles d'une histoire sociale de pauvreté et de souffrance, la « chronique des frustrations et des joies de la quotidienneté » (Benga 2002 : 3005). Le parler est direct et cru. Il affiche un air de provocation par l'agressivité de son intonation, la dureté de ces mots qui laisse percevoir la force de la dénonciation publique de l'ordre social dominant mis en cause. Le « discours est critique, sans concession et évoque l'absence de droits sociaux, l'exclusion et le chômage, le népotisme et la corruption des élites. Mais il fait aussi rêver d'amour, de voyages et de réussite sociale » (Trani 2006 : 335). Les « grins de thé » sont les lieux de répétition musicale de ces jeunes du hip hop. Nombreux sont les rappeurs de la place qui ont émergé sur la scène musicale à partir des « QG ». Ils sont quotidiennement solliciter à faire des prestations musicales dans les centres culturels et les soirées culturelles de la capitale et à l'intérieur du pays. C'est de ces activités qu'ils parviennent à tirer leur révérence quotidienne.

Les « grins de thé » exercent une fonction politique à l'occasion des campagnes électorales. Ils se métamorphosent en cellule de partis politiques pour maximiser au plus vite la rente électorale. La stratégie de mobilisation de la jeunesse par les hommes politiques passe nécessairement par la conquête des « QG » :

> Avec les hommes politiques, nous on les suit pour bouffer, mais on ne vote pas
> pour eux. Moi, j'ai battu la campagne de plusieurs partis politiques. Mais je n'ai pas
> voté. Mon parti, c'est le PDP de Joseph Ki-Zerbo. Le reste, je m'en fous. Nous, on
> profite pendant la campagne, après ça, c'est fini, on ne les voit plus (Soro, secteur n°13).

Il ne s'agit pas pour les jeunes des « grins » d'adhérer aux idéaux ou aux agendas
des partis politiques, mais plutôt d'entrer dans une relation clientélaire avec les
hommes politiques. Leur engagement politique provisoire et conditionnel s'inscrit
dans la continuité de la débrouille quotidienne qui caractérise les pratiques sociales
de ces jeunes. Usant de la ruse, des scénarios sont mis en place par ces jeunes, dans
une relation ponctuelle et éphémère de marchandage électoral avec les hommes
politiques. Se comportant comme des prestataires de service, toutes les tâches de
mobilisation qui leurs sont confiées font l'objet de marchandage politique :

> Le CDP nous a pris pour la distribution des cartes d'électeurs et on nous payait 2000
> F par jour pendant plus de vingt (20) jours. À ce niveau, on était géré par le CDP,
> mais sur le terrain on faisait le travail de mobilisation pour l'ADF alors qu'au fond
> l'ADF ne nous donnait rien (Kambou, secteur n°29).

Au cours du déroulement de la campagne électorale, les « grins de thé » bénéficient
de dons divers des hommes politiques : thé, sucre, tee-shirts, gadgets publicitaires,
argent, etc. En dépit de ces transactions électorales, l'abstentionnisme électoral
caractérise les pratiques politiques de ces jeunes.

Parmi les stratégies de la débrouille que les jeunes engagent dans leur vie
quotidienne, il faut relever celle de la mutation des « grins » en organisation de la
société civile intervenant dans les actions de développement :

> Après la politique, on est rentré dans le monde associatif. On a créé une association
> dénommée SOJES (Solidarité, Jeunesse pour l'Entraide sociale) en 2004. Notre
> objectif était de créer un cadre de rencontre des jeunes pour lutter contre les violences
> faites aux jeunes filles et promouvoir le bien-être des orphelins. On a eu à gérer un
> projet avec le comité national de lutte contre la pratique de l'excision. On a géré un
> autre projet avec l'Ong dénommée « Enfant du monde » pour la prise en charge des
> orphelins. Sur le plan financier, on était un peu rémunéré sur la base des activités
> qu'on menait. Ça nous a aidés à résoudre pas mal de problèmes d'ordre matériel.
> Avec ça, on payait nos scolarités, on aidait nos parents aussi. Le plus lourd financement
> s'élevait à 1 500 000 F pour la prise en charge des enfants (Kambou, secteur n°29).

Ces associations de développement ont permis aux jeunes des « grins » de se
familiariser avec les techniques de gestion administrative et d'élargir leur capital
social par les relations de travail qu'ils entretiennent avec les bailleurs de fond et les
autorités ministérielles. Ces ONG de développement sont des canaux par lesquels
les jeunes des « QG » font leur entrée dans le circuit administratico-politique.

Il est tout aussi important de préciser que les rififis nés des oppositions pendant
le déroulement des jeux de société et les rivalités pour la conquête des jeunes filles

fragilisent par moments la cohésion interne des membres des « grins ». La dislocation des « grins » survient lorsque ses membres prennent pied de façon active dans la vie professionnelle.

Conclusion

En définitive, on a pu constater que les jeunes de la ville de Ouagadougou inventent de nouvelles formes communautaires comme stratégies de négociation de leur existence sociale face à la violence structurelle et à la marginalisation sociale auxquelles ils sont constamment confrontés.

Cette situation dénote indubitablement une crise de l'État-nation en construction, empêtré dans ses contradictions. Cela est dû en partie à l'affaiblissement des mécanismes de contrôle et d'insertion sociale de cet État-nation.

La culture de la rue et l'émergence de nouvelles identités urbaines marquent une rupture avec l'héritage du projet colonial sur la dynamique urbaine. Les nouveaux itinéraires de la réussite sociale chez les jeunes marquent la dynamique transformatrice de l'espace urbain qui révèle une invention du social grâce à l'ingénierie créatrice des jeunes urbains qui n'ont pas toujours les moyens de participer efficacement et équitablement aux différentes formes de l'échange social.

Références

Antoine, Philippe, Razafindrakoto, Mireille, Roubaud, François, 2001, « Contraints de rester jeunes ? Évolution de l'insertion dans trois capitales africaines : Dakar, Yaoundé, Antananarivo », in *Les jeunes, hantise de l'espace public dans les sociétés du Sud ?* Paris : Aube, IRD.

Bahi, Boniface, 2007, *Dérives et réussite sociale en Afrique. Des stratégies juvéniles à Abidjan*, Paris : L'Harmattan.

Sévédé-Bardem, Isabelle, 1997, *Précarités juvéniles en milieu urbain africain. « Aujourd'hui, chacun se cherche »*, Paris : L'Harmattan.

Benga, Ndiounga Adrien, 2001, « Entre Jérusalem et Babylone : jeunes et espaces publics à Dakar » in *Les jeunes, hantise de l'espace public dans les sociétés du Sud ?* Paris : Aube, IRD.

Benga, Ndiounga Adrien, 2002, « Dakar et ses tempos. Significations et enjeux de la musique urbaine moderne (C.1960-années 1990) », in Diop Momar-Coumba (éd.), *Le Sénégal contemporain*, Paris : Karthala.

Callu, Elisabeth, Jurmund, Jean-Pierre, Vulbeau, Alain, 2005, « La « fabrique » de la place des jeunes », in *La place des jeunes dans la cité* tome 2, Espaces de rue, espaces de parole, Paris : L'Harmattan.

Courade, Georges, 2006, *L'Afrique des idées reçues*, Paris : Belin.

De Latour, Eliane, 2001, « Métaphores sociales dans les ghettos de Côte-d'Ivoire », in *Les jeunes, hantise de l'espace public dans les sociétés du Sud ?* Paris : Aube, IRD.

Diop, Momar-Coumba, 2002, *Le Sénégal contemporain*, Paris : Karthala.

Simmel, Georges, 1998, *Les pauvres*, Paris : PUF.

Trani, J.-F., 2006, « Les jeunes sont (et seront) les agents du changement en Afrique ! », in Courade Georges, *L'Afrique des idées reçues*, Paris : Belin.

13

The Value of Socialization in Negotiating Livelihoods among the Youth: A Case of Bugembe Youth Group in Uganda

Tabitha Naisiko

Introduction

As the African continent moves into the 21st century, it is also advancing from an agro-economy to mixed economy. This is characterized by the development of cities as people move from rural areas towards modern facilities in the urban centres, including better markets for their goods, electricity, and running water, which are required for both business and improved livelihoods. This phenomenon has led to a growth in the number of families, and hence a growth in the number of children and youth, in urban spaces. Some of the children and youth have been born and grown up in urban centres while others arrive through rural-urban migration either with their families or on their own. Regardless of how the youth find themselves in urban spaces, increased youth presence, and how to accommodate their interests in the urban centres, is a key concern that deserves urgent attention.

Ogwal-Oyee (2002) categorized the youth in Uganda that need special attention. Among these are out-of-school youth, street youth, youth with disability, young labourers, orphaned youth, girls as a special group, and youth living in areas that have suffered conflict. He missed the youth in schools who also need special attention. All these categories are present in urban centres and negotiate their livelihoods in one way or the other. However, as Hebinck and Bourdillon (2001) advise, it would be productive to consider the negotiations in a given context. They argue that livelihoods should be considered as social constructs, ways of living built by people who make their own value judgements and who choose to follow trajectories to fit their own identities.

Although the youth in urban spaces in Uganda offer commendable services in a bid to negotiate their livelihoods, the general community remains sceptical about them. The socio-economic situations created by urbanization, HIV/AIDs, and several wars have changed the communities. Families have, due to a variety of reasons, failed to socialize their children through household chores and working in gardens as they used to do. In the circumstances, these youth find they have to negotiate their livelihoods on the streets and in market spaces within the towns.

The challenging realities in youth livelihoods in relation to the general populace's social mistrust and doubt about their integrity raises the need to reconsider socialization processes. Not much information is available on the role of socialization and the values it imparts in negotiating livelihoods. Moreover, much available literature reveals moral concerns, connecting youth to such activities as drug abuse, prostitution, increased theft and other crime in their effort to negotiate livelihoods. Perhaps values acquired through socialization could provide a resource for the youth to negotiate their livelihoods in a socially accepted and sustainable manner. On the other hand, such values could be restraints that would hamper the processes of negotiating livelihood. This whole scenario brings up questions such as: Is the socialization process still relevant to these youth? Would not this process instead compromise the youth's efforts in their activities by restricting their autonomy? What do adults say about it and how do the youth respond to it?

Based on field data collected from Bugembe Youth Group in Jinja, Uganda, this chapter addresses the relevance of socialization to the youth negotiating their livelihoods in urban spaces. The chapter considers what adults feel about the values of youth and how the youth respond to them. This leads to a discussion of tension between the youth and the adults, and of ways in which the youth can promote the negotiation of better and supportive livelihoods.

Conceptualizing Socialization in Terms of Youth Livelihoods

Socialization, broadly defined, is the process through which a child or other novice acquires the knowledge, orientations and practices that enable him or her to participate effectively and appropriately in the social life of a particular community. This in reality is a set of densely interrelated processes and is realized to a great extent by means of language, which is the primary symbolic medium through which cultural knowledge is communicated and instantiated, negotiated and contested, reproduced and transformed. Socialization may provide individuals with skills and habits necessary to participate within their own society, which is normally formed through a plurality of shared norms, attitudes, values, motives, social roles, symbols, and language (Baquedano-López 2002:339-361). Socialization is thus 'the means by which social and cultural continuity are attained'.

Since time immemorial, youth have been negotiating their livelihoods, but in different environments. The dominant current reality is urbanization characterized by social problems such as HIV/AIDs, and the failure of governments to provide social services, among other problems and constraints that often make the contemporary urban youth vulnerable. The youth are not only vulnerable to politico-economic exclusion but also social exclusion. The situation of urban youth is characterized by lack of skills, knowledge, relations, and character suitable for social acceptance. The modern urban youth can be portrayed as 'a soldier' paraded on the frontline without a gun or a non-swimmer dropped into a lake. He or she has to survive. While some successfully learn and manage, others fail to cope. The risk of failure is that they turn to socially unaccepted activities for survival.

Although the processes of socialization in Africa have undergone changes due to the impact of modernity, education, and adaptation of foreign religions and cultures, its objective still remains relevant and perhaps more critical. This is because the youth at times lack the coping capacity to confront the world without the social support received through socialization or re-socialization. Besides the cultural paradox of socialization, youth are battling with issues of psycho-social and physical development. They often undergo inner tensions, and need understanding adults to guide or help them. Baquedano-López (2002) and Tienda and Wilson (2002) reveal that socialization has a significant contribution to the normative development of the youth.

Miller (1989:15) too quotes scholars in psychological development including Sigmund Freud (1946), Erick-Erickson (1959), Margaret Mead (1959), James Marcia (1967), Jean Piaget (1947) and Lawrence Kohlberg (1969), all of whom highlight that the youth are entangled in the problems of development and regardless of space and time. Youth development calls for mentoring and integration in the community. Otherwise, there can be a crisis among the youth. They may have resources and energy, but they lack the experience in life that can enable them to live sustainable adulthood. In other words, the successful negotiations of the youth require supportive adults to guide them through socialization. Figure 1 is an illustration of how socialization builds up the required social capital which later enables the youth to access other capitals that enable their livelihoods.

There is literature that gives theoretical justification of the pivotal role of socialization processes and values in the promotion and sustenance of youth livelihoods and normative development; nevertheless, the voices of the youth are lacking. It would be beneficial to hear their voices about the processes and values they are subjected to, in order to inform efforts to support sustainable livelihoods for the youth. The next section will discuss data and responses collected from youth in Bugembe about the roles of socialization in their negotiation of livelihoods.

The data came from a qualitative study that used focus group discussions, key informants, and open-ended questionnaires. It was conducted in December 2009, and included various categories of members of the youth group, the leadership

Figure 1: Conceptual Framework

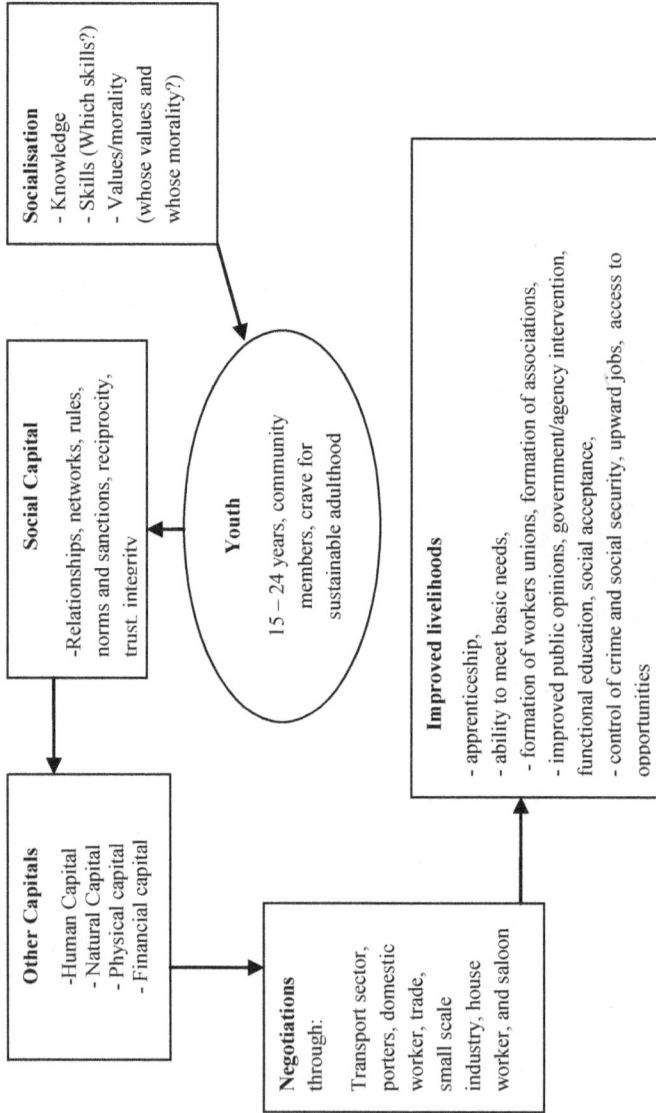

Socialisation
- Knowledge
- Skills (Which skills?)
- Values/morality (whose values and whose morality?)

Social Capital
-Relationships, networks, rules, norms and sanctions, reciprocity, trust. integrity

Youth
15 – 24 years, community members, crave for sustainable adulthood

Other Capitals
-Human Capital
- Natural Capital
- Physical capital
- Financial capital

Negotiations
through:

Transport sector, porters, domestic worker, trade, small scale industry, house worker, and saloon

Improved livelihoods
- apprenticeship,
- ability to meet basic needs,
- formation of workers unions, formation of associations,
- improved public opinions, government/agency intervention, functional education, social acceptance,
- control of crime and social security, upward jobs, access to opportunities

of the youth group and adults related to the youth group. Thirty people participated in the study, including five key informants, five adults/parents, five members of the youth group in school, and five members out of school, all of whom were purposively selected. Thereafter ten members, all students, were randomly selected and given self-administered questionnaires.

The Youthful Population in Bugembe Urban Space

Bugembe Town is semi-urban and was until February 2007 part of the sub-urban environs of the old Jinja industrial town from which it was carved to become a separate township. It is located in the eastern part of Jinja District along the Jinja–Tororo highway, about 4 km from Jinja Municipality, the second largest town in Uganda. Bugembe Town is bordered by Mafubira Sub-County in the north and east, while in the west it is bordered by Jinja Municipality and in the south by the second largest fresh water lake in the world, Lake Victoria. Bugembe Town consists of five wards (parishes) of Wanyama, Katende, Budhumbuli West, Budhumbuli East, and Nakanyonyi, with eight cells (villages).

Based on the provisional census data of 2002, Bugembe Town has an estimated total population of about 30,000. According to the United Nations Human Settlements Programme (2008), Bugembe Town has very high population density with a high youthful, dependant population. Forty per cent of the population is under 15 years of age. The age group of 20 to 30 years, who are included in the category of youth, is relatively high (about 25 per cent) as a result of a strong influx of young people coming from the rural areas looking for job opportunities (see Figure 2).

Figure 2: Age Classes Prevalence by Sex (UIS, Bugembe, 2006)

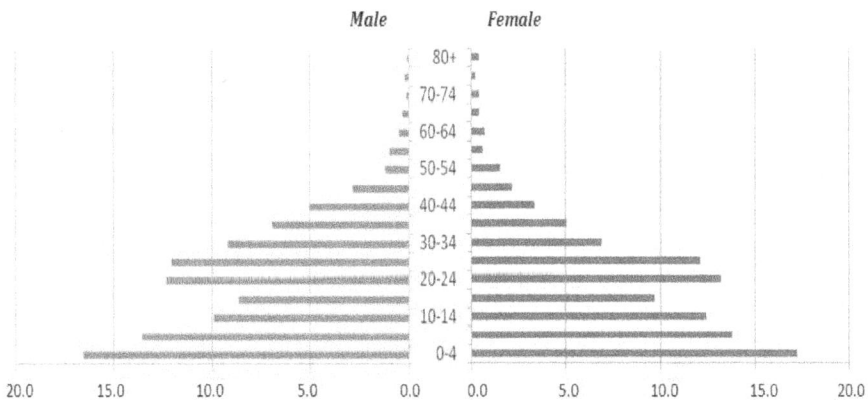

Economic livelihoods are concentrated around Budhumbuli, where the economic activity is high during the day. The market and taxi park are found in this ward though because of the town being along the Jinja-Kampala-Tororo highway, during the day the taxi operation tends to move to the Katende and Wanyama wards for easy capture of the passengers to Jinja Municipality. The major economic activities are buying produce and processing coffee, maize and beans. There are also retail and wholesale shops, bars, restaurants, butcheries and fish stalls. There are no major industries: however, since it is a semi-urban town, many people are engaged in subsistence farming. However, at night most economic activities take place along the Jinja-Tororo highway, where many people converge during evening hours.

Bugembe Youth Centre and the Activities of the Youth Group

Although literature normally concentrates on typically urban youth, the study of Bugembe Youth Group concentrated on youth in a semi-urban area, which means youth with closer links to rural life and family structures than have many urban youth. This is because whether or not in school, they are in close contact with their families and therefore have quick responsive support in case of need. With the town's semi-urban nature, most of the dwellers of the town council rent space in the town, but have homes of origin in the neighbouring villages of Wanyange, Wairaka, Musima, Wakitaka, and Kainhogoga. Some people commute from their villages to work in the town. These sell their agricultural products and other edibles such as bread, doughnuts, pancakes and samosas on a daily basis. Some youth commute from villages to study in the town schools. In other words, there is a continuous movement of people to and from the villages, especially in the mornings and evenings.

Bugembe Youth Centre was established by the Holy-Cross Congregation of Bugembe Catholic Parish in 1994, with the aim of evangelization and developing youth talents. The centre has a youth group whose number is irregular. Youth come and go depending on the activities running in the Centre and its attraction to them. The Centre has on average 40 regular members, though sometimes the number rises to between 80 and 100 during peak times such as school holidays, especially the Christmas holiday. The Youth Centre welcomes all youth regardless of the level of education and religious denomination.

The youth involved in the youth group are mostly students in secondary schools. They range between 14 and 20 years. They tend to leave the group when they join tertiary institutions because this requires them to change geographical location. Those out of school attend the Centre more regularly than the students, and range from 17 years and above. Some appear to be over 30 years old, but often hang around just in case they get an opportunity to earn something through the Centre.

Some youths in the Bugembe group, probably like in other organized groups, suffer exclusion from inclusive sub-groups. The youth are affected by differences in gender, age, literacy, ethnicity, physical ability, and skills within the group. This leads to discrimination and disrespect among some members, which they referred to as 'under-looking' and 'dooling'. There is a need to form cohorts within the group to enable free interaction. This, however, was mentioned as a problem of poor leadership: the youth feel such distinctions would not be affecting the group cohesion if the leaders had appropriate skills.

In answer to questions about the forms and contents of socialization in place to target the youth, they responded by citing the activities of the youth group. Among these were: seminars about spiritual, economic, political and physical life; training on group formation and group dynamics; retreats about discipline, behavioural change with respect to HIV/AIDs; life skills, including computer training; and Music, Dance and Drama (MDD), which involves singing, keyboard, and jazz drumming. The Centre also trains and provides facilities for sports and games, cookery, and art and crafts. With respect to crafts, for example, the youth work together to make items that attract general market in the United States of America. A Christmas card made out of manila paper and banana fibre, would be sold for 500 shillings in Uganda, whereas the same card is sold in the USA for $2, the equivalent of 4,000 shillings. This helps them in creating jobs and income for themselves.

A few of the youth were self-employed in the transport sector as *boda-boda* riders who use motorcycles to transport people to different destinations for a fee. The rest were involved in retail selling. The youth group also takes part in football and of music, dance and drama competitions, which sometimes win them cash prizes. The youth use the Centre to develop talents to join more prominent football teams such as Kakira Sugar Football Club and Nile Football Club. The youth love this group because it brings them publicity.

Some youth members of the Centre initiated an unofficial credit scheme. Every time they meet at the Centre, each contributes 1,000 shillings (half a US dollar), which is paid into a common pool. They refer to this as a 'Merry-Go-Round'. Later, the money is used to lend to a member of the group who is in need at a small interest rate. However, this arrangement often causes conflict when some members defy the rules of the 'scheme'. The arrangement then is left to individual members who are interested.

Often, the Centre works in conjunction with Youth Alive, a Catholic NGO that contributes to HIV/AIDS prevention by conducting programmes for behaviour change. These include advocacy programmes with school administrators and parents, and programmes to develop life skills, build capacity, and offer guidance and counselling. They target children in schools and youth in communities. The implementation of Youth Alive activities follows the strategies of advocacy for space and time to support behaviour change programmes in schools; peer education; group and individual counselling; positive formation of peer groups and clubs; talent identification and development through music, dance, drama, and sports galas; family life; and education to improve family health.

The youth in Bugembe Youth Group enjoy the activities of Youth Alive because these activities are fully sponsored. Unlike Bugembe Youth Centre, Youth Alive has sponsorship from several organizations, including Youth Alive Africa, CARE International, USAID, Irish Aid, and CORE Initiative (Communities Responding to the HIV/AIDs Epidemic). With this availability of funds, the Bugembe Youth feel motivated to participate in the programmes with the hope of benefiting from the prizes through participation in festivals and competitions. In this regard, Bugembe Youth Group is proud to have won the national music festival organized by Youth Alive and officiated by President of Uganda in July 2006.

The youth joined the group precisely because of the opportunities it offers. They understood the activities in the youth group as part of socialization, not in the sense of reproduction of African culture, but rather of being social and interacting with others, and also a means through which they develop their talents or potential livelihood skills.

Limitations of the Youth Centre

Although the youth highlighted the activities of the Youth Group as forms of socialization and rated them important in their efforts to negotiate their livelihoods, they also pointed out that there are factors that inhibit their ability to access what the Centre offers. Some of these factors are brought out in the rest of this section.

Church leaders who were in charge of the youth group were sometimes slow in making decisions. The youth felt that they consequently lost out on some opportunities. The bureaucracy among adults negatively affected the youths' progress, especially on issues like releasing money or giving them approval to implement a particular activity.

The youth felt that politicians neglected them and did not give them access to the national cake through participation in government programmes. This affected the activities they got involved in at the Youth Centre. Considering that through national programmes such as the National Agricultural Advisory and Development Services (NAADS), government endeavoured to avail publicity, storage and markets for the products of farmers' groups, youth pointed out that they too at times had products that lacked markets. The youth felt that the government should get involved in the youth affairs and facilitate their products' access to better markets.

The youth felt that the Parish, as the proprietor of Bugembe Youth Centre, should support the group with financial and material resources to develop its activities. Several youths mentioned poverty, lack of capital and lack of materials and support as problems limited the centre when there was a requirement to give the youth seed money or initial capital to start business.

Lack of skilled personnel to help the youth organize their group and their lives was another factor that affected the youths' responsiveness. Sometimes the youth convened when there were no skilled persons to teach them. This limited their prospects to learn modern skills and opportunities that would accrue from the technical know-how of the facilitators such as writing project proposals, advocacy, networking and lobbying for resources even at national level. Probably the issue of poor leadership would not arise if they had adequate professional support.

The youth cited personality problems as another factor that inhibited their participation in the Centre's activities. The personality problems included some youths being disrespectful; others lacking self-esteem probably due to their financial status and education level; rumour mongering; permissiveness; and peer influence among youth regarding how to react towards good or bad decisions. On the other hand, good relations characterized by cooperation and self-respect were mentioned as good for socialization.

Low motivation from elders was mentioned as one of the factors that affected their responsiveness to the group activities. This took the form of home ties and mistrust from their parents, who were worried that the youth would learn bad manners such as sexual promiscuity, gambling, and being disrespectful of them due to the influence of the youth group. Such mistrust denied the youth opportunities to attain new ideas and life skills. The restrictiveness of the parents at times made the youth, especially students, feel alienated from the group activities. School programmes were also seen as affecting their participation in the centre's activities, as some youth complained of insufficient time to attend the youth group meetings.

Roles of Socialization in Negotiating Livelihoods

The youths' perception of socialization did not differ much from the conventional perception rooted in the acquisition of survival skills and being functional in the society. However, the youth's perception put emphasis on the need for socialization to be dynamic and contextual, and always sensitive to modern demands such as ICT, sports and other skills. The youth upheld the socialization process at the Bugembe Youth Centre as important because it promoted friendship, and imparted skills, including those obtained in business courses such as book-keeping, marketing, bee-keeping, making candles and soap, and information on issues to consider when taking and using loans. The training helped them to start their own businesses. It also enabled some youth to find future careers as footballers and musicians. The centre promoted self-reliance and satisfaction. They avoided begging. They also learnt to live in a cosmopolitan community by respecting each other and acquired techniques of approaching different people.

In spite of the seemingly negative picture that was painted by their voices, the youth still found socialization important to their lives. It helped them to become responsible members of the community. They emphasized the need for discipline and integrity as one of the benefits of socialization and a requirement in negotiating livelihoods. The youth affirmed that social capital was necessary in their negotiation of livelihoods. They also proved correct the assumption in the study's theoretical framework that socialization lay a foundation for social capital. It later opened the youth to other kinds of capital, such as financial and physical resources, which would bring them opportunities. However, they argued that the socialization process should put into consideration the new techniques of forging through and managing life. There was need for professional skills to make them feel accepted and build their esteem in the community.

Youth Opinions about the Need for Socialization in Today's Society

Having explored the contents and uses of socialization, all the respondents confessed that they still needed the socializing activities of the Youth Centre. They said the Centre was necessary because they thought it was a 'get together thing': they found new friends, learnt and got help to overcome stress, boredom and idleness. One lady said:

> You know why I think that it is necessary: there are moments when you get a big problem and you find yourself a misfit in the society where you live to the extent that it can even cause you make a scandal. Then you talk to yourself that let me go to the Centre and join others. While you are there, you laugh, sing, and even forget the torturous moments you are undergoing. That is why it is necessary. You also get physically fit.

In addition to the Centre being a stress-releasing place, the youth also say that they obtained funds to support themselves and avoid being thieves. They cultivated popularity in church by becoming active members of the congregation and taking up roles such as reading during mass and singing in the youth choir. Often when there were functions at the church, such as weddings or festivals, the youth group took an active role in offering catering services, decorating the premises, and animating the liturgy. They hailed socialization at the Centre because it helped them develop their talents, earn a living, and plan for the future. To them, the Centre provided an opportunity to socialize as they had previously defined it. A 27-year-old primary teacher, once a very active member of the group, but who was upgrading in a National Teachers College by the time of this research, had this to say:

> The youth group is very helpful. They are now an established group: it has taken root. Many people have managed to be somewhere. Many people have been empowered even at national level, e.g., Jose Chameleon [a renowned singer of pop

music]. Even here in Bugembe, like me, am a guild Speaker of Aduk and I will be the leader to of the University. Some people have reformed for example Christine.[1] You knew her, what can I lie about her?

Christine was a secondary school teacher who had earlier dropped out of school to cohabit with her partner. Her change of behaviour and later completion of studies was attributed to the counselling she received from the youth centre.

The youth also confessed ignorance of some issues concerning life. As one remarked, 'There are many things that youth do not know and would like to know them, socialization is needed because the youth need to utilize them.'

Socialization at the Centre was seen as a learning process. It helped them identify their talents, learn skills, change their morals positively, develop their spirituality, and develop their self-esteem. As far as Bugembe Youth Centre was concerned, the youth were appreciative of free training in different activities. However, to the youth, there was need for it to move according to their needs and what they found attractive.

On the other hand, some respondents, especially parents, accepted the need for socialization such as took place at the Centre, but with some reservations. Having noted the way the youth themselves perceived it, the parents complained that some youth and the leaders of the youth group only thought of economic achievements. This was because most attention was paid to income generation through talent development, skills development and project establishment. In the process, some parents argued, the youth became spoiled with money.

While the search for money was imperative to the youth, some of them felt that they were being exploited by the group leaders and the organisers in the course of socialization. For instance, when they joined group activities that involved generating money and sharing it amongst themselves – such as making decorations for parties, offering catering services, and singing at occasions – some thought they were exploited and underpaid. Some commented that such activities of the youth group were a waste of time and they were threatened by the tendency for some youths to succumb to the temptation of coupling up when leaving late in the evenings after, say, football or choir practices.

Discussion of Findings

The voices of the youth revealed perceptions of 'socialization' that were slightly different from the classical sociological concept. The youth also spoke of the challenges they faced during the processes of socialization. Like other youth in general, the youth of Bugembe disclosed their reality as coloured by prejudices from the community, more especially at home, that made them feel that the socialization process was marred by pre-conceived ideas about them. They complained of home ties, restrictions from the parents, and mistrust among the public, the bureaucracy, and the adults they dealt with. All these served to discourage them from achieving their goals at the Centre.

The tension between the adults and the youth seems to influence the youths' perception of term 'socialization'. For both those in school and out of school, the initial idea of socialization in relation to the youth group always meant 'to socialize', that is taking part in social activities or behaving in a friendly way to others. This perhaps was the core motive for the youth to join the group. Accordingly, they repeatedly recommended that more social activities such as seminars, retreats and parties, be organized at the Centre alongside the training. However, when the academic meaning of 'socialization' was explained, the youth observed that the Centre should train them in skills required for functioning successfully in society. Here they mentioned skills in ICT, cookery, music, dance and drama (MDD), self-help projects in agriculture, arts and crafts, as wells as general knowledge and ethical behaviour.

Their responses also revealed that socialization should be integrated with income generation. For instance, they wanted MDD as well as sports for income generation. The youth wanted socialization to be integrated with skills development towards economic empowerment for self-sustenance. In contrast with the traditional understanding of socialization which concentrated on making one functional in the community, the study revealed that monetary income was basic to surviving in the contemporary society. The youth also understood that there were several options for making money besides the traditional modes of employment or trade. They saw that they could use their talents to earn a living. There was need to allow them develop such talents even if they were in school.

The youth underlined their conviction that there was an inseparable connection between successful socialization and supportive adults. However, they pointed out that often the adults were not supportive to the youth in several ways. It was revealed that the concerned adults, particularly parents, sometimes failed to trust the youth and refused to approve their choices of activities: they were critical and did not allow the youth freedom to decide. The youth sometimes feel betrayed by their parents who discouraged them from taking up some activities they might have excelled in.

The youth also felt betrayed by adults who used youth for personal gain. They gave an example of the politicians who used them to look for votes with the promise that they too would be helped to obtain jobs, financial capital, and political positions at lower levels. While the youth participated with enthusiasm, they ended up being used. There was need to uplift the integrity of both sides, such that the blame of indiscipline should not fall on the youth alone but on adults too.

The youth cited bureaucracy as a hindrance to their negotiations. For instance, youth under organized groups like the Bugembe Youth Group, said they used groups as a combined effort or collective voice to have their programmes drawn and advocate for their needs. However, the adults in the administrative structures placed conditions which were difficult to fulfil. This frustrated the youths' efforts when they spent much of time 'chasing things' they never received because of the bureaucracy. In this regard, the youth claimed that the adults in the agencies ignored them whenever it came to their cause.

Prospects of Successful Socialization in the Contemporary Society

Although there are some challenges in relation to socialization and youth negotiations, there is a need to acknowledge that the situation can improve basing on the fact that both the adults and youth value socialization. The study revealed that socialization is still important to the youth. It lays social foundation, discipline as well as opportunity for the youth to negotiate their livelihood. However, there is a lot of room for improvement required in areas of communication, organizational skills of the youth agency and skilled personnel in working with them.

The voices of the parents revealed that they were not aware of the activities their children were engaged in. Aidah[1], one of the church leaders had this to say:

> Issues to do with socialization have changed. The aunts and uncles are no longer playing their roles. For me I train mine [youth] in religious affairs, household chores….I do not associate with the youth, so I do not know about them. I just see them at the Centre and also hear that some involve in promiscuity….However, what I know is that when people work together, they develop spiritually and physically

This response implies that there is an information gap between parents and the youth with regard to the activities they are involved in. The parents demand that the youth agency keeps them abreast of the activities they are involved in. On the other hand, youth sometimes complained that parents were at times non-supportive. The prospect of the activities of the Youth Centre then lies in efficient communication with the parents. It is only then that the parents will be informed and convinced to support their youth in their various activities to enable them succeed in their struggles.

There is also a need to define the way forward of the youth negotiations. This should be directed towards self-sustenance of some sort. Perhaps the proceeds of the youth negotiations do not reflect their efforts and so the parents think it is a waste of time; yet it exposes them to the vulnerability of learning bad manners. The youth need to help to become self-reliant in using the proceeds of their negotiations, or at least share their proceeds with the families. Otherwise, the parents revealed that they could not support their youth when all they brought home were problems and expenditure.

There is also a need for youth agencies to streamline their leadership activities to address the problems of different members of the group. It was revealed that some of the youth, like those who have disabilities who were in school and those out of school, did not benefit from the activities of the youth group equitably. This indicates that the agencies dealing with the youth need to put into consideration the diversity of problems and interests of those who comprise the youth groups.

Besides inclusiveness as group members, the youth also felt that they are citizens and so ought to benefit from government programmes such as Savings and Credit Cooperative Organisations (SACCOs) and NAADS. However, these organizations do not favour the youth in rural towns. For instance, a group benefits from a SACCO only after it is fully registered, which requires a minimum of 30 members. As soon as a SACCO is certified, its members are trained by the Uganda Cooperatives Savings and Credit Union (UCSCU). Thereafter the group is recommended to borrow money through the Uganda Post Bank. Often it is women's groups that are able to register and benefit from a SACCO. The irregularity of the membership, in addition to most youth lacking regular sources of income, makes it difficult for the youth group to fulfil the requirements and to register the group with a SACCO. Government officers in charge of 'Prosperity For All' programmes should devise strategies to bring the youth on board.

There are financial resources in the government that could benefit the youth, but do not under current management. Consequently, many youth suffer challenges of lack of initial capital and access to markets. Despite constrained resources, the youth are benefiting in various ways from the Bugembe Youth Centre. It would be beneficial for public and private resources to combine, and for the government to extend the implementation of some programmes to private agencies like the Bugembe Youth Centre.

The problem at hand in this context is the failure to link up the youth to the available national resources. This is a weakness of the Uganda National Youth Council (UNYC), which was established by the National Youth Council Statute 1993 with the objectives of organizing the Youth of Uganda into a unified body; engaging them in activities that are of benefit to them and the nation; protecting them against any kind of manipulation; consolidating their role in national development in the economic, social, cultural and educational fields; as well as promoting relations between Youth organizations in Uganda and International Youth organizations and other bodies with similar objects or interests. The limitations mentioned by the youth in Bugembe could potentially be resolved through proper co-ordination with the UNYC. The Council is in position to advocate and lobby for the interests of the youth in areas of micro-finance. Nanyongo and Nsubuga (2004) revealed that the government releases money, including Youth funds, known as Youth Entrepreneur Scheme (YES):

> Over the past decade, the Government of Uganda via the Ministry of Gender, Labour and Social Development (MGLSD) has implemented and/or supported various micro credit schemes aimed at fighting poverty in the country. Most of

these schemes focused on the provision of revolving funds for micro credit to households at the grass root level. Examples include the Poverty Alleviation Project (PAP), Entandikwa Credit Scheme (ECS), Rural Farmers Scheme, Cooperative Credit Scheme, and the Youth Entrepreneurs Scheme (YES). In addition, the Government has supported credit activities within the framework of other multi-purpose projects, including the Micro projects Programme, Danida Credit scheme.

This indicates that there are provisions for the youth to realize successful negotiations. There are, however, no links between the Youth Centre and the organizations such as YES to enable them access national resources. Furthermore, due to lack of skilled personnel, it is unlikely that the Youth Centre can access the required information and make proper advocacy and lobbying for the resources. Another prospect of the youth Centre therefore lies in availability of trained and technical personnel.

Having learnt that the traditional modes of socialization are no longer appropriate in socializing youth in contemporary cities, the youth suggested some ways forward. They mentioned Straight Talk, which is perceived as a modern form of making the youth informed in a friendly way. This is not, however, a new method of communication. Straight Talk Foundation (STF) originated from Straight Talk newspaper that was first published in 1993 and funded by UNICEF. Today, Straight Talk Foundation (STF) is a health communication NGO that promotes Communication for Social Change through print, radio, and face-to-face interventions for adolescents and important adults, such as teachers and parents, in the lives of adolescents. STF produces 53 radio shows a week in 14 languages and about a dozen publications (some monthly, some termly) and conducts interactive face-to-face work in schools and communities.

Although the respondents still have respect for their traditional/cultural modes of socialization, they realise that the modern forms are very convenient and open them to opportunities. On this note, Straight Talk needs to be concretized as a mode of socialization. This requires that the proprietors of Straight Talk liaise with the grassroots organizations, such as the churches, and with parents and politicians in order to widen the scope of their operation. This can probably enable other agencies and actors in the lives of the youth to disseminate their information through Straight Talk, which is popular to them.

The failure of uncles and aunts to play their roles in socializing the youth implies that the traditional social structure is no longer functional. During socialization and rites of initiation to adulthood in several African communities, the youth used to be incorporated into social support groups called age-sets. In the current context, there is a need for the parents and other adults to realise that the youth still need social support, which can be realised through the youth groups. There is a need for parents to support these new modes of socialization and support for their youth.

Conclusion

The study concluded that the socialization offered by the Bugembe Youth Centre is important for the youth when they are negotiating their livelihoods. Socialization is about psycho-social empowerment and it is dynamic and changes according to developments in society. Regardless of time and space, the youth need to be socialized as a way to enhancing their coping capacity. The study affirms that the youth need support from parents, community, and government and non-government organizations. There is no harm in the adults getting involved in the affairs of the youth as long as there is dialogue and respect for each other. The study also revealed that the youth need to be helped to show tangible results out of the proceeds of negotiation. Otherwise, the adults may continue to mistrust and fail to support the efforts of the youth in their efforts. The youth need to be socialized with updated knowledge; skills and exposure to enable them become functional in the community and live meaningful lives.

Note

1. Informants' names in this chapter are pseudonyms.

References

Baquedano-López, Garrett and Patricia, 2002, 'Language Socialization: Reproduction and Continuity, Transformation and Change', *Annual Review of Anthropology*, Vol. 31, pp. 339-361.

Hebinck, Paul, and Bourdillon, Michael, 2001, 'Analysis of Livelihood', in *Women, Men and Work: Rural livelihoods in South-Eastern Zimbabwe*, Paul Hebinck and Michael Bourdillon, eds, Harare: Weaver Press, pp. 1-12.

Miller, Patricia H., 1989, 'Theories of Adolescent Development', in *The Adolescent As Decision-Maker: Applications to Development and Education*, in J. Worell and F. Danner, eds, London: Academic Press, pp.13-44.

Nannyonjo, Justine and Nsubuga, James, 2004, Recognising the Role of Micro Finance Institutions in Uganda, Kampala: Bank of Uganda.

Ogwal-Oyee, Fred, 2002, 'Life Skills for Ugandan Youth', in *Youth in Cities. A Cross-National Perspective*, Martin Tienda and William J. Wilson, eds, New York: Cambridge University Press, Pp. 247 – 266.

Tienda, Martin and Wilson, William J., 2002a, 'Comparative Perspectives of Urban Youth Challenges for Normative Development', in *Youth in Cities. A Cross-National Perspective*, Martin Tienda and William J. Wilson, eds, New York: Cambridge University Press, pp. 3 – 20.

Tienda, Martin and Wilson, William J., 2002b, 'Prospects and Retrospect: Options for Health Youth Development in Changing Urban Worlds', in *Youth in Cities. A Cross-National Perspective*, Martin Tienda and William J. Wilson, eds, New York: Cambridge University Press, pp. 269 – 277.

Tienda, Martin and Wilson, William Julius, eds, 2002c, *Youth in Cities. A Cross-National Perspective*, New York: Cambridge University Press.

14

La « prostitution alimentaire » juvénile à Yaoundé

Achille Pinghane Yonta

Introduction

Le phénomène de la prostitution constitue encore une préoccupation majeure dans les recherches. La difficulté à cerner cette réalité dans toutes ses dimensions naît du fait qu'elle est en interrelation avec plusieurs faits sociaux de telle sorte qu'on ne saurait l'appréhender de manière isolée. De ce fait, une concaténation de facteurs pourrait expliquer ce phénomène. À la suite de Paulette Beat Songue (1986 : 4) :

> la prostitution est un contrat dans lequel la partie donnante offre ses services sexuels contre une rémunération matérielle. (...) Pour attribuer le qualificatif de prostitué à un individu, il faudrait que celui-ci ait habituellement des rapports sexuels rémunérés.

Les jeunes n'échappent pas à cette réalité qui, non seulement peut trouver son essor tant dans les mobiles extrinsèques que intrinsèques, mais aussi pourrait s'inscrire de manière générale dans la recherche des moyens de subsistance. En ce sens, se prostituer serait donc une réponse aux difficultés quotidiennes que rencontrent les jeunes.

Cette réflexion est le fruit d'une enquête réalisée à Yaoundé sur une base purement qualitative. À partir des entretiens approfondis menés auprès des jeunes rencontrés dans les zones de prostitution formelle et des jeunes (filles et garçons) commerçants ambulants dans les quartiers, cette réflexion s'appuie sur l'analyse stratégique de Michel Crozier (1977) en vue de ressortir les stratégies que développent au quotidien les jeunes dans la recherche de la satisfaction de leurs besoins, de ressortir les contraintes socioéconomiques que subissent les jeunes, et enfin les marges de manœuvre dont ils disposent dans le système social. C'est pour cette raison qu'elle essaye de ressortir les facteurs, les catégories des personnes qui interagissent dans ce phénomène, le cadre légal et socioéconomique de cette pratique. Une classification peut être faite à ce niveau : la prostitution formelle ou officielle et la semi prostitution dite informelle et moins affichée. De par les stéréotypes sexistes portés sur le phénomène de la prostitution, cette analyse s'attarde plus sur les filles conformément aux représentations sociales qui pousseraient à penser que seules les filles se prostitueraient. Or, la prostitution (en tant que fait social au sens durkheimien du terme, et même fait social total selon l'appréhension de Marcel Mauss) ne peut se lire que dans les interrelations entre les trois composantes que sont les filles, les garçons et les éléments de l'environnement socioéconomique.

Le cadre social, économique et infrastructurel de la prostitution juvénile

Par cadre social, économique et infrastructurel de la prostitution, nous devons entendre l'ensemble des structures et activités qui rendent possible la pratique de la prostitution dans la ville de Yaoundé au Cameroun. Avant de traiter des infrastructures qui favorisent l'expansion de l'économie du sexe dans notre zone d'étude, il convient de nous appesantir sur la composante sociale de la prostitution juvénile.

Les acteurs de la prostitution

Plusieurs catégories sociales interviennent dans le phénomène de la prostitution et la transforment en un système. Entre autres, se démarquent les prostitué(e)s, les parrains de l'activité, les commerçants…

L'existence de la prostitution formelle est conditionnée dans une zone précise par la présence de cette catégorie sociale qu'on désigne sous l'appellation variée de : travailleuses du sexe, prostituées, filles de la joie, « bordelles », péripatéticiennes. La prostitution doit sa survie à ces filles de la rue habillées de diverses manières : en petite tenue, en taille basse, en petite culotte, en pagne, en « *kaba ngondo* », en collant, et qui laissent généralement entrevoir certaines parties sensibles du corps, question d'« exposer la marchandise » et d'attirer la clientèle. Cette catégorie est de niveau supérieur dans la mesure où les filles affichent leur activité et ne se cachent guère. C'est pour cette raison qu'elles sont appelées « filles du poteau ». Toutes les classes d'âge se retrouvent parmi ces prostituées, à la seule condition que le corps soit déjà mâture pour une telle pratique. Ce sont donc ces filles et ces femmes de la rue qui réussissent à braver l'hostilité de la nuit noire, non sans le soutien de leurs parrains, pour exercer cette activité génératrice de revenus. D'un point de vue légal, soutient Régis Vénacio Loumingou-Sambou (1999 : 128), « le droit de la femme de travailler la nuit dans les secteurs du commerce et des services a engendré une prolifération des métiers et des postes d'emploi convenant spécialement aux femmes ».

L'enquête menée à Yaoundé a donné lieu de constater que la permanence de la prostitution dans des zones précises est due en partie à la présence, dans ces lieux, d'une catégorie sociale que nous qualifions de parrains de la prostitution. En réalité, ces parrains sont constitués généralement des tenanciers des auberges, des bars, à coté desquels on peut ajouter les bandits. Pour les identifier, il suffit d'interroger les prostituées ayant un certain capital d'ancienneté. Un fort réseau de complicité règne entre les prostituées et les bandits, elles sont parfois des membres actifs des gans de voleurs.

En effet, ces parrains fonctionnent comme de véritables « anges gardiens » des prostituées de qui ils tirent des bénéfices. Les prostituées de Yaoundé jouissent auprès des parrains d'un droit de protection et de sécurité, certes conditionné, mais efficace. De ce fait, pour reprendre cet adage bien connu, « derrière une grande bordelle se cache un grand bandit ». Autrement dit, ce sont eux qui, à une heure avancée de la nuit, les accompagnent jusqu'au lieu où elles doivent emprunter soit une moto, soit un taxi pour regagner leur domicile.

Pour que l'économie du sexe prospère, il faut la présence de deux catégories d'acteurs incontournables : l'offreur (la prostituée) et le demandeur (le client) de la prostitution. Voilà pourquoi la notion de clientèle sera nécessairement prise en compte dans l'analyse des acteurs de la prostitution juvénile féminine. Il s'agit principalement d'une clientèle masculine. En effet, l'observation permet de noter que les prostituées interpellent presque toutes les personnes qui passent par des périphrases telles : « on part… », « allons baiser », « chéri, piquer… », « allons couper », « chéri je vais te faire ça bien au point où tu reviendras », « un coup ». De plus, cette clientèle est variée et est constituée d'hommes en civil tout comme d'hommes en tenue (militaires, gendarmes, policiers) qui fréquentent ces lieux arborant les tenues de service non pas toujours pour assurer leur fonction régalienne, mais aussi pour bénéficier des services des prostituées. Ces acteurs justifient parfois leur présence par la recherche des informations sur des gans de voleurs, ou encore par des missions d'enquête. Qu'ils soient en tenue ou en civil, leur présence peut être comprise en ce sens comme une stratégie qu'usent les agents secrets des forces de maintien de l'ordre pour démanteler certains gans de criminels, étant entendu qu'il existe une symbiose entre ces groupes déviants et les prostituées. Mais le port de la tenue serait un handicap à cette tâche, ce qui pousse à accréditer les thèses de l'existence des « filles à soldats » pour ne pas dire des prostituées pour soldats. Aussi est-il curieux de remarquer que dans les grandes villes du Cameroun en général, la présence des regroupements des hommes en tenue est synonyme de l'existence d'un point focal pour prostituées. De ce fait, la cartographie des grandes zones de prostitution à Yaoundé en particulier et au Cameroun en général montre un rapprochement entre celles-ci et les camps militaires et policiers, ce rapprochement va dans le sens où les deux activités iraient toujours de pair.

De la semi prostitution à la prostitution

Au cours de la collecte des données sur le terrain, les prostituées ont procédé à une spécification des périodes de forte demande assimilable aux « crues » et de faible demande « étiage ». Les périodes de crue dépendent de la date de paiement des salaires des employés de la fonction publique. Ce qui pousse à croire que ce secteur d'activités entretient d'étroites relations avec le secteur public dans la mesure où les fonctionnaires n'échappent pas à la prostitution, ou encore dès que l'État injecte de l'argent dans l'économie nationale, tous les secteurs en bénéficient.

Une autre période de crue est celle des vacances. Au Cameroun, pendant les vacances, les jeunes du secondaire et même du primaire se déplacent vers les grandes métropoles afin de se « débrouiller » dans le petit commerce de jour et même de nuit. Pour ceux qui exercent de jour, pour se divertir dans les soirées, ils se retrouvent de plus en plus dans ces zones de prostitution car ce phénomène est pour ces derniers étrange, nouveau, et attire curiosité et passion. Certains choisissent de mener leur activité de nuit et se retrouvent généralement dans ces lieux très « ambiancés » où il y a beaucoup de boites de nuit, de bars, et forcément beaucoup de personnes, de clients. Dans l'espoir de vendre leur marchandise, ils se trouvent plus en train d'observer les prostituées pour qui ils finissent par créer une admiration dans leur système de pensée, admiration qui, associée aux stratégies des prostituées, finit par les conduire à l'acte. Les propos du jeune Stanis (14 ans), rencontré dans une zone de prostitution (Mini-ferme, Yaoundé) à minuit sont révélateurs :

> Après la remise des bulletins, je suis venu à Yaoundé pour me débrouiller dans le petit commerce. Je vends la cigarette, les préservatifs et les bonbons. En journée, j'aide ma tante dans les travaux et je n'ai que la nuit pour vendre… La zone de Mini-ferme est propice car je suis en sécurité ici et je vends aussi bien. J'ai des clients prostituées qui prennent les préservatifs chez moi régulièrement et certaines préfèrent payer à la fin de la semaine le total de leur consommation… Une fois, une d'entre elles m'a proposé à la fin de la semaine de passer à l'acte sexuel avec elle en compensation de ce qu'elle me devait, j'ai refusé et à partir de ce jour, elle n'achète plus les préservatifs chez moi.

Certaines prostituées déclarent que pendant les vacances, beaucoup de jeunes connaissent leur premier rapport sexuel en ces lieux, et pour elles, ces jeunes paient sans « réfléchir », donc les prostituées exploiteraient leur naïveté. Les plus courageux, une fois passés à l'acte, stimulent les autres et, de ce fait, éloignent la peur, la frustration de ces derniers. Cette situation aboutit à la conséquence que beaucoup de jeunes passent leur temps à travailler pour l'argent d'un « coup », c'est-à-dire d'un passage chez une prostituée.

En ce qui concerne les filles, les mêmes mouvements de migrations de vacances s'observent. Dans certains lieux de prostitution, quelques jeunes filles offreuses de service déclarent être en vacances chez leurs aînés qui opèrent dans la même activité. On assiste de ce fait à une certaine reproduction sociale. Cette catégorie de jeunes filles prostituées est très sollicitée dans la mesure où les hommes la qualifient de « naturelle », « fraîche », de « non gâtée ». Certains clients pensent réduire le degré de risque de contracter une maladie en recherchant ces jeunes, qui, pour eux, sont à leurs premiers rapports et par conséquent, présentent moins de risque. « Quand je viens ici (Nvog ada, autre site de prostitution), c'est pour rechercher le « jus frais », c'est-à-dire les jeunes écolières. Quand elles ne sont pas là, je rentre chez moi » (Raymond, 42 ans).

Dans les vacances, le nombre de prostituées ne cesse de croître. Autour des zones de prostitution se développent des activités génératrices de revenus telle la vente du poisson braisé, les « call box ». La féminisation de ces activités oblige un questionnement dans la mesure où certains responsables (mères) entraînent leurs filles dans ces zones pour les aider dans le service, ainsi quand elles braisent, celles-ci se chargent de servir dans les bars. Les effets de l'alcool auxquels s'associe le désir de satisfaire la libido stimulent les individus à ne plus se contenter uniquement du poisson, mais aussi de la servante. La « force financière de frappe » est si forte que ces dernières résisteraient difficilement, surtout dans un contexte de vie précaire. Il en est de même pour les « call boxeuses ». Cette activité de prostitution est très difficile pour elles dans les débuts, mais après une période, elles s'habituent et en deviennent dépendantes au point d'en faire leur première source de revenus.

De retour dans les villes secondaires et dans les campagnes, ces jeunes, filles et garçons, ayant été habitués non seulement à un rythme de rapports sexuels intense mais surtout à la contrepartie, le type de relation qui sévissait dans ces zones se déstructure au profit de nouvelles plus contractuelles, c'est-à-dire capitalistes. De cette situation pourrait aussi s'expliquer la naissance des points de prostitution dans les campagnes ou dans les villes secondaires. De ce fait, les faits a priori urbains se retrouvent en milieu rural, il s'ensuit une difficile définition du milieu rural à partir de certaines activités. L'urbanisation du milieu rural sur ce point et bien d'autres est si forte et croissante qu'il faudrait redéfinir les critères de distinction du rural par rapport à l'urbain.

Un autre phénomène de prostitution qui ne cesse de prendre de l'ampleur est celui mettant aux prises les jeunes et les « grandes dames ». Les épouses des hommes d'affaires et des hommes politiques, en raison des multiples occupations de leurs époux ou encore de la dégradation des rapports dans le foyer, se trouvent de temps à autre abandonnées à elles mêmes, n'ayant personne à leur côté pour satisfaire leur besoin affectif. Pour résorber ce problème, elles recherchent des jeunes garçons à qui elles offrent tout ce dont ils ont besoin et entretiennent des rapports sexuels avec ces derniers. De plus en plus, bon nombre d'étudiants voient leur loyer et leur ration alimentaire assurés par ces dames. Les « grandes femmes » célibataires ou veuves n'échappent pas à cette logique. Ce phénomène peut aussi s'expliquer par les écarts d'âge au mariage dans la société camerounaise. A un certain âge, le mari ne peut plus satisfaire aux exigences sexuelles de sa (ses) jeune (s) épouse (s). De ce fait, recourir à un jeune célibataire est la solution idoine car les hommes mariés ne peuvent pas toujours être disponibles. Ce phénomène n'est pas seulement l'apanage des femmes, dans les circonstances similaires, les hommes recourent aux jeunes filles pour répondre à leur besoin affectif.

Dans les différents quartiers des villes, les jeunes filles, pour assurer leur pain quotidien se livrent à la vente des articles de beauté par la procédure de porte à porte avec toutes les conséquences qui peuvent en découler. Pour certaines, elles remplissent des commissions familiales par les mêmes techniques pour vendre les vivres, de la nourriture. Le fait de proposer des articles dans les domiciles, dans les cités des étudiants, poussent certaines personnes à leur proposer un autre marché : celui de la semi-prostitution. Ceux-ci procèdent généralement par la proposition suivante : « j'achète toute ta marchandise et en retour, ici et maintenant, tu entretiens des rapports sexuels avec moi » ; ou encore : « qu'as-tu gagné depuis que tu vends aujourd'hui, et si je t'offrais le double pour que tu passes deux heures avec moi ». Même si elles résistent une à deux fois, elles finissent par céder à cause de la précarité de leur statut et du contexte socioéconomique dans lequel elles évoluent. À ce niveau, l'objet de commerce officiel est la nourriture et l'objet officieux le corps, d'où le qualificatif de « prostitution alimentaire », on se vend en même temps que la nourriture. Cette réalité ne cesse d'inquiéter dans la mesure où le nombre d'enfants qui se livrent à ce commerce de porte à porte ne cesse de croître dans un contexte de lutte contre l'exploitation des enfants ou du travail des enfants. Sylvain Sorel Kuate Tameghe (1999 : 112) soutient :

> L'environnement économique a largement contribué et contribue à l'exploitation des enfants par le travail de deux manières complémentaires qui appellent néanmoins des commentaires distincts. Il s'agit de la quête d'un supplément de revenus par les ménages d'une part, et, d'autre part, de la recherche de l'amélioration de la production et des marges brutes de bénéfices par les ménages ou les employeurs.

De manière générale, « quand il y a des filles dans la rue, … elles sont pratiquement toutes prostituées, que ce soit de façon permanente ou, au moins, occasionnelle », (Bompard et Marguerat 1996 : 74)

Quelques facteurs explicatifs

Le relâchement du tissu familial qui implique la chute du contrôle des parents sur les jeunes constitue dans plusieurs cas le principal facteur explicatif de l'essor de la prostitution chez les jeunes. Bon nombre d'enfants se retrouvent dans la prostitution à cause du manque d'affection familiale, de la dégradation des relations entre les parents, entre parents et fils ou filles. Les membres des familles vivent de plus en plus dans des situations de hautes tensions. Yves Marguerat (2003 : 18) soutient cette analyse en écrivant que cette situation est « le produit de la déstructuration des familles …, qui entraîne un conflit entre parents et enfants, une atmosphère de violence domestique, ouverte ou sournoise, que les plus audacieux fuiront dans la rue ». À la suite des mots de Julie (29 ans), la situation de plusieurs filles s'explique par les tensions familiales :

> Ce que je vis aujourd'hui est le résultat des conflits que mon père avait régulièrement avec ma mère… Pour finir, les deux se sont séparés et je suis allée avec ma mère. Tout a commencé par la privation de liberté qu'elle m'imposait alors qu'elle n'était jamais là. Elle recevait chaque fois des hommes (des amants) et ne voulait guère qu'un garçon me rende visite… Nous avons discuté plusieurs fois et en fin de compte, j'ai décidé de me séparer d'elle pour aller rejoindre mon père. Il a décidé de ne pas m'accepter car j'avais choisi de défendre ma mère lors de la séparation. C'est pour cette raison que je vis seule et je me débrouille.

Le mot « débrouille » renvoie en réalité à je me prostitue pour avoir de quoi manger.

Cette situation est assez importante dans la mesure où les jeunes ne cessent de tenter de reproduire les comportements de leurs parents, de procéder à des copies dans un contexte où ces derniers n'arrivent plus toujours à cacher leur intimité en raison de l'étroitesse des maisons d'habitation. Dans certaines zones précaires à Yaoundé (Elobi, les marécages…), on dénombre plusieurs familles qui vivent dans une seule chambre avec un lit à étages et où les enfants se couchent au premier niveau et les parents au second. Cette réalité inhibe chez les enfants dès le bas âge des sentiments affectifs et sexuels. Le manque du contrôle social à son tour offre la possibilité aux jeunes de disposer de leur temps à leur guise sans licence ni tabou, surtout avec l'accroissement du phénomène des enfants confiés. De plus, les enfants se voient attribuer les chambres dont les ouvertures donnent sur la cour, ce qui leur donne toutes les possibilités dans leurs actions.

Les média constituent un facteur non négligeable. De par la prolifération des vidéogrammes pornographiques, d'une accessibilité très facile quel que soit l'âge, et par la mise à la disposition des jeunes des appareils (téléviseurs, VCD/DVD…) par les parents, sans compter qu'à partir des faibles coûts de ces derniers sur les marchés et donc bon nombre de jeunes s'en procurent aisément, le poids de ces éléments est non négligeable dans l'explication de ce phénomène. Certaines chaînes radio/télé ouvrent des tribunes aux jeunes pour poser leurs problèmes affectifs alors qu'ils ne disposent pas toujours des spécialistes pour leur répondre. Sous un autre angle, presque toutes les séries télévisées ont pour thématiques centrales, l'amour, le sexe et ce sont ces dernières qui captivent l'attention de la jeunesse. Les propos du jeune Prosper (17 ans) sont révélateurs :

> Pour me distraire, je regarde les films pornographiques quand mes parents ne sont pas là. J'achète moi-même ces vidéogrammes et je les cache dans ma chambre. C'est à partir de ces films que j'ai su ce qu'est l'amour, le sexe. Cette expérience me permet d'intervenir régulièrement dans les émissions telles : « À cœur ouvert »,

« Sentimental », « Cœur brisé »... qui passent dans les radios de Yaoundé. C'est très bien, car les jeunes filles et garçons posent anonymement tous leurs problèmes affectifs et les autres auditeurs réagissent à partir de leurs propres expériences ou encore des situations similaires qu'on regarde chaque fois dans les séries télévisées.

Le type d'habillement des acteurs de ces séries constituent pour la jeunesse des modèles et suscitent accommodation et imitation. Pour ces derniers, c'est être à la page, c'est-à-dire s'habiller, selon leur vocabulaire, en VCD (Ventre et Cuisse Dehors), DVD (Dos et Ventre Dehors), DN (Dos Nu), SD (Sein Dehors). Cette exposition du corps attire forcément curiosité et suscite dans les cerveaux des désirs, d'ailleurs que les jeunes qui se parent de ce type de vêtements sont bien conscients des effets, c'est ce qu'ils recherchent. Ils se remettent en question dans les cas où leur habillement n'attire pas curiosité et convoitise. Sur ce point, la prolifération des média en milieu urbain constitue une source de déperdition pour la jeunesse.

La situation de pauvreté généralisée dans les familles pourrait aussi expliquer ce phénomène. Dans la mesure où certaines familles n'arrivent pas toujours à satisfaire les besoins fondamentaux (scolarité, santé, nutrition) de leurs enfants, à les hisser au même rang ou presque que leurs camarades, les tentations se multiplient et finissent par devenir des contraintes. Par exemple, dans les cours de récréation, certains enfants affamés se voient offrir régulièrement des beignets par leurs camarades. À terme, les premiers deviennent dépendants des seconds et peuvent de ce fait céder à toute proposition. De ce fait, la vulnérabilité de certains enfants tire sa source dans la pauvreté non seulement de ces derniers, mais surtout de leurs familles. Paulette, fille de 17 ans en classe de seconde relate :

> J'ai connu mon premier amour (première relation sexuelle) en classe de quatrième. Depuis longtemps ce garçon m'offrait à manger à toutes les pauses, les récréations. Il est d'une bonne famille. Mes parents ne me donnent pratiquement rien, d'ailleurs c'est à peine que nous mangeons chez nous deux maigres fois par jour. Ce garçon m'aide beaucoup et je ne pouvais pas résister à sa demande, je ne pouvais compter sur personne d'autre.

La recherche de la satisfaction des désirs corporels est souvent à la base du début des rapports sexuels. De par l'orgueil de certaines personnes, leur cupidité, la multiplication des partenaires dans certains cas stimulent plus d'expériences en la matière et plus d'envie. À l'opposé, le manque d'expérience provoque chez plus d'un la frustration, des lacunes à combler. La sélection des partenaires se fait sous la base des critères bien précis. Les jeunes filles/garçons recherchent toujours un quelconque intérêt dans leurs relations. De manière générale, à la suite de Marie Paule Thiriat (2000 : 86) :

> Avec l'accroissement des difficultés économiques, il est probable qu'un nombre croissant de jeunes filles commencent précocement à avoir des relations sexuelles

pour des raisons financières. Le phénomène de « suggar daddies » (parallèlement à celui de « suggar mommies ») où les relations sexuelles s'échangent contre des cadeaux ou un soutien financier permettent de poursuivre des études (et autres) semblent prendre de l'ampleur en milieu urbain. (…) Les jeunes femmes entretiennent concurremment des relations matérielles (le chèque), des relations amoureuses (le choc) et d'autres socialement plus gratifiantes (le chic).

Les couples en milieu urbain ont l'habitude de retourner dans leur village d'origine prendre des petites filles aux fins de baby-sitting. Dans certains cas, la rémunération est directement versée chez leur parent resté au village. A ce moment, ces dernières ne jouissent pas du fruit de leur labeur et parfois ne trouvent pas toujours de solutions à leurs problèmes de jeunes filles. C'est pour cette raison qu'un ami, à mesure de répondre à ces besoins, est le bienvenu. Au cas où elle est assez grande, elle peut se passer pour « maîtresse » de son employeur. Cette réalité oblige les femmes à exiger de leur époux le recrutement des mineures pour les travaux de baby-sitting ou encore des garçons. Mme Nganda déclare :

> Il faut beaucoup se méfier des hommes avec les baby-sittings, elles sont dans plusieurs cas des coépouses officieuses. J'ai travaillé dans quatre familles comme baby-sitting, j'ai eu des relations sexuelles avec deux chefs de famille afin de préserver mon emploi et me prémunir des menaces de leurs épouses. Ma rémunération était parfois triplée officieusement, la dame envoyait ma vraie rémunération à mon père et le monsieur s'occupait de moi. Quand la dame a découvert, elle a exigé un garçon pour me remplacer. J'ai été remerciée dans une autre famille parce que je n'avais pas céder aux avances du chef de famille, seul un monsieur ne m'a fait des avances.

Cadre socioéconomique et infrastructurel de la prostitution des jeunes

Quelles structures favorisent la permanence de cette activité ? Deux catégories d'acteurs ont été retenues en fonction de leur niveau de participation. De ce fait, une composante socioéconomique majeure et une autre mineure peuvent être décelées. Au niveau de la composante socioéconomique majeure, l'attention est portée sur toutes les activités dont l'incidence sur l'économie du sexe est directe. Il s'agit des bars et des auberges. Le bar est le lieu de « fermentation » idéale du désir qui conduit à l'auberge. La relation entre le bar et la prostitution a été soulignée par Valentin Nga Ndongo (1975 : 93-94) en ces termes :

> C'est dans les bars populaires que la prostitution se pratique ouvertement et sur une grande échelle. … En général, la prostituée préfère aller au bar le plus proche de sa chambre, bar où elle finit par se faire remarquer de tout le monde, et s'assurer ainsi une clientèle régulière.

Sous un autre angle, Josiane Nomsi Tagne (1999 : 86) soutient qu'on trouve certaines jeunes filles qui dansent nus pour gagner de l'argent. « À Yaoundé par exemple, le « mimao » et le « madrigal », deux anciens snacks bars détenus jadis par les expatriés, aujourd'hui aux mains des Camerounais, poursuivent cette activité avec toutes les autorisations requises à cet effet ».

Les auberges interviennent dans le système en ceci qu'elles sont le lieu où prostituées et clients consomment l'acte sexuel. Dans certains milieux tels mini ferme à Yaoundé, la « passe » ou encore un « coup » vaut en moyenne mille francs CFA (1000 F CFA) dont cinq cent francs pour la prostituée et cinq cent francs pour le propriétaire de l'auberge ; à cet effet les propriétaires des auberges disposent des jeunes gestionnaires qui sont prostrés à l'entrée et sont chargés de pointer le nombre de fois que chaque prostituée est entrée avec un client. C'est sur la base de ce décompte que la prostituée payera les frais de location du lieu de consommation de l'acte sexuel. De ce fait, plus les prostituées ont des clients, plus les auberges voient leurs entrées financières s'accroître. Certaines prostituées préfèrent les forfaits de loyer en termes de nuitée. Ces gestionnaires sont dans la plupart des cas des jeunes de moins de 25 ans, ce qui pousse à s'interroger sur leur personnalité et, sur leur niveau de participation dans le système prostitutionnel. À côté de cette composante majeure, certaines activités se développent autour du commerce du sexe dans les points focaux.

Par composante socioéconomique mineure, nous entendons cet ensemble d'activités économiques qui se déroulent autour des sites de prostitution. Les vendeurs de porc, de « soya », les tenanciers de café-restaurants, les boutiquiers, les vendeurs de cigarettes, les « calls boxeurs », les « motos taximen », qui, chacun à sa manière soutiennent cette activité soit en apportant des ressources de sécurité, des ressources énergétiques, alimentaires, commerciales, soit pour des moyens de communication et de transport. Chacun de ces éléments contribue à la survie du système prostitutionnel. Les personnes qui exercent dans ces différentes activités sont dans la plupart des cas des jeunes qui recherchent les moyens de subsistance, d'autant plus qu'un (e) homme/femme « responsable » ne peut se retrouver à ces heures et de manière régulière en ces lieux. La recherche des moyens de survie oblige les jeunes à se livrer à toute sorte d'activité quel que soit le prix, l'essentiel pour ces derniers étant de pouvoir en tirer un profit économique capable d'assurer leur ration alimentaire. Seulement que, ces derniers, à force de constituer un maillon du système prostitutionnel, finissent par prendre une part active, c'est-à-dire par devenir prostituées ou clients.

Cadre légal et pratique de la prostitution

La prostitution est un phénomène social prohibé par la loi camerounaise. Dans cette perspective, l'Ordonnance n° 72/16 du 28 septembre 1972 dispose en son article 343 que : « est punie d'un emprisonnement de six mois à cinq ans, et d'une amende de 20 000 à 500 000 francs toute personne de l'un ou de l'autre sexe qui se livre habituellement, moyennant rémunération, à des actes sexuels avec autrui ». L'article 294 de cette même Ordonnance dispose :

> est puni d'un emprisonnement de six mois à cinq ans et d'une amende de 20 000 à 1 000 000 de francs, celui qui provoque, aide ou facilite la prostitution d'autrui ou qui partage même occasionnellement le produit de la prostitution d'autrui ou reçoit des subsides d'une personne se livrant à la prostitution.

Le rapport entre forces de l'ordre et prostituées est vu comme le rapport de la sanction à la connivence. En effet, si la prostitution peut être considérée comme une déviance à partir du cadre légal susmentionné, déviance au sens de Gilles Ferréol (2002 : 45) pour qui elle « désigne les comportements (individuels ou collectifs) qui, s'écartant de la norme, créent des dysfonctionnements et donnent lieu à une sanction », alors les forces de l'ordre devraient constituer une entrave à l'essor de cette activité. À partir du moment où elles se positionnent dans ce système, aux dires des prostituées, comme les principaux clients, ces derniers se résignent de leurs missions. Curieusement, dans ces lieux de prostitution, les agressions sont récurrentes à la différence que les prostituées sont très rarement attaquées. Ce qui pousse à penser que ces dernières disposent d'un système de sécurité où les forces de l'ordre participeraient à leurs protections dans le but de bénéficier des éventuelles remises. C'est pour cette raison que la présence régulière des patrouilles de gendarmerie et de la police en ces lieux ne constitue guère un obstacle au commerce du sexe. D'ailleurs, pour Ouédraogo, repris par André Soubeiga (2002), « l'émergence de la prostitution en Afrique remonte à la période coloniale en même temps que l'apparition des garnisons militaires ».

Conclusion

Au terme de cette analyse qui avait pour objectif d'étudier les facteurs sociologiques susceptibles de rendre compte de l'essor et de la permanence de la prostitution juvénile en dépit d'un cadre légal et normatif réprimant ce phénomène, force est de constater que maints éléments contribuent de manière significative dans ce système prostitutionnel. Non seulement le milieu social est totalement favorable, mais surtout l'existence d'un cadre infrastructurel et économique s'associe au relâchement du tissu familial, de la chute du niveau de contrôle des parents sur les jeunes, de la pauvreté ambiante, pour expliquer l'essor et la permanence de la prostitution des jeunes dans un contexte où ces derniers ne cessent de capitaliser la ressource sexe dans la recherche des moyens de survie au quotidien.

La prostitution, à l'analyse, est un « fait social total » dans la mesure où non seulement elle est extérieure aux individus, mais surtout dans la mesure où elles imposent des contraintes aux jeunes et embrassent tous les autres aspects de la vie socioéconomique et politique. Prétendre qu'on pourrait éradiquer la prostitution juvénile, qualifiée de prostitution alimentaire, dans la société camerounaise serait faire preuve d'irréalisme d'autant plus qu'il faudrait restructurer tous les aspects de la société, revoir le système social qui continue à être favorable pour le développement de cette acticité.

Références

Bompard, Françoise, et Yves Marguerat, 1996, « Le temps, l'argent et le sexe : Note sur la psychologie de l'enfant de la rue en Afrique noire », *Cahiers de Marjuva*, France, pp. 72-74.

Crozier, Michel et Erhard Friedberg, 1977, *L'acteur et le système*, Paris, Seuil.

Ferreol, Gilles, 2002, *Dictionnaire de sociologie*, Paris, Armand colin/VUEF, 3ᵉ édition.

Kuate Tameghe, Sorel Sylvain, 1999, « À la recherche des causes de l'exploitation des enfants par le travail », in *Formes contemporaines d'esclavage*, Études et documents de l'APDHAC, Yaoundé : Presses de l'UCAC, pp.101-114.

Loumingou, Sambou, et Régis Venacio, 1999, « Le travail de nuit des femmes », in *Formes contemporaines d'esclavage*, Études et documents de l'APDHAC, Yaoundé, Presses de l'UCAC. pp. 115-135.

Marguerat, Yves, 2003, « À la découverte des enfants de la rue d'Abidjan : Des visages et des chiffres pour les comprendre », in Yves Marguerat (sous la dir de), *Garçons et filles des rues dans la ville africaine : Diversité et dynamique des marginalités juvéniles à Abidjan, Nairobi, Antananarivo : Rapport de l'équipe de recherche Dynamique du Monde des Jeunes de la Rue : recherches comparées*, Paris, EHESS, pp. 15-36.

Nga Ndongo, Valentin, 1975, Ethnosociologie du « bar » à Yaoundé, mémoire de Diplôme d'Études Supérieures de Sociologie, Université de Yaoundé, Cameroun.

Nomsi Tagne, Josiane, 1999, « L'exploitation sexuelle des enfants dans la ville de Yaoundé », in *Formes contemporaines d'esclavage*, Études et documents de l'APDHAC, Yaoundé, Presses de l'UCAC, pp.77-99.

Beat Songue, Paulette, 1986, *Prostitution en Afrique, l'exemple de Yaoundé*, Paris, L'Harmattan.

Soubeiga, André, 2002, Prostitution et sida à Ouagadougou, in *http://books.google.com/books?id*

Thiriat, Marie Paule, 2000, « Les pratiques matrimoniales, au principe des systèmes de genre », in Michel Bozon et Thérèse Locoh, *Rapport de genre et question de population : Genre, population et développement*, Paris, INED, pp. 81-94.

15

The Trajectories of Survival of the Mungiki Youth in Nairobi

Susan M. Kilonzo

Introduction

The numerous socio-economic challenges facing the youth in developing nations today have meant that youth must find new approaches to address these challenges and utilize what is available in their surroundings to enable them survive. This is especially the case in the congested, poor living conditions of the sub-urban regions. In most of the developing nations, youth burgeon has been associated with increased crime in both urban and rural areas, activities that can be linked to unemployment and low literacy levels. In their effort to live within the limits of their surroundings, some youth in Kenya have formed groups, within which they identify and pool their efforts for wider recognition, besides enhancing their survival techniques in the midst of economic hardships. Some of these groups have been labelled as gangs, criminal groups and dangerous sects. Members of these groups, therefore, do not readily negotiate livelihoods with the general public but rather with their sect leaders, and they are sometimes known to make deals with political leaders to protect their interests.

Youth gangs may function as residual social institutions when other institutions fail, and provide a certain degree of satisfaction, order and solidarity for their members. Such gangs are present in both socialist and free-market societies and in both developing and developed countries. To exemplify, the Japanese Yazuka, the Chinese Triads, and the Italian Mafia are organized criminal gangs with youth street affiliates or aspirants (Irving 1990:172). Youth and children have been linked to some of these groups. For instance, the Japanese Ministry of Justice reports that 52,275 gangsters were arrested in 1983. The number of juveniles identified as members of gangster organizations who entered Japanese reformatory schools in 1983 was 713 or 12.3 per cent of the total 5,787 juveniles. In the African continent, juvenile and youth membership in criminal gangs has been evident.

Writing on youth gangs, Irving observes that today's gangs are a violent and insidious new form of organized crime. Heavily armed with sophisticated weapons, they are involved in drug trafficking, witness intimidation, extortion, and bloody territorial wars. Dowdney (2003), studying the involvement of youths in gang violence in Rio de Janairo, argues that many children who are armed with guns have few other options economically, educationally, and in terms of protection and status. Jensen (1999:76) in his research on the discourses of coping with violence in South Africa's Cape flats mentions that no government has been able to solve the socio-economic crisis of her people or the high levels of crime and violence, and this inability has always been very highly resented. Jensen, borrowing from a number of researches and interviews, explains that the type of violence within a given group is dependent on a number of factors including age, gender, class, housing, and race.

Different groups have been used to perpetrate crime and violence to benefit their members, and as Stephen Ellis (1999) explains, in the context of the discernible drift away from Western modernity towards the re-traditionalization of society, which anthropologists and social analysts have identified in contemporary Africa, youths have adopted diverse aspects of traditional cultures, including initiation rites and religious beliefs and practices, as ideological foundations of their resistance. These characteristics are typical of the Mungiki sect in Kenya. In adopting these features, the Mungiki sect followers claim to be fighting the 'ills' of the state.

On a different twist, African states have at certain times used such groups to perpetrate crime and violence, especially when this is deemed beneficial to a particular group of leadership in the government. The membership of these movements largely constitute youth, and though in some cases they are in conflict with the existing legal frameworks, they have found refuge under existing corrupt leadership in some African governments, who shield them but on certain conditions. The crimes perpetrated by these movements deserve theoretical and practical analysis. As we explore the nature of these movements, we are not ignorant of the fact that there exist economic crises in most of the African countries, with the youth facing the blunt effects of poverty, unemployment, and non-literacy.

As a contribution to this volume on negotiating livelihoods, this chapter takes the extreme perspective in which the youth may not be keen to negotiate the challenges facing their livelihoods with the public, but do negotiate partly with their leaders and the state, in which case they engage the ruling authorities through their ideologies. The chapter therefore questions whether these ideologies have helped the group to succeed in sorting out the social and economic crisis faced by the youth, and considers survival mechanisms employed by this group. The trajectories of engaging the government and different religious groups in Kenya in their endeavour to survive in the city will be discussed. These highlights will read deeper into the social and economic activities of disfranchised youth, and whether we can use these to exonerate the Mungiki of what the public and the governing authorities have claimed to be criminal activities. This is because, as Mkandawire (2002:181) observes, a disturbing feature of some of the post-independence armed rebel movements in Africa have been the extremely brutal and spiteful forms of violence that they have unleashed and inflicted on fellow citizens.

The situation and nature of the research behind this chapter did not allow much attention to the first-hand views of Mungiki. However, I managed to solicit information from six sect ex-members who insisted that their names should be concealed for security purposes and therefore the names used in the text are pseudonyms. I also listened to conversations held on radio and television programmes and watched documentaries from both Kenyan and European journalists on the activities of the group. These were integrated with the personal experiences and observations to provide an analysis of the findings presented.

Conceptualizing Youth Criminality: A Focus on Mungiki

Cities in sub-Saharan Africa have experienced the fastest population growth and most of the future population growth in the region is expected to occur in the urban areas (Fotso 2007). Fotso explains that rapid urbanization has been occurring amidst stagnating or declining economies, in which case local and national authorities are unable to provide decent living conditions and basic social services, which are already strained. Between 1980 and 2000, the urban population in sub-Saharan Africa grew by almost 4.7 per cent per year according to the United Nations, and per capita gross domestic product according to World Bank dropped annually by 0.8 per cent (2007:208). Consequently, a rapidly increasing proportion of urban dwellers in sub-Saharan Africa are living in overcrowded slums and shanty towns amidst filthy conditions: uncollected garbage, unsafe water, poor drainage and sewers. This poses a challenge not only to their health, but also to their psychological wellbeing. Within these demeaning living conditions, there have arisen needs for social and economic security for groups of people who identify with each other in the quest for survival and protection. The massive powers of these groups have been the main cause of stability and resistance, as well as their continued growth in membership. Moreover, the malleable nature of such movements perplexes the public on their objectives.

Musambayi (2005:507) notes that mobilization and contestation over economic spaces, and the resultant voluntary servitude, have the effect of engendering instrumentalized violence that tends to narrow associational space as variegated social groups turn against one another at the behest of the state. Musambayi explains that this process means rolling back of the logic of stateness, especially the state's need to dominate the means of violence in the society.

This chapter draws examples from the renowned Kenyan Mungiki sect. The focus is on the malleable nature of the sect, a characteristic that has helped the group change its appearance in the Kenyan public space, hoodwinking both the legal frameworks and the common citizen only to emerge at different times with what has been conceived as dangerous ways of surviving in the public space. On the one hand, we need to reckon: in the words of Loffman (2008:126), 'Understanding conflict does not simply involve engaging with the historical reasons for it. For processes of violence to be properly understood, and to have meaning for readers, the local must be examined in conjunction with the national.' Accordingly, to comprehend the criminal activities behind any youth group, it is necessary to explore the contribution of the state. Some authors have argued that the involvement of Mungiki in criminal activities can be attributed to the push by the state (see the works of Klopp 2002; Ruteere 2008; and Kagwanja 2005). For this reason, Mungiki might justify their unlawful actions because of the failure of state.

Brief History

Early in the history of Mungiki, as Wamue (2001) propounds, it was a paragon of retraditionalization of society, in which the leaders used traditional forms of mobilization and beliefs as instruments for restoring moral order and empowering the dispossessed. However, Anderson (2002) has argued that when the movement stepped outside its rural base and ventured into the milieu of Kenya's urban estates, shanties, and slums, it absorbed some criminal elements and was transformed into a large violent gang that was gradually co-opted by sections of the ruling elite to serve its patrimonial interests.

Mungiki is believed to have been started in the late 1980s by two cousins, Maina Njenga and Ndura Waruinge, when they were still young boys in secondary school. Under this leadership in the late 1980s, the movement split from *Hema ya Ngai wi Mwoyo* 'Tent of the Living God' led by Gonya wa Gakonya in Laikipia (Wamue 2002). Initially the movement took a religious perspective by trying to enhance African culture as a way towards 'liberation' (refer to Gecaga 2007). In the early 1990s, during the land and ethnic clashes of the Rift Valley Province, the movement, mainly composed of the youth aged between 15 and 30, fought for the land rights of the Gikuyu. This saw the first metamorphosis of the 'religious sect' into a militaristic group. According to Waruinge[1], the co-founder of the sect, Mungiki therefore operated as a defence force against the predominantly ethnically Kalenjin militias that attacked Gikuyu settlements (also see Wamue 2001). In the late 1990s, the group metamorphosed from a rural religious sect with political overtones into an urban militia. They began to dominate the *Matatu* (public transport) industry in Nairobi. Using the *Matatu* industry as a spring-board, the group moved into other areas of commerce, such as garbage collection, construction, and even protection racketeering. They did not, however, shed their first image of religiosity: this continues to be used as a tool to recruit members to the sect.

Wamue explains that Mungiki comes from the word *muingi-ki*, meaning 'we are the public', which Githogo (2000) compares with the Mau Mau, who in the 1950s and 60s would identify themselves as, 'it is us'. *Muingi* is a term derived from the word *nguki* which means *irindi* (crowds) and reflects a belief that destiny entitles people to particular place of their own. Wamue describes Mungiki as heir to a long tradition of religio-political revivalism that dates back to the early stages of anti-colonial resistance, which in turn was characterized by a total rejection of modernity. The mandate of Mungiki, then, was to call people to return to Gikuyu's indigenous beliefs and practices, and condemn the white man's culture. Mungiki leaders developed the sect's teachings (*kirira*) and used especially the Old Testament teachings which form the sect's Bible (*Gikunjo*) to justify these teachings. They condemned social immorality such as prostitution and called for a return to female genital mutilation, which they justified by noting that when the practice was taken seriously in the traditional communities, there was no immorality and subsequently no HIV and AIDS. They used this ideology forcefully to circumcise women both in the villages and in the city streets. They also stripped naked women who wore trousers and miniskirts.

The initial recruitment process entails the use of *Gikunjo*, and there is some level of acceptance by the initiates that the movement is inclined to Gikuyu traditional religion. Those who accept to receive *Kirira* become followers and initiate others by teaching them the way of Mungiki. A sect ex-member[2] explained that in most cases, the sect's criminal activities are not revealed to the initiates until they take the final oath. In taking the oath of secrecy, members agree not to reveal the secrets of the group and at this stage they go through very brutal physical attacks by the sect elders, which are meant to harden them. They swear not to deviate but to protect 'those of their own', meaning sect members. They swear to choose to protect the sect's secrets and members over their families.

Mungiki has metamorphosed to conceal their identity. Mungiki's religiosity and their initial call for people to return to the Gikuyu traditional cultures has since been replaced by other faces as the following sections reveal. However, they still claim to maintain their religiosity, which is evident in the recruitment procedures.

A Religious Sect?

Mungiki trace their roots to religion, and specifically the Gikuyu Traditional African Religion, more specifically a splinter sect, the Tent of the Living God. Kagwanja (2003) argues that Mungiki's ideological bloodline can be traced from such revivalist movements as *Dini Ya Msambwa, Legio Maria, Akorino* and more recently Tent of the Living God – African-initiated churches and movements that are very common in the Kenyan public space. The common thread that joins these movements is that they have rallied their followers behind traditional values to challenge the orthodoxy of the mainstream churches as well as injustices by the state. To Kagwanja, this well-intentioned movement, whose concern was the restoration of moral order, was only infiltrated and given a bad tag by the KANU regime in the run up to the 2002 general election.

However, the Mungiki legend, according to Makokha (2000), has grown out of the mysterious and little understood ideology and theology of the group. Its members have a god (Ngai) on Mount Kenya (Kirinyaga) whom they worship and to whom they pray. So far no written doctrines about Mungiki as a religious sect have been availed to the public, but Mungiki publicly advocate a return to 'African traditions'. Githongo (2000) explains that Mungiki advocates cultural and religious revival and this has alarmed church leaders and fervent Christians, who have occasionally denounced the activities of the sect.

Mungiki baptizes new members in a river, and with fire. After the initiates are immersed in a river, they walk through smoke as the elders chant certain traditional religious words. Their holy communion is tobacco-sniffing. There are rituals performed, and religious practices used by Mungiki members, which according to Smart's (1968) criteria would warrant Mungiki being classified as a religious sect. The dimensions as explained by Smart include: myths, rituals, social institutions, doctrines, ethical teachings and religious experiences. All these are typical characteristics of the sect. They baptize their converts who also take oaths and swear by saying, 'May I die if I reveal our secrets.' They also perform rituals such as offering of sacrifices, which are believed to protect members; sniffing tobacco; praying while facing Mount Kirinyaga; and keeping unshaven hair (dreadlocks). Their dress code is the African garb made from animal skin. Although some of them have been spotted wearing animal skins, to conceal their identity, this regalia has been used only on special occasions.

Their faithfulness to their religiosity has, however, been determined by the political circumstances of the country. This implies that they change their religious affiliations at different times to camouflage their identities. One interviewee revealed that they rent church buildings on Sundays after a Christian group has held a Sunday service.

In early 2000, many of the Mungiki members converted to Islam, including the co-founder Ndura Waruinge, who was named Ibrahim Ndura Waruinge (according to Panafrican News Agency 2000). However it was realized that this was in a bid to deceive the government. In December 2000, Waruinge and 50 sect members attended a Church service before being arrested, and this was a clear act of camouflage. This act met great criticism from Sheikh Banda who pointed out that Islam would not allow hypocrisy. A few days later, Waruinge was released from police cells and he proclaimed that he was saved. He changed his name to Ezekiel Ndura Waruinge and started his own church. In October 2009, when Maina Njenga, the national chair, was released from jail, he was prayed for and converted to become a Christian at the Jesus is Alive Ministries, a church headed by Dr Bishop Margaret Wanjiru, the Assistant Minister of housing and the member of parliament of Starehe Constituency in Nairobi. He promised to disband Mungiki. However, in early November 2009, the police arrested 200 Mungiki sect members involved in criminal activities in one of the Nairobi estates. In December the same year, police arrested several sect members in Murang'a District, whom they claimed were extorting money from the public service vehicle operators.

Militaristic Group?

The failure of the state to address the core issues of land and ethnic clashes that led to formation of civil militia groups in the early 1990s (see Klopp 2002; Ndegwa 1997 and Odhiambo 2003, who have tried to analyze the origin and causes of land and ethnic clashes in Kenya) might be used to explain how Mungiki youths joined the 'drift into collective social deviance' characteristic of the 1990s. This was an era in which vigilantism and the privatization of violence increased and was profitable. This violence was privatized in consultation with politicians and with their approval. Politicians sought after and employed the services of private militia to execute their political missions, and cripple individuals and groupings within the political opposition.

In 1991, when ethnic clashes broke out in the Rift Valley province, which to a great extent were instigated by the political wing (Klopp 2002), Mungiki metamophorsed from being a religious sect to fight for '*Vizazi vya wapiganaji uhuru*' – the descendants of freedom fighters – who were the Gikuyus living in Rift Valley Province, especially in Molo and Kuresoi regions. They fought other vigilante and militia groups including the Kalenjin warriors. At this time, as rightly observed by Turner and Brownhill (2001), Mungiki could be linked to *Muungano wa Wanavijiji* (the organization of villagers), established among the slum dwellers of the city to fight eviction and protect tenants from exploitation. In the face of land privatization programmes sponsored by the World Bank, which tend to increase rather than alleviate landlessness, the urban-based *Muungano wa Wanavijiji* and the massive Mungiki have arisen to address, among many other realities, the immediate needs of the impoverished for land. There are a wide range of researches that have documented land and ethnic squabbles in Kenya.[3] The squabbles have always left reports on deaths and displacement of Kenyans.

From the ethnic clashes, in which Mungiki tried to protect the Gikuyu, the realization was that a great damage had been caused and many Gikuyus had been displaced, rendering them landless. Mungiki had a large number of followers composed of the youth who had participated in the land and ethnic clashes. With the challenges of landlessness and homelessness on the one hand, and the strengths of a crowd on the other, Mungiki then transformed into an urban sect, moving into the capital city, Nairobi, in the late 1990s, violently demanding conformity to Gikuyu traditions (particularly targeting women). After their arrival in the city, with time they realized there were more open ways of gaining financial support. Emerging during Moi's repressive system as an expression of youth resistance and voice of moral ethnicity, Mungiki was co-opted and transformed into a deadly instrument of political tribalism and terror, as Kagwanja (2005) argues. The group agreed to be used by the KANU government.

Economic Ventures for Mungiki's Survival

One of the perceived reasons why Mungiki moved into the city is the economic challenge in the areas where ethic clashes had been eminent in the early 1990s. Once they became an urban militia, they not only took over the *Matatu* (public service vans) industry, but also found their way into the informal settlements. Mungiki operates most extensively in Nairobi slums, where poverty and crime are pronounced. Before the ethnic clashes after the contested 2007 election in Kenya, Mungiki had organized itself to extort money from slum residents. Every resident in the slums had been paying a sum of money to the organization, in exchange for protection against theft and property damage. The gang also 'manned' public toilets and charged a fee for their use. These activities mark 'small' sources of money. Their major source of income is the *Matatu* industry. They collect money from drivers and conductors of public transport. It has been reported that those who have failed to honour Mungiki's demands have fallen victims of dreadful wrath. In May 2007, the *Matatu* operators raised an outcry complaining that Mungiki extorted most of their profits. They were forced to part with Kshs. 200 ($2.5) for every trip made. After the outcry, Mungiki embarked upon a murderous campaign. Members of public would wake up to severed heads on poles, and body parts strewn in bushes in attacks blamed on Mungiki. This drew an armed response from Kenyan security forces, which stormed the Mathare area and killed 100 of its members. These killings did not deter the members of the sect from extorting money from *Matatu* owners. In January 2007, it had been estimated that the sect netted Kshs 90 million (approximately 1.3 million dollars) a day nationwide and this had sparked the May-June 2007 battles with *Matatu* operators (Reuters 2007).

Besides these sources, Mungiki also sources money from small businessmen and women. In Kihuro division in Central Kenya, the business operators would part with Kshs 50 while the homesteads would pay Kshs 100, said to be security fee. Those who did not comply with these demands were objects of violence from the sect members. The sect members also killed policemen who interfered with their extortion of money from the public.

Mungiki members provide at a cost services of garbage collection, toilet cleaning, illegal power installation, and house security. Those who defy orders to pay face the risk of attack by group members. These are services that should freely be provided to the slum dwellers by the government.

Lately, the movement has been extorting money from peasant farmers in Central Province. They have also been forcefully recruiting youth to the movement and those who defy are subjected to the terror by the members. This was evident on 20 April 2009 when the gang slashed dead 29 young men in Kirinyaga and Nyeri East districts of Central Province, who had attacked and killed three sect members believed to have been forcefully recruiting young men from the said districts (*Daily Nation*, Nairobi 2009).

The structure of the movement and how the activities of the organization are managed are also mesmerizing. An interview with one of the sect ex-members indicated that the members themselves hardly benefit from the collections, although they may withhold some of the proceeds. The sect leaders benefit the most. They live in expensive mansions in Nairobi's affluent areas. The collections are also used to train more initiates and bail out the arrested sect members. The interviewee indicated that before one is fully initiated, he or she can ask for favours from the sect and they are granted. However, once they become sect members there are no more favours. One is supposed to serve the sect wholeheartedly. An ex-member of Mungiki, Mungai (not his real name), compared joining the group to 'stepping on a burning cooker and having a hot cooking plate placed on one's head'. The fear is that one cannot deviate from serving the group. On the other hand, involvement in these activities is risky because members are continuously on the run from the arm of law. Members are supposed to protect each other from the public (which is seen as an enemy), and in the process, the group uses terror to scare the public. The ex-member indicated that the initiated members are meant to support the leaders. To Mungai, some members are leaving the sect because they are used as tools to commit violence and to obtain money for the leaders. He gave an example of the leader Maina Njenga, who then was in prison, and said that his family lived like royalty in Komarock (an estate in the outskirts of Nairobi). He commented that ex-members lived under fear of attack from the current members. He also pointed out that the sect would never be completely eliminated because it had accumulated many followers over the years and even if the leadership wanted to dissolve the organization, the members might not yield because in one way or another, it was a source of livelihood for disfranchised Gikuyu youth.

Political Movement

The group has a flag of red, green, black, and white in that order from top to bottom; red symbolizes blood, black the African people, green the land, and white is the symbol for peace (Wamue 2001). They claim to spearhead African socialism and that their other professed goals are to fight bad governance and social ills facing society and to establish a just nation. They claim to have the Mau Mau blood – that the Mau Mau fought for land, freedom, and religion, and so do they. Wamue, however, emphasizes that the Mau Mau did not achieve all their goals. Further, Waruinge has argued that 'Kenya today is controlled by the International Monetary Fund, the World Bank, the Americans, the British, and the Freemasons. It cannot initiate its own development. All these have promoted tribalism, nepotism and individualism, rather than socialism' (http://en.wikipedia.org/wiki/mungiki, accessed 19 May 2008).

With their ideology of socialism, it is expected that the members would take a keen interest in the less fortunate in the society, and fight the present social and economic crises in the country. Socialism developed in part in response to what were perceived as the failures of liberal individualism, emphasizing instead the values of social and economic equality and social cooperation. It saw social and economic inequality and exploitation as arising from the institutions of private property and capitalistic competition, for which liberal individualism was held to provide the ideological support. The socialist critique argues that the liberal individualist values of liberty and political democracy remain empty or merely formal if the material means of well-being are lacking or are so inequitably distributed that some individuals are totally dependent on others for their livelihood (Gould 1988). Socialist theory emphasizes the centrality of social and collective interest – whether as class interest or as human solidarity – as a motive for action. Thus socialist theory proposes social and economic equality and social cooperation as norms for the good society. Mungiki's wrath and vengeance as released on innocent citizenry, and especially the poor in the slums and peasant farmers in the village, however, did not indicate socialism.

From a different perspective, Kagwanja explains that KANU used Mungiki in 2002 to ensure that the 'Uhuru Project', in which Uhuru Kenyatta the son of Jomo Kenyatta (first President of independent Kenya) was Moi's (the then President) preferred presidential candidate. Waruinge went so far in his support to claim that Uhuru Kenyatta was himself a Mungiki. During this time the Mungiki also expanded their revenue-making activities. They controlled *Matatu* trade in Nairobi, supplied illegal electricity in the slums, and stepped into the space left by the failure of the police force in Kenya to provide private security. Unfortunately for Moi and Uhuru, Kibaki of National Alliance Rainbow Coalition won and as Kenya crossed the post-Moi era, Mungiki entered a new phase of becoming a fully-fledged criminal group. Less than a month after the elections, violence erupted leading to deaths of over 40 people in different estates of Nairobi. This triggered the new government to ban the group in 2002 (Murunga 2008).

There were allegations at that time that Mungiki members had strong links to old KANU government and to some MPs in Kibaki's government. These allegations were given some support six years later in April 2008 when a group of politicians calling themselves elders from Central Kenya appeared publicly to demand the release of the National Director of Mungiki, Maina Njenga. This was after two other leaders of the movement, including Njenga's wife, had been shot dead by the police. Njenga Karume (former Minister of Defence), Elias Mbau (Member of Parliament of Maragua), Joseph Kamotho (former Member of Parliament of Mathioya), Jane Kihara (former Member of Parliament), and Nyaga (an ODM affiliate) all demanded the release of the leaders of the outlawed sect and initiation of dialogue between the government and the sect.[4] The ex-member Mungai claimed that some of the political leaders were sect members. He noted that these leaders did not attend *k)gano* (sect meetings) but always sent money to the leaders secretly. This enabled them to use the sect for their political ambitions when a need arose.

The demands for the release of leaders were made amidst fears that the sect members would revive the post-election violence that had ended in the month of March 2008, and which had led to ethnic cleansing in several parts of the country. At the end of March 2008, and up to mid-April, the sect members had paraded themselves as Kenya National Youth Alliance, and descendants of freedom fighters. Through their leader, the late Gitau Mwangi, who had been declared by Mungiki as the group's spokesperson (Waruinge and Njenga were in custody), they indicated that they were defending their rights which had been violated by the police, who were out to destroy them. Deceiving Kenyans by using different names for the movement, they named senior police officers such as Erick Kiraithe (a police spokesperson) and warned them of dire consequences if the police continued to kill the group members, who were then alleged to be over one million and spread in all parts of the country.

Following the demands of the politicians that the group leaders should be released, the public, through human rights groups and the media, raised questions on the existence of this group. How could such a group comprising mainly youths, most of whom were non-literate, display such organization, with calculated and targeted moves directed to either the government or the citizens? At one point, the sect leaders threatened to make publicly known their political organizers, who were alleged to be in the government. In April 2008, there were claims from Mungiki that they had been promised their leaders would be released but that the promises had been broken. This was the reason they had to release their anger on police and the fellow citizens as a way of communicating to the politicians who made the promises.

In September 2008, after four months of quiet, the group re-appeared in Nakuru, the fourth largest town in Kenya, and the headquarters of Rift Valley province. Parading as the Progress Party Alliance, the movement held a political rally in the town without government permit (in breach of the law that any public gathering, especially one political in nature, must acquire a prior permit), with the late Njuguna Gitau (a Mungiki spokesperson) addressing the public in the presence of the police.

In April 2009, it took a massacre by the Mungiki sect to awaken the government. As already noted, Mungiki youth killed 29 men in Kirinyaga and Nyeri East districts of Central Province in one night. .From the massacre, the then police spokesperson through the media pointed out that the political leaders linked to Mungiki were to be named, and that the police had several files containing names of those affiliated to the group and who were yet to be approached and probed. The government argues that there is need to enhance community policing, but there are indicators that some police are members of the group. In the arrests made lately (4 November 2009) in Ndandora estate in Nairobi, one of the 200 suspects was an area chief (the administrator in charge of a division). The study having explained and given evidence that some of the political leaders are affiliated to the sect, it might be a challenge for the government officials to be trusted by the citizens and community members on issues concerning security in as far as Mungiki is concerned. This is a group that has existed for over three decades with the government doing very little to tame its terror activities. On the other hand, amidst the socio-economic challenges in Kenya, the youth have to survive in one way or another. For me, the activities of Mungiki are just an indicator of the hardships facing the youth in the country, and therefore, they manifest one way in which the disfranchised youths have tried to show the government there is need to   deal with the problems facing the youth; otherwise crime will be inevitable.

Towards Understanding Youth Movements: Exonerating Mungiki?

Lonsdale (1986:130) argues that although youth rebellion was a feature of the Mau Mau war against British colonialism in the 1950s in Kenya, with the disintegration of the multi-ethnic nationalistic coalitions immediately after independence, youth identity like ethnicity was instrumentalized and transformed by patrimonial politics into a weapon in the hands of elders. Kagwanja (2005) explains that at the height of the Nyayo era (1982-1990) President Moi revitalized the KANU youth wing as a powerful instrument for monitoring and punishing public dissent and asserting his authority. Terror and extortion were perpetrated by party youth on commuter buses, taxis, and kiosk businesses supported by a patron-client relation in a classic demonstration of the state using criminal methods to defend the status quo. Kagwanja further argues that founded by the youth in late 1980s, Mungiki could be seen as a true child of the age of resistance to Moi's patrimonial rule and a sign of the increasing use of generational politics as an idiom for the accountability of state power. Further, he underscores the fact that between 1991 and 1998, violence linked to tribal militias such as the Maasai Morans, Kalenjin warriors, Chinkororo of Kisii, Sungusungu in Kuria (who were later to extend their tentacles to Kisii land) and Kaya Mbombo of the Digos of Coast, claimed an estimated 3,000 lives and displaced nearly half a million Kenyans. These observations lead to the likely conclusion that Mungiki and related groups were founded to respond to the 'ills' of a state that could not protect the vulnerable in the society.

In a study of children in the drugs trade in Rio de Janeiro, Dowdney points to similarities between children involved in violence and child soldiers: they comprise armed factions, with military weapons that control territory, people and resources within the *favelas*, and operate within a command structure (2003:10). There are parallels with Mungiki, who changed from a rural militaristic group to an urban militia for economic gain, and use weapons but for a different cause. The group is financially stable and can manage members' activities. Once they emerge in a given locality, they take charge and freeze business activities and curtail people's movement.

The incident described above of the massacre of *Matatu* drivers and conductors in May-June 2007, came after President Mwai Kibaki had warned the sect members of dire consequences for unlawful acts. This was an indication that the sect members' demands from the public transport industry had been defied since most of those who suffered were drivers and *Matatu* conductors. It was also an indicator that the sect did not have any respect for the government leaders, not even the President.

In an effort to propagate their 'religion', Mungiki have publicly displayed their loathing for Christianity and other forms of religion that do not conform to the traditional religion that they advocate. For instance, in November 2006, Waruinge declared war on the Freemasons building, referring to the members as a devil worshipers. He observed that most of the members were politicians. A group of 400 sect members with match boxes and petrol in their hands had marched along Nyerere Road singing songs and occasionally sniffing tobacco on their way to the premises where the Freemason temple is located. They chanted, 'We will burn it down.... It promotes devil worship,' but were dispersed by police before they could torch the building. In retaliation, they burned down Muranga and Nyahururu police stations, which are miles away from Nairobi (http://whow.kumekucha.com, 16 August 2008). This is an indication that the group is coordinated in various parts of the country, and deterrence in one city does not indicate complete paralysis of the sect.

Mungiki have therefore devised mechanisms that are meant to benefit the sect as they seek to make known their demands to the government. It is unfortunate that their violence takes the lives and destroys property of innocent citizens, though to Mungiki this is meant to send a word to the government. The section that follows contrasts the activities of Mungiki with their ideology of socialism.

Activities Versus Ideology

The history of the formation of Mungiki as indicated by one of the leaders, Waruinge, was to fight for the rights of the poor and disenfranchised, and especially to propagate socialism in a state that encouraged individualism and capitalism after the introduction of structural adjustment programmes in Kenya. An observer of Mungiki activities would state otherwise about the objectives of the group. Take, for instance, the 2002 Kenyan general elections when, through their leader Waruinge, the movement agreed to be used by the KANU government to obtain the Gikuyu vote in support of Moi's chosen successor Uhuru Kenyatta. A group that had opposed the government since its inception was used by the same government as a campaigning tool.

Second, it is evident that, since 1996, when they became urban-based, Mungiki have been extorting money from slum dwellers. If their objectives were to propagate socialism and fight for justice, especially for the poor, why would they then demand money for security, garbage collection, sanitary fees, and for power installation from the poor slum dwellers? Why not target the rich in the community? Their brutal attacks on *Matatu* drivers and conductors, who happen to be employees, is questionable. Most of the *Matatu* operators in Nairobi are Gikuyus and the question is: if Mungiki have Gikuyu roots are in search of equality and are 'fighting for the descendants of freedom fighters', why then would they attack 'their own'? Why would they seek to provide security in central province villages, which are mainly occupied by the Gikuyu ethnic grouping? Kenya is made up of over 42 tribes and so the Gikuyu youth are not the only marginalized group.

Mungiki are wise to be hands-on in whatever is happening in the political arena. The knowledge of political issues has therefore enhanced their arguments, and they have subsequently used politics tactfully to argue out their cases. If it were about socialism *per se*, then the agenda would be a call to all to embrace their ideology, with a clearly laid down constitution and not ethnic kind of affiliation.

The group uses politicians and the politicians as well use them to promote their interests and achieve their ends. This is the reason why despite the killings of innocent Kenyans by Mungiki their 'sponsor' politicians would call for the release of the leaders of the outlawed sect. Following Maina Njenga's release from the jail, and his pledge that he would disband Mungiki and call on the political leaders that support the group to stop it so as to bring to an end the unlawful activities of the group, the eyes now are focused on the future of this sect.

Projected Future of Mungiki

Mungiki is a group that emulates the Mau Mau, though with a different objective. The Mau Mau was purposely fighting for independence. Mungiki is not. It is evident from the above discussion that Mungiki's actions in the Kenya public space are meant to enable them survive economically. However, the problems of land, poverty and unemployment in Kenya are not likely to be solved in the near future. They continue to affect the youth more than any other group. Mungiki, and any other similar groups, such as the Kisii vigilante groups, and Sabaot Land Defence groups that are formed to enable the members negotiate their livelihoods, are likely to persist for long in the country. Apart from being well established in terms of numbers, which are relatively well spread in three of the most populated Kenyan provinces, Mungiki has well-controlled and reliable sources of income. When all this added to the advantage of political support, Mungiki emerges as a group that is likely to remain strong.

Mungiki seems to be a well-organized group with focused leaders who know the political situation, and who have used religion to conceal their affiliation to the group. This kind of coordination makes it difficult for the country's security agencies to completely wipe out the movement. From the government's perspective, it will take a strong-willed leader to completely crack Mungiki and stop the terror that this group wreaks on the general public. It is also noted that the strategies of Mungiki cannot be used to enhance socialism. The Marxian principle proposes, and as further propounded by Geras (1994), that 'the liberation of the working class must be won by the working class'. Any great decisive movement must originate not in the initiative of a handful of leaders, but in the conviction and the solidarity of the masses. It must be made from the depth, out of the self-conscious efforts of an active politically vigorous populace.

Conclusion

Mungiki is just one example of youth gangs that have violated the rights of citizens through unlawful activities. This is, however, linked to the socio-economic challenges that most youth in developing countries face. The issue here is not to justify their misdemeanour, but to call for a deeper insight and for more research on related groups. A variety of theoretical and methodological problems have hindered the development of adequate knowledge about youth sects and movements. Variables and categories in such studies have not been clearly defined and distinguished. There has been a failure to distinguish norms and behaviours, sub-cultures and gangs, gangs and delinquent groups, different ethnic movements' patterns, and variability in their problems and patterns in different cities over time (Irving 1990). Such groups may be an endemic feature of urban culture that varies over time in its form, social meaning, and anti-social character. Observational studies, on the other hand, have been time-limited. Conspicuously absent have been studies of socialization of youth gangs compared with other non-youth gangs or other sub-cultures or groups. These are possible avenues of constructive research on related groups or groups with characteristics that are similar to Mungiki's.

Notes

1. Waruinge is believed to be the co-founder of Mungiki. History indicates that he founded the group with Maina Njenga (the national director, who after his jail term is now claiming to have seen the light and endeavours to reform Mungiki), when they were young boys.
2. An interview with Njeru (not his real name) an ex-Mungiki sect member on 29 November 2008, who indicated that he is living in fear after he deviated from the group because the members of the group might 'come for his head' any day.
3. Klopp 2002; Odhiambo 2003; Turner and Brownhill 2001; Lynch 2006. In the presentation of research findings, all these researches acknowledge that the land clashes faced in most parts of the Rift Valley are politically instigated, or happen with full knowledge of political leaders. The areas affected by these clashes have been used as grounds to appropriate political ambitions and at times by some political leaders to seek revenge. It is also realized that land and related ethnic clashes started in the Rift Valley especially before the very first multi-party elections. The need for Moi together with his allies too stay in power saw the introduction of the *Majimbo* system, which led to ethnic divisions and squabbles over land. All these issues are well articulated by the noted scholars and the government is also aware of such, yet very little is done to rectify the situation.
4. Caroline Mutoko & Maina Kiai, Oral Interview about Mungiki on Kiss 100, FM Radio, on 30 April 2008.

References

Anderson, David, 2002, 'Vigilantes, Violence and the Politics of Public Order in Kenya', *Journal of African Affairs*, Vol, 101, pp.531-555.

Dowdney, L., 2003, *Children of the Drug Trade: A Case Study of Children in Organized Armed Violence in Rio de Janeiro*, Rio de Janeiro: 7 LETRAS.

Ellis, Stephen, 1999, *The Mask of Anarchy: The Destruction of Liberia and the Religious Dimension of African Civil wars*, London: C. Hurst & Co.

Fotso, Jean, 2007, 'Urban-rural differentials in child malnutrition: Trends and socio-economic correlates in SSA', *Journal of Health and Place*, Vol.13, pp.205-223.

Gecaga, Margaret, 2007, 'Religious Movements and Democratisation in Kenya: Between the Sacred and the Profane' in G. Murunga and S. Nasong'o, eds, *Kenya: The Struggle for Democracy*, London and New York: CODESRIA and Zed Books.

Geras, N., 1994, 'Democracy and the ends of Marxism', in Michael Moran, ed., *Democracy and Democratization.*, London: Routledge.

Githogo, John, 2000, 'Why won't the State Clip Them Dread-locks?' *The East African*, Nairobi, 15 November 2000.

Gould, C., 1988, *Rethinking Democracy: Freedom and Social Cooperation in Politics, Economy and Society.* New York: Cambridge University Press.

Irving, Spergel, 1990, 'Youth Gangs: Continuity and Change', in *Crime and Justice*, Vol.12, pp.171-275.

Jensen, Steffen, 1999, 'Discourses of violence: Coping with violence on the Cape flats', *Social Dynamics*, Vol. 25, No.2, pp.75-97.

Kagwanja, Peter, 2003, 'Facing Mount Kenya or Facing Mecca? The *Mungiki*, Ethnic Violence and the Politics of the Moi Succession in Kenya 1987-2002', *African Affairs*, Vol.102, pp.25-49.

Kagwanja, Peter, 2005, '"Power to Uhuru": The Youth Identify and Generational Politics in Kenya's 2002 Elections', *African Affairs*, Vol.105, No. 418, pp.51-75.

Klopp, Jacqeline, 2002, 'Can Moral Ethnicity Trump Political Tribalism? The Struggle for Land and Nation in Kenya', *Journal of African Studies*, Vol. 61, No.2, pp.269-294.

Loffman, Reuben, 2008, 'A History of Violence: The State, Youth and Memory in Contemporary Africa', *African Affairs*, Vol.108, No.430, pp.125-133.

Lonsdale, John, 1986, 'Political Accountability in African History', in Patrick Chabal, ed., *Political Domination in Africa: Reflections on the Limit of Power*, Cambridge: Cambridge University Press.

Lynch, Gabrielle, 2006, 'Negotiating Ethnicity: Identity Politics in Contemporary Kenya', *Review of African Political Economy*, Vol.107, pp. 49-65.

Makokha, K., 2000, 'The Mungiki Mystique Just Shattered to Pieces', Nairobi: *The Nation*, 27 October 2000.

Murunga, Godwin, 2008, 'Crime and Entitlement' *The East Africa Magazine*, 12-18 May.

Musambayi Katumanga, 2005, 'A city under siege: Banditry & modes of accumulation in Nairobi, 1991-2004', *Review of African Political Economy*, No. 106, p. 505.

Mkandawire, Thandika, 2002, 'The terrible toll of post-colonial "rebel movements" in Africa: Towards an explanation of the violence against peasantry', *Journal of Modern African Studies*, Vol.40, No.2.

Ndegwa, Stephen, 1997, 'Citizenship and Ethnicity: An Examination of Two Transitional Movements in Kenyan Politics', *Journal of American Political Science Review*, Vol.91, No.3, pp.599-616.

Odhiambo, Atieno, 2003, 'Ethnic Cleansing and Civil Society in Kenya 1969-1992', *Journal of African Contemporary Studies*, Vol.22, No.1, pp.29-42.

Ruteere, Mutuma, 2008, *Dilemmas of Crime, Human Rights and the politics of Mungiki Violence in Kenya*, Nairobi: KHRI.

Smart, Ninian, 1968, *The Religious Experience of Mankind*, New York: Collins.

Sussane, Mueller, 2008, 'The Political Economy of Kenya's Crisis', *JEAS*, vol. 2, No.2, pp.204-210.

Turner, Terisa and Brownhill, Leigh, 2001, 'African Jubilee: Mau Mau Resurgence and the Fight for Fertility in Kenya, 1986-2002', *Canadian Journal of Development Studies*, Vol22, pp.1037-1041.

Wamue, Grace, 2001, 'Revisiting our indigenous shrines through Mungiki', *African Affairs*, Vol.100, No.400, pp.453-467.

www.ingramcontent.com/pod-product-compliance
Lightning Source LLC
Chambersburg PA
CBHW060034030426
42334CB00019B/2315